Immanuel Kant

Anthropology

From a

Pragmatic Point of View

Translated by Victor Lyle Dowdell

Revised and edited by Hans H. Rudnick

With an Introduction by Frederick P. Van De Pitte

SOUTHERN ILLINOIS UNIVERSITY PRESS
CARBONDALE AND EDWARDSVILLE
FEFFER & SIMONS, INC.
LONDON AND AMSTERDAM

FRANCISCAE CATHARINAE

UXORI MEAE

HUNC LIBRUM

PIA VENERATIONE

DEDICO

Library of Congress Cataloging in Publication Data

Kant, Immanuel, 1724–1804.
  Anthropology from a pragmatic point of view.

  Translation of Anthropologie in pragmatischer
Hinsicht.
  Includes bibliographical references and index.
  1. Man. 2. Psychology—Early works to 1850.
I. Title.
B2794.A572E5   150   77–10819
ISBN 0-8093-0623-9

COPYRIGHT © 1978 by Southern Illinois University Press

CONTENTS

Anthropology from a Pragmatic Point of View

Part One: ANTHROPOLOGICAL DIDACTIC

First Book: *On the Cognitive Faculty*

Second Book: *On the Feeling of Pleasure and Displeasure*

Third Book: *On the Faculty of Desire*

CONTENTS

PREFACE

KANT's *Anthropology from a Pragmatic Point of View* has been the object of about forty years of continuous work for Victor L. Dowdell and of more than five years for Hans H. Rudnick. The result of our work has gone in various stages of completion through many hands, for advice and further improvement. The *Anthropology* in its present form, revised word by word, phrase by phrase, and sentence by sentence, appears to have reached the level of accomplishment that can be optimally achieved.

The lack of a complete English translation made Dr. Dowdell begin this work as a labor of love more than a generation ago. The strongly felt conviction that Kant's *Anthropology* had to be made accessible to the English reader brought Dr. Dowdell, Dr. Rudnick, and Southern Illinois University Press together for this venture.

The *Anthropology* has to be understood as Kant's study of man, and man has to be understood in this context as part and parcel of an all-encompassing nature. The *Anthropology* was published at the end of Kant's life, although Kant had regularly lectured on this subject since the fall semester 1772 / 73 at the Albertus University of Königsberg. From a humanist's perspective the *Anthropology* can be interpreted as the capstone of Kant's entire philosophical system. It differs clearly in character from his three famous *Critiques*. The *Anthropology* provides the reader with a new and significant angle to Kant's personal character and the motivating forces of his philosophy. The *Anthropology* is the ideal introductory text to acquaint the student with Kant's way of thinking. The formidable intellectual giant of the categorical imperative here reveals his more human traits. We learn about Kant's personality, his way of life, his experiences, his reading, and above all, his image of man, which seems to be pertinent to the social problems of modern man.

In this work Kant comes as close as possible to combining the

qualities of English and Continental philosophy. The power of
the intellect and the attraction of the imagination both merge into
a system of common human concern which has more relevance
today than it has ever had before. Kant has the answer to the
question of how man should live in order to enjoy a humane life
on an overpopulated planet on the verge of self-destruction. He
writes about the evolution of man within the framework of an
ecologically responsible system. He speaks to us from the end of
the eighteenth century. We learn about his world, but we also feel
how strongly his thought still influences us today. He is the
originator of the critical attitude which prevents us from becoming dogmatic and intolerant. His thinking frees us from dog-
matism and slavery to ideas. He asks the question "What is man?"
all through the *Anthropology,* and, while he does so, it becomes
obvious that Kant himself is also a human being with prejudices
and "hang ups" similar to everybody else's.

   The text of this translation is based on the definitive edition
of the *Anthropologie in pragmatischer Hinsicht* as prepared by Oswald Külpe for the Königlich Preußische Akademie der Wissenschaften. The *Anthropology* is volume 7 (Berlin: Reimer, 1907)
of *Kants gesammelte Schriften.* In order to provide the most accurate translation, and to supply the critical reader with relevant
information about the different versions of available texts, notes
have been provided at the end of this translation. These notes
have been prepared by Dr. Dowdell when factual statements
within the text were concerned, whereas Dr. Rudnick has provided those notes that refer to different textual versions and
related problems of translation.

   The most clarifying and helpful source for a clearer understanding of Kant's sometimes very enigmatic passages has been
the text of the only existing manuscript of the *Anthropology.* This
manuscript was written by Kant in, approximately, 1796 or 1797
and is held by the Rostock University Library. The text of the
Rostock manuscript is not completely identical with the first edition of the *Anthropology* which was published in 1798 (A edition).
The manuscript of 1796 / 97 has been of particular help to the
editor in reconstructing Kant's original intentions and preparing
the textual notes, since the genesis of the *Anthropology* could be
traced from Kant's deletions, emendations, and remarks on the

margins of the manuscript. As far as these marginalia had any relevance to the understanding of the text, or if they were characteristic of Kantian thinking, they have been incorporated into the notes by the editor.

The B edition of 1800, which is a stylistically revised version of the A edition, served as the basis for Külpe's edition of the *Anthropology* in the *Akademie Ausgabe*. Ernst Cassirer's edition of the *Anthropology* (prepared by Otto Schöndörffer) and the B edition (1800) were the most helpful compilations and sources besides the Rostock manuscript. Bracketed numbers within the text of this present translation refer to the respective page numbers of the *Anthropology* as found in volume 7 of the *Akademie Ausgabe*.

It was decided, with the regrets of the editor, that the great number of italicized words found in Kant's original text should not be reflected in this translation in italicized form. Technical terms in Latin which were frequently given by Kant in parentheses have not been translated into English; however, other, mostly proverbial, quotations from Latin which Kant used in order to make succinct elucidating or summarizing statements have been translated for the reader's convenience. Brackets used in this edition indicate references or phrases added by the editor. The parentheses are mostly Kant's, except when translations have been provided by the editor or when Kant's words in the original German are quoted in the text.

To express gratitude to all who have helped in one way or another would involve an exceedingly long list of names. Yet, we must name Allen Webster Brown, Marie Josephine Hartford Bryce, Frances Catherine Kivell Dowdell, Florence K. Dowdell, and Harold Martin, as well as many renowned professors of philosophy, among whom are Foster Partridge Boswell, Walter S. Gamertsfelder, Frank Thilly, Ernest Albee, Harold Smart, John E. Smith, Lewis White Beck, Paul A. Schilpp, and Willard Enteman.

V. L. D.
H. H. R.

January 1977

INTRODUCTION

Frederick P. Van De Pitte

WHEN Kant began lecturing on Anthropology in the winter of 1772–73, he correlated a good deal of material that he had already been using in his lectures on Ethics, Metaphysics, and Physical Geography. An examination of these earlier lectures indicates that he had been reading the travel reports of famous voyagers, and whatever scientific material was available on anthropology for a number of years—at least since 1755 or 1756. Perhaps at first this interest was merely a pastime, a vicarious participation in great adventures by one who had very little experience with travel, but a great deal of curiosity about the various peoples and places of the world. The purely scientific aspects of anthropology would, of course, be interesting in their own right to one trained in science as he had been. For while Kant's course work at the University of Königsberg (1740–46) had given him a sound background in metaphysics and morals, as well as physics and mathematics, there is good reason to believe that his primary orientation was, and for a long time remained, in the area of the exact sciences. Soon, however, his interest spread to all aspects of anthropology, and he ultimately decided that it should be ranked among other studies as a regular academic discipline. Yet, in this early period there is no reason to believe that Kant recognized the essential role that anthropology was to play in his own development.

It would be impossible in a brief outline to give an accurate account of the progress in Kant's thought prior to the writing of the great *Critiques*. But one can understand a great deal by keeping in mind the one dominant interest which became more and more pronounced in this period—his concern for the proper method to be employed in metaphysics. And perhaps the traditional oversimplification of the history of philosophy in this period will serve well enough to indicate the character of this problem. The "rationalist" philosophers (from Descartes forward) had employed essentially a mathematical method, depending upon reason with its clear and distinct ideas for the true source and criterion of knowledge. The "empiricists," on the other hand, maintained that reason was miscast in this role, and that while it could effectively compare and evaluate information, only experience could serve as the genuine source and criterion of knowledge. It was Kant's virtue that he avoided both these extremes.

Gradually he came to the awareness that metaphysics could not follow the method of pure mathematics. Mathematics has ideal entities as its objects, and the principle which it follows is that of ground and consequence. Metaphysics, in contrast, has real, existing entities as its objects, and its principle is that of causality. Thus, while mathematics can proceed synthetically, moving from definitions by purely rational arguments to certain conclusions, metaphysics must proceed analytically in an attempt to clarify what is given indistinctly in experience. Kant concludes, therefore, that "the true method of metaphysics is basically the same as that introduced by Newton into natural science and which had such useful consequences in that field."[1] Roughly this would mean that speculation must be based upon experience, and always checked against experience. It was Kant's special use of this method that saved him from falling into a simple empiricism.

But while this procedure might avoid the errors of the extreme rationalist-empiricist dichotomy, it came accompanied with its own set of inherent difficulties. The traditional objects of metaphysics (God, freedom and morality, and the immortality of the soul) are not objects of experience in any ordinary sense of the term. The adoption of this new method would seem to frustrate the very purpose of metaphysical investigation. Not just a new method, but a revised conception of the task of metaphysics was being formulated.

An additional difficulty resulted from the fact that metaphysics requires absolute certainty. With the mathematical method this had been thought to be assured by the principle of contradiction, and the rigorous process of logical argumentation from basic definitions. But if metaphysics now was to begin in experience, where would it find the fixed principles in terms of which it could build with assurance? As Kant himself expressed it, the variations in taste and the different aspects of man give to the flow of experience an uncertain and delusive character. "Where shall I find fixed points of nature which man can never shift and which can give him indications as to the shore on which he must bring himself to rest?"[2] It is a curious and remarkable fact that both of these problems—the revised conception of metaphysics and the fixed points which could serve as a reliable guide—were resolved under the influence of Jean Jacques Rousseau.

Some of the most important works of Rousseau were published during this transitional period in Kant's life. *Julie ou la nouvelle Héloïse* appeared in 1761; the *Contrat social ou principes du droit politique* in 1762; and this was followed in the same year by *Émile ou de l'Education*. Combined with the earlier essay on the arts and sciences, *Si le rétablissement des sciences et des arts a contribué à épurer les moeurs* (1750), these provided Rousseau's full conception of human nature, and it is certain that these views profoundly impressed Kant.[3]

In his home as a youth, and in his early school years, Kant had been given a rigorous moral training. The dignity of man and the essential importance of morality had not simply been preached to him—it was a living fact in the home due to the extraordinary example of his parents. But for some years, during and after his university training, Kant was caught up in intellectual pursuits and the acquisition of knowledge for its own sake. He thought for a while that such knowledge constituted the real worth of mankind, and despised the common people who know nothing. But then, as he said, "Rousseau set me right. . . . I am learning to honor men, and I would regard myself as of much less use than the common laborer if I did not believe that this speculation can give a value to everything else to restore the rights of mankind."[4] It must be noted as well that this encounter with Rousseau was not merely a brief infatuation, or momentary inspiration—it was a profound and lasting revelation which eventually resulted in the elaboration of a complete philosophical program.

In the announcement of Kant's lectures on ethics for 1765–66 we find the statement that he will set forth the method by which man must be studied, not in the varying forms in which his accidental circumstances have molded him, or in the distorted form in which even philosophers have almost always misconstrued him, but that which is enduring in human nature, and the proper place of man in creation.[5] Rousseau is not mentioned at all, but Kant speaks of this new method of investigation as a "brilliant discovery of our time, which, when considered in its full scheme, was completely unknown to the ancients."[6] There can be no doubt that he is referring to the work of Rousseau—especially when we turn again to comments in his notes. There he mentions explicitly that just as the theories of Newton had brought order, regularity, and great simplicity into our conception of the universe, so Rousseau had provided the key which would permit a neat and orderly philosophy of man. "Rousseau was the very first to discover beneath the varying forms which human nature assumes the deeply concealed nature of man and the hidden law in accordance with which Providence is justified by his observations."[7]

Rousseau had made Kant realize (as Cassirer has so nicely pointed out) that "what is truly permanent in human nature is not any condition *in which* it once existed and *from which* it has fallen; rather it is the goal *for which* and toward which it moves."[8] Thus it is vitally important to understand not simply what man is or has been, but what he can, and therefore ought to, become.

From this time forward, Kant realized that man's rational capacity alone is not sufficient to constitute his dignity, and elevate him above the brutes. If reason only enables him to do for himself what instinct does for the animal, then it would indicate for man no higher aim or destiny than that of the brute, but only a different way of attaining the same end.[9] However, reason *is* man's most essential attribute, because it is the means by which a truly distinctive dimension is made possible for him. Reason, that is, reflective awareness, makes it possible to distinguish between good and bad, and thus morality can be made the ruling purpose of life. Because man can consider an array of possibilities, and which among them is the most desirable, he can strive to make himself and his world into a realization of his ideals.

This insight is simple and clear—but it opened enormous possibilities for the speculative mind of Kant. In the past, metaphysics had been *mere* speculation, full of chimerical insights which could only increase the amount of folly and error in the world.[10] But now Kant realized that metaphysics could proceed in terms of clearly defined absolute principles derived from man's potential. The moral dimension of man would serve as the most important element in the projected structure, but since reason is the essential condition for morality, its potential must be determined first. The force of this latter consideration was so strong when it first struck Kant that he seems to have considered it to be the main (and perhaps the *only* task) of metaphysics. In his notes we find: "One might say that metaphysics is a science of delimiting human reason."[11] And again: "Metaphysics is useful in that it abolishes illusion which can be dangerous."[12] But from this time on Kant moves gradually toward his mature view of metaphysics as serving a dual role: First in establishing the limits of reason, and thereby eliminating the misconceptions of previous rationalist systems; and secondly, in laying the foundations of pure philosophy—of physics with respect to the material order, and of morality with respect to the intelligible order. This may be expressed differently by saying that the two branches of metaphysics, of physics and of morality, encompass the two aspects of man's nature, since he is a member of both the physical and the intelligible worlds. And to set limits to, and define clearly, the kinds of experience he can have in these two spheres is at the same time to determine the full range of experience open to him, and thus the limits of reality with which he can and should be concerned. It may at first seem curious, but it is perfectly legitimate to assert that, with respect to a rational entity, to determine the full range of its possible experience is precisely to determine its "nature."

Kant realized at this time that knowledge of God based upon speculative principles is inferior to that achieved through morality and faith,[13] and that in general it is far better to base religion on morality than to do the reverse.[14] He saw, as well, that true virtue is the fulfillment of one's duty toward humanity (one's self as well as others) and that this virtue must be based upon principles which are not speculative rules, but the consciousness of a feeling which lives in every man's breast. "I hope that I express this completely when I say that it is the feeling of the beauty and worth of human nature."[15] As his moral philosophy developed, Kant eliminated this psychological element of feeling, basing morality entirely on man's awareness of the moral law—the sole fact of pure reason.[16] But what is important to note in this early period is that Kant had clearly determined that the traditional objects of metaphysics can be dealt with adequately without employing the traditional form of speculative metaphysics. Natural theology and religion were to be based upon morality, and morality in turn was to be based upon the concept of the inherent dignity and worth of human nature.

The importance of this commitment is clear when it is realized that such a philosophic scheme leaves nothing for metaphysics (or pure philosophy) except the analysis of the essential (a priori) aspects of that human nature on which—or in terms of which—the rest of the system will be built. And it is not surprising, therefore, that this is precisely what Kant's Critical Philosophy attempts to do. It is often forgotten that Kant's critique of pure reason is not restricted to a critique of pure speculative reason. While that task is the purpose of the first *Critique,* the second and third *Critiques* continue to develop the critical analysis of man's pure cognitive faculties. The intention of the *Critique of Pure Reason* is to establish the conditions which alone constitute experience as a unified, coherent awareness. At the same time, consequently, it determines the limits of possible experience. But this is experience in the scientific sense of *fact.* The *Critique of Practical Reason* has as its primary purpose to establish that there is a *pure* practical reason,[17] and the nature of the moral experience imposed on man by the moral law. These two works, therefore, set out the general nature of man as a rational being.[18] His sensuous nature is an existence under empirically conditioned laws, and from the standpoint of reason, therefore, it is heteronomy. But his supersensuous nature consists in his existence according to laws which are independent of all empirical conditions, and these laws belong to the autonomy of pure reason.[19] Autonomy, of

course, is self-legislation—the power which man has to impose upon himself values which he recognizes and accepts. But precisely the fact that he can and does impose such values on himself constitutes the essential nature of morality. It forces man to postulate freedom as a fact of his own moral experience—and it is *freedom* which is the key to the true nature of man, and which Kant employs as "the keystone of the whole architecture of the system of pure reason and even of speculative reason."[20]

But at this point man may appear to be a curious dual personality. One element of his nature is enmeshed in the causal necessity of a purely mechanical order of physical nature. The other is absolutely free and requires him to impose moral order on his world. Can he really bring both aspects of his nature into a unified and coherent pattern? It was a recognition of this difficulty within his system that prompted Kant to write the *Critique of Judgment*, "as a means of combining the two parts of philosophy into a whole."[21] In this third *Critique* Kant employs reflective judgment and the principle of teleology to link together the speculative dimension of man presented in the first *Critique* with the practical or moral dimension revealed in the second. Teleology, or purposiveness, is seen as an interpretive principle by which reflective judgment supplements the constitutive role of the categories in organizing nature. It is understood to reveal nothing new in the order of objective fact—but only how a mind such as man's *must* interpret the world of nature with which it is confronted. And because nature is conceived in this way as not hostile to purposeful activity, and even fully comprehensible only when we assume it, we are encouraged to believe that we can effectively impose our own purposeful activity upon nature—realizing the ends which morality demands. Thus, it is a fact that our mind necessarily imposes a teleological interpretation on reality which serves as the ultimate principle of unity and integrity in the Kantian system. Only in this way can mechanical causality and causality through freedom be conceived of as compatible, and man's physical and intelligible aspects be brought into harmony.

But it would be wrong to think of Kant's system merely in terms of its neat logical structure. And the third *Critique* must be seen as a great deal more than an ingenious device by which Kant

could impose organic unity on this structure. In it we find revealed the principles according to which man can achieve aesthetic awareness; can grasp natural objects as organic wholes,
rather than mere mechanical entities; and can comprehend the
whole of nature as an organic, interrelated system. Moreover,
here Kant shows how man is able to grasp his own dichotomous
nature (and the two spheres in which he expresses that nature) as
a unified whole—and how he is able to impose conceptual unity
on his own development within this integrated system, so as to
project his fulfillment and destiny as a realistic goal. It is clear in
this context, and in *Religion Within the Limits of Reason Alone,* that if
Kant's *method* involves the investigation of the a priori principles
of human nature, his *purpose* is to establish the destiny which these
principles reveal, and to provide the prescription by which that
destiny can be attained.

It must be acknowledged that much of what has been said
here does not sound like the normal description of Kant's
thought as it is encountered in a summary of the history of
philosophy. But neither the spirit nor the letter of Kant's work is
violated by this formulation.[22] In fact, once the suggested perspective is adopted, there are several additional arguments to
support it. Several times in his correspondence Kant speaks of his
Critique of Pure Reason as a propaedeutic—a necessary introductory measure which will pave the way for the proposed metaphysics of physics and of morals.[23] He also says that this new
system will provide a firmer foundation for philosophy, and one
which would be more advantageous for religion and morality. In
the first *Critique* itself, he mentions that in a system of philosophy
there can be only one highest end; and other ends, while essential,
must nonetheless be subordinated to that highest end as a means
for its achievement. The first *Critique* is clearly the means in this
context, while the ultimate end "is no other than the *whole vocation
of man,* and the philosophy which deals with it is entitled moral
philosophy."[24] This statement is not a casual or ill-considered
comment, but rather expresses a fundamental commitment on
the part of Kant—one that we find both early and late in his
writings. In 1765 we find among his notes: "If there is any science
which man really needs, it is the one I teach of how to fulfill
properly that position in creation which is assigned to man, and

from which he is able to learn what one must be in order to be a man."[25] We find in the Introduction to his *Anthropology* that Kant recognizes as *science* only those disciplines which are organized philosophically. Thus the description which he offers here is precisely that of a philosophically ordered study of man and his place in reality—or a philosophical anthropology. And when, in the same place, Kant describes his "pragmatic" anthropology as a study of what man can and should make of himself, how can we fail to recognize it as dealing with the "whole vocation of man"? All of Kant's philosophy is ordered to a single purpose: By means of an analysis of the essential principles of human nature, it discloses his proper destiny, and indicates how he must work toward its fulfillment.

If this is true, then Kant's *Anthropology* is a much more important work than has traditionally been recognized. It will involve a rough outline of his entire system, and serve as an excellent introduction to his complex thought. Unfortunately the *Anthropology* was the last major work that was edited by Kant himself, and his age and the state of his health compelled him to do little more than correlate his lecture notes for publication. The richness and intensity which the younger man had imparted to this material in the classroom was lost forever when he retired. And, of course, Kant himself acknowledged that the lectures were on a popular level—full of examples and humorous elements to provide a light and varied fare. But these facts should not cause one to conclude, as some writers have, that the *Anthropology* is not worthy of serious attention. In this work we find clues of several kinds which help us to understand both Kant and his system more completely.

First, and of primarily historical interest, we find a great deal of information about Kant as a man. There is much evidence to confirm the comments of his biographers: concerning his great love for the classics, and his voracious reading of contemporary works in science and literature—even the purely entertaining novels of the period, such as those of Fielding. There are many expressions of personal taste, and evidence of a great deal of concern for correct form in matters of social intercourse. And finally, there is the combination of great shallowness and equal profundity in this extraordinary man. One is amazed at the uncritical views which are expressed about women, and about certain religious and racial groups. Nor can one fail to note the contrast between such views and the emphasis upon the correct use of man's reflective capacity, awareness of duty, and proper conduct toward our fellowman. But Kant *was* a man of goodwill, and any failure on his part to live up to the moral ideal must be ascribed to a lack of experience which permitted his prejudices to remain undetected.

From the philosophic standpoint, however, information about Kant as an individual is the least interesting aspect of the *Anthropology*. Here it is more important to seek out definitions, comments and distinctions which will throw light on other aspects of Kant's work. And there are a good number of these. In the first portion of the work there are several interesting comments on the precise interrelation of the distinct cognitive faculties. The statements on affinity in section 31 are particularly helpful to one who has found this notion rather obscure in the first edition of the *Critique of Pure Reason* where it plays such an important role. The distinction between propensity and inclination (sections 73 and 80) helps one to understand more clearly certain of the more concrete aspects of Kant's moral theory. The extended discussions of imagination and of genius cannot help but throw light on the inadequate treatment which these vital aspects of man receive in other contexts. And the notion that the faculty of taste, in which the sensible and intelligible elements of cognition are conjoined, can serve as the ground for the external advancement of morality (section 69) is surely one which will help the student of Kant to bring together some of the apparently loose ends in his system.

This last point, of course, brings us back to our primary point of emphasis. There can be no doubt that the most important philosophic impact of the *Anthropology* is in its ability to clarify for the student of Kant the precise purpose which his philosophic system is intended to fulfill, and the manner in which the parts of that structure are related. Kant sees himself not only as indicating to man the kind of program of self-education which must be undertaken if he is to fulfill his destiny, but also as having removed the primary impediments to that education, and having

outlined the social and political programs which would enhance
and promote it.

It would not be surprising if the contemporary reader were
to judge the anthropology of Kant a curious anthropology indeed. But that is only because the English-speaking world has too
long restricted its consideration to a purely empirical anthropology. Such an anthropology can, of course, only describe man as
he has expressed his nature in the course of historical events. But
this will only give us the various roles that man has played, the
various masks that he has worn from time to time. We will still
know nothing of his essential nature, and of what man ought to
be. Kant's formulation, on the other hand, is a prescriptive, and
even a *creative* anthropology—it emphasizes man's responsibility
to become what he can be, that is, to fulfill his potential. This
prescription is based upon a combination of pure a priori principles, and an enormous amount of carefully considered empirical
data. And if it is incorrect in certain of its conclusions (as any
scientific work is likely to be in retrospect), it is by no means
incorrect in its general conception of man—or for that matter, of
anthropology. Anthropology must be the study of what man is
and has been, in order that he may more efficiently direct his
energies toward fulfilling his potential in the future. And Kant
realized as clearly as we do today that there is no way to know
where this development will end. In the *Critique of Pure Reason* he
says:

> What the highest level might be at which humanity may have to
> come to rest, and how great a gulf may still be left between the
> idea [of human perfection] and its realization, are questions
> which no one can, or ought to answer. For the matter depends
> upon freedom; and it is in the very nature of freedom to pass
> beyond any and every specified limit.[26]

European scholars have since Kant's time kept up a continuous flirtation with the notion of a genuinely philosophical
anthropology—and a bibliography on the topic would require an
entire volume in itself. But curiously enough it has only been
within the last fifty years or so that this particular aspect of Kant's
work has been given important emphasis—by writers like Max

Scheler, Martin Heidegger, and Ernst Cassirer. Gradually, however, there has been an increase of interest in the area, and it now seems likely to take on major proportions. In a recent bibliography of works on Kant[27] there were more articles and books on anthropological topics than on any other theme in his work (i.e., more than on anything other than the individual *Critiques* themselves). Of course, very few of these works were in English, since little of Kant's anthropological thought had been translated, and there was apparently an unwillingness to work with it in the original. But now that Kant's major anthropological work has been made available in English, one may hope to see a significant increase in enthusiasm for the task. Of course, a great deal of work remains to be done in this area. There are two large volumes of "anthropological notes" in the Akademie Edition of Kant's work. Careful scholars have been making isolated references to these notes for years, but their significance is far from exhausted. And when the task of correlating and evaluating this material has been completed, there still remains the need for a detailed commentary on this aspect of Kant's work. There is a rather brief contribution to this cause by J. H. von Kirchmann in the old *Philosophische Bibliothek* series. But this is perhaps the only commentary available. Michel Foucault had planned a work which would relate the *Anthropology* to Kant's critical works,[28] but unfortunately his interests in other areas of thought have forced him to cancel the project. Thus there is a surprising amount of work left to be done on the anthropological aspects of Kant's thought, and the present translation will be valuable indeed if it encourages its readers to contribute their energies to the task.

ANTHROPOLOGY

From a

Pragmatic Point of View

Introduction

ALL cultural progress, which represents the education of man, aims at putting acquired knowledge and skill to use in the world. The most important object of culture, to whom such knowledge and skill can be applied, is Man because he is his own ultimate purpose. To recognize him, according to his species, as an earthly creature endowed with reason deserves to be called *knowledge of the world,* even though he is only one of all the creatures on earth.

A systematic doctrine containing our knowledge of man (anthropology) can either be given from a physiological or a pragmatic point of view. Physiological knowledge of man aims at the investigation of what Nature makes of man, whereas pragmatic knowledge of man aims at what man makes, can, or should make of himself as a freely acting being. He who ponders about natural phenomena, for example about the causes for the faculty of memory, can make sense (in the Cartesian fashion) of the traces of impressions which keep lingering in our brain; but, in doing so, he has to admit that he is a mere spectator in this game of his imagination and that he has to leave everything entirely to Nature, since he knows neither the cerebral nerves and filaments nor their operation when they carry out his intentions. Such speculative theorizing is a sheer waste of time. If, however, he distinguishes between those observations which have been found to hinder and those which have been found to promote memory in order to amplify it and make it more efficient, and if he needs for this purpose a better knowledge of man, then we are involved in a section of anthropology with pragmatic purpose, and this is precisely what concerns us here.

[120]   Such an anthropology, understood as *knowledge of the world,* has to be continued after formal education is over. It is not yet properly called pragmatic so long as it contains extended knowledge of the *things* in the world, such as animals, plants, and minerals in various lands and climates. It is properly pragmatic only when it incorporates knowledge of Man as a citizen of the world. Hence even knowledge of the races of man, which are regarded as products of the play of Nature, is not yet pragmatic, but only theoretical knowledge of the world.

Idiomatic expressions such as "he knows the world" and "he knows his way about the world"[1] are widely separated in meaning. The first implies only the understanding of the game which he has witnessed, whereas the second implies actual participation in it. The anthropologist finds himself in a very unfavorable position for judging the so-called *high society,*[2] the world of aristocrats, because the aristocrats are too close together among themselves and too distant from everybody else.

Travel is among the means of enlarging the scope of anthropology even if such knowledge is only acquired by reading books of travel. One must, however, have gained his knowledge of man through interaction with one's fellowmen* at home if one wishes to know what to look for abroad in order to increase one's range of the knowl-

---

*   A large city like Königsberg on the river Pregel, the capital of a state, where the representative National Assembly of the government resides, a city with a university (for the cultivation of the sciences), a city also favored by its location for maritime commerce, and which, by way of rivers, has the advantages of commerce both with the interior of the country as well as with

edge of man. Without such a program (which presupposes knowledge of man), the anthropology of the citizen of the world will remain very limited. Universal knowledge will always precede local knowledge[3] as long as it is to be arranged and guided by philosophy, without which all acquired knowledge can provide nothing but fragmentary groping, and no science at all.

All responsible endeavors, however, to attain such a science encounter considerable difficulties inherent in human nature itself.

[121] *1.* A man who notices that he is being observed or scrutinized will either appear disturbed (embarrassed), and will therefore not be able to behave as he really is, or else will conceal himself because he does not want to be known as he really is.

2. Also, if he wants to observe himself, he will reach a critical point with regard to his emotional state where, generally, no further concealment is possible; that is to say he is not consciously watching himself when impelling forces are in action, and that he is observing himself *when* the impelling forces are at rest.[4]

3. Conditions of time and place, when lasting, result in habits which, it is said, constitute second nature, which makes man's judgment of himself more difficult. Therefore he is not sure what to think of himself and what he is to think of those with whom he comes into contact. Consequently, any change of the condition into which man was placed by fate, or into which he, as adventurer, has placed himself makes it more difficult to raise anthropology to the rank of a formal science.

---

neighboring countries of different languages and customs, can well be taken as an appropriate place for enlarging one's knowledge of people as well as of the world at large, where such knowledge can be acquired even without travel.

Finally, although there are no real sources available for anthropology, there are such aids as world history, biographies, and even plays and novels. Since the last two are not based upon experience and truth, but upon fiction, permitting the presentation of man as if in a dream through exaggeration of character and situation, they seem to teach nothing of the knowledge of man. But such characters as are created, for instance, by Richardson and Molière, still had to be derived in their basic traits from observance of the actual doings of Man. Exaggerated as these traits may be in degree, they must still conform to human nature.

A pragmatic anthropology which has been systematically devised and which can be understood by the general reading public (because of reference to examples which can be checked by every reader), has the advantage that the completeness of headings, under which observed human characteristics of practical consequence have been subsumed, offers many occasions and challenges to the   [122] reading public to study each particular characteristic in order to classify it accordingly. Any study of a certain characteristic will attract the attention of specialists in the same area and, because of the unity of the design, they will be integrated into a comprehensive whole. Thus the development of a science which is beneficial to the human community will be furthered.*

* In my occupation with *pure philosophy,* which was originally undertaken of my own accord, but which later belonged to my teaching duties, I have for some thirty years delivered lectures twice a year on "knowledge of the world," namely on Anthropology (in the winter semester [1772/73—Trans.]) and Physical Geography (in the summer semester [1756—Trans.]). They were popular lectures attended by people from the general public. The present manual contains my lectures on anthropology. As to physical geography, however, it will not be possible, considering my age, to produce a manual from my manuscript which is hardly legible to anyone but myself.

ANTHROPOLOGY

Part One

Anthropological Didactic

On the Art of Knowing the Interior

as well as the Exterior of Man

First Book

On the Cognitive Faculty

ON BEING CONSCIOUS OF ONE'S SELF

[127] § 1. THE fact that man is aware of an ego-concept raises him infinitely above all other creatures living on earth. Because of this, he is a person; and by virtue of this oneness of consciousness, he remains one and the same person despite all the vicissitudes which may befall him. He is a being who, by reason of his preeminence and dignity, is wholly different from *things,* such as the irrational animals whom he can master and rule at will. He enjoys this superiority even when he cannot yet give utterance to his ego, although it is already present in his thought, just as all languages must think it when they speak in the first person, even if the language lacks a specific word to refer to this ego-concept. This faculty (to think) is understanding.

It is noteworthy, however, that the child who already speaks fairly well begins to use the pronoun *I* rather late (perhaps after a year), in the meantime speaking of himself in the third person ("Carl wants to eat, go, . . ." etc.). A light seems to dawn upon him when he begins speaking in the first person. From that day on he will never again revert to the third person. At first the child merely *felt* himself, now he *thinks* himself. The explanation of this phenomenon might be rather difficult for the anthropologist.

The observation that a child does neither weep nor smile until after it is three months old appears to be based on the development of certain notions of offense and injustice,[1] which point toward reason. In this period, when his eyes [128] begin to follow bright objects which are held before him, we have the crude beginnings of a process of broadening perceptions (the apprehensions of sensory awareness) into a recognition of objects of the senses, that is, of experience.

When the child tries to talk, his mangling of words makes him so lovable to mother and nurse, and makes both of them so well-disposed that they hug and kiss him continually.[2] They also thoroughly spoil the little tyrant by catering to his every wish and desire. That the little creature is lovable in the period of the development of his human nature must be credited to his innocence and the candor of his still stumbling utterances which are free from guilt or deceit. Yet the child's charm must also be credited to the natural inclination of nurses to care for a creature that flatteringly submits itself completely to the will of someone else. The child does so because he knows that a playtime, the best time of all, will be granted, and in this way the teacher, who now becomes a child again, enjoys once more the pleasures of childhood.[3]

The teacher's memory of his own childhood does, however, not reach back to that time, since the time of early childhood is not a time of experiences but rather a time of mere sporadic perceptions which have not yet been unified by any real concept of an object.[4]

ON EGOISM

§ 2.   FROM the day that man begins to speak in the first person, he brings his beloved self to light wherever he can, and his egoism advances unrestrained. If he does not do so openly (for then the egoism of others may oppose him), his egoism expresses itself

covertly and with[5] seeming self-abnegation and pretended modesty in order to ensure for himself a superior
value in the judgment of others.

Egoism may be thought of as containing three pre-
sumptions: that of reason, that of taste, and that of practical interest, that is, it may be logical, aesthetic, or practical.

The logical egoist considers it unnecessary to test his
judgment by the reason of others, as if he had no need of
a touchstone *(criterium veritatis externum)*.[6] However, it
is so certain that we cannot dispense with this means of
ensuring ourselves of the truth of our judgment, that this
is perhaps the most important reason why learned people
insist so emphatically on the freedom of writing. If this
freedom   [129] is denied, we are deprived of an effective means of testing the correctness of our judgment,
and we expose ourselves to error. It should not even be
said that a mathematician is privileged to make judgments on his own authority, for if the perceived and
verified agreement between the judgments of one
geometer and those of all others who devote themselves
with talent and industry to the same subject did not
prevail, then even mathematics would not be free from
having somewhere[7] fallen into error. There are also[8]
certain cases where we do not trust solely in the judgment of our own senses, where we find it necessary to
inquire of other people if they seem[9] to have had the
same *impression* as ours, for example, whether the ringing
of a bell was real or only in our ears. And although, when
philosophizing, we are not even permitted to appeal to
the judgments of others for establishing our own (as the
jurists do in appealing to those well-versed in law), every
writer who finds that no one agrees with his clearly
expressed and important views is suspected by the public[10] of being in error.

Therefore, it is a risk to hold a view which conflicts
with public opinion, even if it is deemed to be reasonable. Such a display of egoism is called paradoxical.

Boldness does not lie in running the risk that the view is untrue, but rather in the risk that the view might be accepted by only a few. Preference for the paradoxical is logical obstinacy in which a man does not want to be an imitator of others, but rather prefers to appear as an unusual[11] human being. Instead of accomplishing his purpose, such a man frequently succeeds only in being odd. But, because everyone must have and maintain his own intelligence (*Si omnes patres sic, at ego non sic.—* ABAILARD),[12] the reproach of being paradoxical, when it is not based on vanity or the desire to be different, carries no bad connotations. Opposite to the paradoxical is the commonplace, which sides with the general opinion. But with the commonplace there is as little safety, if not less, because it lulls the mind to sleep, whereas the paradox awakens the mind to attention and investigation, which often lead to discoveries.

The aesthetic egoist is satisfied with his own taste, even though others may dislike, criticize, or even ridicule his verse, his painting, or his music. He deprives himself of the progress toward improvement when he isolates himself [130] and his own judgment; he applauds himself, and he seeks art's touchstone of beauty only in himself.

Finally, the moral egoist limits all purposes to himself; as a eudaemonist, he concentrates the highest motives of his will merely on profit and his own happiness, but not on the concept of duty. Because every other person has a different concept of what he counts as happiness, it is exactly egoism which causes him to have no touchstone of a genuine concept of duty which[13] truly must be a universally valid principle. All eudaemonists are consequently egoists.

Egoism can only be contrasted with pluralism, which is a frame of mind in which the self, instead of being enwrapped in itself as if it were the whole world, understands and behaves itself as a mere citizen of the world. The above is all that belongs to anthropology. The consideration of the contrast between egoism and pluralism from a metaphysical perspective lies beyond the scope of the science with which we are dealing here. If the question were only whether I, as a thinking being, have any reason to assume that beside my existence there exists a totality of other beings (called the world) with whom I am in relation, then it is not an anthropological but merely a metaphysical question.

Note On the Formality of Egoistic Language

The language used by the head of state, when speaking of himself to the people, is nowadays in the plural (We, King by the Grace of God . . .). The question arises whether the meaning of this is not rather egoistic, that is, indicative of the speaker's own authority; the same meaning is expressed by the King of Spain when he refers to himself as *Io, el Rey* (I, the King). It appears to be a fact, however, that such formality in speaking about the highest authority was originally to indicate condescension (We, the King and his Counsel, or Estates). But how does it happen that the reciprocal form of address, which was formerly expressed in the old classical languages by the familiar Thou[14] in the singular, should later be indicated by the formal You in the plural[15] when spoken by various (chiefly German) peoples? For the sake of giving greater distinction to the person addressed, the German [131] language uses two distinctive expressions, namely *he* and *they*[16] (as if it were not a form of address at all, but a story about someone[17] absent, be it one person or more[18]). This has finally led, to complete the absurdity, to the use of such expressions as Your Grace, Right Honorable, Right Noble, High-and-Noble, in which the speaker, rather than pretending to humble himself before the person addressed, shows deference instead to the abstract quality of his station. Probably all this is the result of feudalism which saw to it that[19] the degree of respect due the socially more distinguished not be violated in a hierarchy extending from the royal dignity down through all the stages until even human dignity itself ceases and only man remains, that is, down to[20] the position of serfdom, where a man is addressed by his superiors as *you*,[21] or down to the position of a child who is not allowed to have its own way.

ON BEING ARBITRARILY CONSCIOUS OF ONE'S IDEAS

§ 3.   THE effort to become conscious of one's sense impressions [ideas] is[22] either the perception (*attentio*) or the abstraction (*abstractio*) of a sense impression of which I am conscious within myself. Abstraction is not just a neglect and cessation of perception (since that would be distraction [*distractio*]), but rather it is a considered act of the faculty of cognition; it is a sense impression of which I am inwardly conscious, keeping it separate from other sense impressions in my consciousness. Therefore, one does not speak of abstracting (separating) something, but of abstracting from something, that is, abstracting a definition from the object of my sense impression, whereby the definition preserves the universality of a concept, and is thus taken into the understanding.

For a man to be able to make an abstraction from a sense impression, even when the sense impression forces itself on his senses, is proof of a far greater faculty than just paying attention, because it gives evidence of a freedom of the faculty of thought and sovereignty of the mind in having the condition of one's sense impressions under one's control (*animus sui compos*). In this respect the faculty of abstraction is much more difficult, but also more important than the faculty of perception when it encounters sense impressions.

Many people are unhappy because they cannot en-

gage in abstraction. Many a suitor could make a good
marriage if he could only shut his eyes to a wart   [132] on
his sweetheart's face or to a gap where teeth are missing.
But it is a peculiarly bad habit of our faculty of perception
to observe too closely, even involuntarily, what is faulty
in other people. Likewise, it is bad manners to fix one's
eyes on the spot where a button is missing from the coat
of a man who is directly in front of us, or upon a missing-
tooth gap, or to call attention to a habitual speech defect,
or to make the other person feel uneasy by staring at him
and thus ruining any possibility of personal relations with
him. If the essentials are good, it is not only fair but wise
to shut one's eyes to the shortcomings of others, as well
as to our own good fortune. The capacity to abstract,
however, is a power of mind[23] which can only be acquired by exercising it.[24]

ON SELF-OBSERVATION

§ 4. NOTICING (animadvertere) oneself is not the
      same thing as observing (observare) oneself.
Observation is a methodical compilation of perceptions
which we have experienced. Such perceptions furnish
material for the diary of an *observer of the self*[25] and they
may easily lead to wild imaginings and insanity.

The perception (attentio) of oneself when dealing
with others is necessary, but it must not be obvious in
daily intercourse; if it is noticeable, it makes conversation
awkward (a hindrance) or affected (a mockery). The opposite of both is a free and easy manner (air dégagé), the
self-confidence that one's behavior is not going to be
criticized unfavorably by others. He who pretends to
judge himself as if he were standing in front of a mirror,
and he who speaks as if he heard himself speak (and not
simply as if someone else heard him), is a kind of actor.
He wishes to appear as someone, and so he feigns a
semblance of his own person. However, on this account,

he suffers in the estimation of other persons who perceive his attempt because it arouses the suspicion that he intends to deceive. Candid behavior (a manner which causes no such suspicion) is called natural behavior (although it does not exclude all fine art and the cultivation of taste).[26] Such behavior pleases because of its simple *truth* in expression. But when sincerity appears to proceed from simplicity, that is, because a mode of perception has been neglected which has already been established as a rule, then simplicity is called naïveté.

[133]   The naïve[27] manner of revealing one's self as evidenced when a girl is approached by a man for the first time, or when a peasant, unfamiliar with urbane manners, entering the city for the first time, provokes, because of the person's innocence and simplicity (caused by the lack of the art of pretense), a benevolent smile from those who are already well versed and adept in this art. Such a smile is not a condemnation, since honesty and sincerity are still respected; it is a good-natured and kindly ridicule at inexperience based on the evil art of pretense, indicative of our already corrupted human nature. It is an art which should be lamented rather than ridiculed, especially if one compared it with the idea of a still uncorrupted human nature.* It is a momentary joy, as when a cloudy sky breaks open for an instant and lets a sunbeam through, only to close up at once as if to avoid hurting the purblind eyes of egoism.

But the real purpose of this section is the previous warning against engaging in deliberate observation and studied compilation of an inner history of the involuntary course of our thoughts and feelings. The warning is given because deliberate observation is the most direct path to illuminism and terrorism in the confused belief that we are open to higher inspiration and, without our help, who

---

*   In reference to this, the familiar verse of Persius can be parodied as follows: *Naturam videant ingemiscantque relicta.* [That they may look on Nature, and sigh because they have lost her—Ed.]

knows why, are subject to unknown interior[28] forces. In such a situation, without noticing it, we make pretended discoveries of what we ourselves have introduced into our own minds, like a Bourignon, with flattery, or a Pascal,[29] with terrifying and frightful implications,[30] or as was the case with Albrecht Haller,[31] an otherwise splendid mind, who while writing the extensive and much-interrupted diary of his spiritual life, finally came to the point of asking a famous theologian, his former academic colleague Doctor Less,[32] whether in his extensive store of divine learning he could not find any consolation for his anguished soul.

To scrutinize the various acts of the imagination within me, when I call them forth, is indeed worth reflection, as well as necessary and useful for logic and metaphysics. But to wish to play the spy upon one's self, when those acts come to mind unsummoned and of their own accord (which happens through the play [134] of the unpremeditatedly creative imagination), is to reverse the natural order of the cognitive powers, since then the rational elements do not take the lead (as they should) but instead follow behind. This desire for self-investigation is either already a disease of the mind (hypochondria), or will lead to such a disease and ultimately to the madhouse. He who has a great deal to tell of inner experiences (for example, of grace, of temptations, etc.) may, in the course of his voyage to self-discovery, have made his first landing only at Anticyra.[33] Inner experiences are not like external experiences of objects in space, wherein the objects appear[34] side by side and permanently fixed. The inner sense sees the conditions for its definition only in Time and, consequently, in a state of flux, which is without that permanence of observation necessary for experience.*

---

* If we consciously imagine for ourselves the inner action (spontaneity), whereby a concept (a thought) becomes possible, we engage in reflection; if we consciously imagine for ourselves the susceptibility (receptivity), whereby a perception (*perceptio*), i.e., empirical observation, becomes possi-

[135] ON THE IDEAS WE HAVE WITHOUT BEING AWARE OF THEM

§ 5. To have ideas and still not to be conscious of them seems to be a contradiction; for how can we know that we have them unless we are conscious of them? This objection has already been raised by Locke,[35] who on that account rejected the existence of such a type of ideas. Nevertheless, we can be indirectly conscious of having an idea, although we are not directly conscious of it. Such ideas are called obscure,[36] the others are clear, and when their clarity extends to the components of the whole idea and their combination, then they are called distinct ideas either of thought or of perception.

Whenever I am conscious of seeing a person in the distant meadow, though I am not aware of seeing his eyes, nose, mouth, and so forth, then I really only conclude that this thing is a person. If I were to say that I did not have any idea at all of these perceptions (simply because I was not conscious of perceiving these and other

---

ble, we engage in apprehension; however, if we consciously imagine both acts, then consciousness of one's self *(apperceptio)* can be divided into that of reflection and that of apprehension. Reflection is a consciousness of the understanding, while apprehension is a consciousness of the inner sense; reflection is pure apperception, and apprehension is empirical apperception; consequently, the former is falsely referred to as the inner sense. In psychology we investigate ourselves according to our perceptions of the inner sense; but in logic we make the investigation on the grounds of what the intellectual consciousness supplies us with. Here the self appears to us as twofold (which would be contradictory): (1) the self, as the subject of thinking (in logic), which means pure apperception (the merely reflecting self) of which nothing more can be said, except that it is an entirely simple perception. (2) The self, as the object of the perception, consequently also part of the inner sense, contains a multiplicity of definitions which make inner experience possible.

To ask whether or not a man conscious of different inner mental changes (either of his thoughts or of fundamental principles assumed by him) can say that he is the selfsame man, is an absurd question. For he can be conscious of these changes in the first place only on condition that he represents himself, in the different situations, as one and the same subject. The human ego is indeed twofold as regards its form (manner of representation), but not with respect to its matter (content).

parts of the person), then I would not be able to say that I saw a person. It is these partial ideas that contribute to the entirety of the head or of the person.

Sense perceptions and sensations of which we are not aware but whose existence we can undoubtedly infer, that is, obscure ideas in both man and animals, constitute an immeasurable field. The clear ideas, on the other hand, contain infinitely few instances of sense perceptions and sensations which reveal themselves to consciousness. It is as if just a few places on the vast map of our mind were illuminated. This can inspire wonder at our own being; for a higher power would need only cry, "Let there be light" and then, without further action (if, for instance, we take an author and find out all that he has stored in his mind), there would be laid open before the eyes half a universe. Everything that the eye reveals when strengthened by the telescope (perhaps directed toward the moon) or by the microscope (directed upon infusoria) is perceived by the naked eye, for these optical instruments[37] do not bring more rays of light and subsequently more pictures into [136] the eye. The pictures reflect themselves upon the retina without such ingenious instruments. They simply enlarge the images so that we become conscious of them. The same thing is true of the sensation of hearing, when the musician plays a phantasy on the organ with his ten fingers and two feet, while at the same time he is speaking to someone standing beside him. Within a few seconds a host of ideas is awakened in his soul, and every idea requires special judgment as to its appropriateness, since a single stroke of the finger, not fitted to the harmony, would immediately be heard as a discord. Yet the whole comes out so well that the improvisator must often wish to have preserved in a score many a passage which he has performed in this happy fashion, but which he could not have performed so well with real diligence and attention.

Because obscure ideas can only be perceived by man passively as a play of sensations, their theory does not belong to pragmatic anthropology but to physiological anthropology with which we are not properly concerned.[38]

We often play with obscure ideas, and we have an interest in removing objects that are liked or disliked by the imagination. But still more often we ourselves become an object of obscure ideas, and our understanding is unable to rescue itself from absurdities which were caused by those ideas, although we recognize them as an illusion.

Such is the case with sexual love where no benevolence is intended but only the enjoyment of its object. How much cleverness has been wasted in throwing a delicate veil over man's desires,[39] but revealing still enough of man's close relation to the animal kingdom so that bashfulness results. Blunt expressions are replaced by euphemisms in polite society even though they are transparent enough to inspire a smile. Here the imagination may well walk in obscurity, and it requires an uncommon skill if, in order to avoid cynicism, one does not risk falling into absurd purism.

On the other hand, we are often enough the victims of obscure ideas which are reluctant to vanish even when understanding [137] has thrown light upon them. To arrange for his grave in his garden or under a shady tree, in a field or in a dry plot of ground, is often a very important affair to a dying man, even though he knows that if he chooses the one, he has no reason to hope for a nice view; and if he chooses the other, he has no reason to worry about catching a cold.

The saying, "Clothes make the man," holds true in a certain measure even for an intelligent man. The Russian proverb says: "One receives a guest according to his clothes, and accompanies him according to his understanding." But understanding cannot prevent the obscure impression that a well-dressed person is a person of a certain importance, but the preliminary judgment may be revised later.

Even studied obscurity is often used purposely to reflect profundity and thoroughness in much the same way as objects seen at dusk or in a fog always appear to be larger than they actually are.* Skotison (make it obscure) is the catchword[40] of all mystics in order to lure with fictitious obscurity those who dig for the hidden treasures of wisdom.[41] But generally the reader welcomes a certain degree of mystery in a manuscript, because he thereby becomes aware of his own intellectual power in resolving the obscure into clear thoughts.[42]

ON DISTINCTNESS AND INDISTINCTNESS IN RELATION TO THE CONSCIOUSNESS OF ONE'S IDEAS

§ 6.   THE awareness of one's ideas, sufficient for distinguishing one object from another, is   [138] clearness.[43] Awareness which makes the composition of ideas clear is called distinctness. Distinctness alone makes it possible for an aggregate of ideas to become cognition, whereby order is established from manifold ideas, because every conscious combination presupposes a unity of awareness which in turn supplies the rule for the unity. One cannot contrast clear ideas with confused ones (*perceptio confusa*); rather, they must be contrasted with the indistinct (*mere clara*) ideas. Whatever is con-

---

*   But in looking at an object in daylight, it is apparent that what seems lighter than surrounding objects also seems larger, e.g., white stockings display fuller calves than black ones. A fire in the night, burning on a high mountain, appears to be larger than one actually finds it to be upon inspection. Perhaps we can also explain in this way the apparently larger size of the moon [MS and Cassirer; B: the apparent size of the moon—Ed.] as well as the apparently greater distance between stars close to the horizon. In both cases shining objects appear to us as being high in the sky. They are objects close to the horizon seen through an obscuring layer of air; and what is dark is judged smaller because of the light which surrounds it. In target practice, therefore, a dark target with a white circle in the center would be more advantageous for shooting than a white target with a dark center.

fused must be compounded, for within the simple there is neither order nor confusion. Confusion is the cause of indistinctness, not its definition. In every complex idea *(perceptio complexa)*, and thus in every cognition (which requires both perception and concept), we see that distinctness depends upon the order according to which contributory ideas are combined (merely considering form) which order gives rise either to a logical division into primary or secondary *(perceptio primaria et secundaria)* ideas or a real division into principal and accessory ideas *(perceptio principalis et adhaerens)*. Distinct cognition results from order. One can see that if the faculty of cognition is to be called understanding (in the most general sense of the word), it must contain the faculty of apprehending *(attentio)* given ideas in order to produce perception; furthermore, it must contain the power of separating what is common to more than one object *(abstractio);* in order to produce the concept, it also must contain the faculty of deliberation *(reflexio),* in order to produce cognition of an object.

We say that he who possesses these powers to a superior degree has a head; and he who has a small measure of these faculties is called a simpleton, because he always allows himself to be guided by other persons. But we call him a genius who makes use of originality and produces out of himself what must ordinarily be learned under the guidance of others.

He who has learned nothing of what must be taught in order to be knowledgeable is called an ignoramus, if he has been expected to know because of his claim to be a man of learning. Without such a claim he may still be a genius. He who cannot think for himself, though he can learn much, is limited (warped). One can be a person of vast learning (a machine for the instruction of others, teaching what one has once been taught) and still be limited in reference to the rational [139] use of his actual knowledge. The pedant is the one whose conversation on what he has learned betrays academic constraint and consequently a lack of independent thought. This is so whether he is a scholar, a soldier, or even a courtier. Of all kinds of pedants the most tolerable is the learned pedant, because we can still learn from him. On the other hand, in a courtier scrupulousness in formalities (pedantries) is not merely useless, but, in view of the pride inevitably exhibited by the pedant, also ridiculous since it is the pride of an ignoramus.

The art, or rather the skill, of speaking in the socially proper tone, and appearing up-to-date, especially when the conversation is about science, is falsely called popularity, but should rather be called polished superficiality because it frequently cloaks the paltriness of a narrow-minded person. Only children can be fooled by this. Addison had the Quaker say to the constantly talking officer who was traveling with him in the coach: "Thy drum is a symbol of thee, it soundeth because it is empty."[44]

In order to judge men according to their cognitive faculty (according to their understanding as such) we make a division into two classes: those to whom must be attributed common sense *(sensus communis),* which certainly is not common *(sensus vulgaris),* and men of science. People with common sense are familiar with the principles relating to practical application *(in concreto).*[45] Scientific people are familiar with the principles themselves prior to their application *(in abstracto).* The understanding, which belongs to the first cognitive capacity, is sometimes called horse sense *(bon sens),*[46] whereas the understanding belonging to the second cognitive faculty we call perspicuity *(ingenium perspicax).* It is noteworthy that we interpret horse sense, which is generally considered only as practical cognition, not just as an understanding which can exist without cultivation, but rather as an understanding to which cultivation can be a hindrance if it is not conscientiously followed through. Some praise this understanding fanatically and represent[47] it as a storehouse of treasures hidden in the depths of the mind.

Sometimes we even interpret the dictum of horse sense as an oracle (the genius of Socrates) which is more accurate than anything that erudite wisdom has to offer. So much is certain, that, whenever the answer to a question rests upon general and innate rules of the understanding (the possession of which is called native intelligence), we may be sure that seeking for studied and artifically established principles [140] (school learning), and forming a conclusion accordingly, is less reliable than gradually coming to a conclusion from the grounds of judgment which lie in the dark recesses of the mind. This may be called logical tact, in which reflection looks at the object from many angles and produces the correct result without being aware of the acts occurring within the mind during this process.[48]

Horse sense, however, can demonstrate this superiority only with regard to an object of experience. In this way it not only grows in knowledge but even extends experience itself; not, however, in a speculative, but only in an empirico-practical respect. For in the speculative employment of understanding, scientific principles a priori are required, while in the empirico-practical[49] employment of understanding it is possible to have experiences, that is, judgments, which are continually confirmed by experiment and result.

ON SENSIBILITY IN CONTRAST TO UNDERSTANDING[50]

§ 7. WITH respect to the state of its ideas, my mind is either active, and shows a capacity (*facultas*) for accomplishment, or it is passive, and continues in a receptive capacity (*receptivitas*). Cognition contains a union of both states of ideas. The possibility of having such a cognition bears the name of cognitive faculty, a term derived from its most important part, namely, the activity of the mind in combining or separating ideas.

Ideas with respect to which the mind is passive, and by which the subject is therefore affected (whether it affects itself or is affected by an object), belong to the sensual cognitive faculty. But ideas which involve a pure activity (that is, thinking) belong to the intellectual cognitive faculty. The first is called the lower; the other, the higher cognitive faculty.[51]* The sensual cognition has the character [141] of passivity toward the inner sense of awareness, while intellectual cognition has the character of spontaneity[52] of apperception, that is, of the pure consciousness of the act which constitutes thought and appertains to logic (a system of the rules of the understanding). Passivity, in turn, belongs to the field of psychology (a summary of all inner perceptions under the laws of nature). Psychology is the foundation of inner experience.

Remark

The object of an idea, which comprises only the manner in which I am affected by the object, can be recognized by me only as it appears to me. All experience (empirical cognition), the inner not less than the outer, is nothing but the cognition of objects as they appear to us, not as they are (when considered by themselves). Not

* To posit sensibility only in the obscurity of ideas, and intellectuality in distinctness, and thereby merely positing a formal (logical) distinction of cognition instead of a real (psychological) distinction, which not only refers to the form, but also to the content of thinking, has been a great mistake of the Leibniz-Wolff school. The error consisted in attributing a deficiency (as to clarity and constituent ideas) to sensibility and thus associating it with indistinctness, whereas the nature of rational ideas was understood to be distinct on the grounds that sensibility is something very positive and an indispensable ingredient of rational ideas for the process of producing cognition. Leibniz is really the one to blame. As a Platonist, he posited innate, pure perceptions of understanding, called ideas, which are encountered, though only obscurely, in the human mind. By applying our intellectual awareness to the analysis and elucidation of Platonic ideas, we are said to arrive at the cognition of objects as they really are.

only the quality of the idea, but also the quality of the subject and its susceptibility is important in determining the kind of sensual perception on which the thought process concerning the object (the concept of the object) bases itself. The formal character of this receptivity cannot be borrowed from the senses; it must be given a priori, that is, it must be a sense perception which remains after everything empirical (the content of sense perception) is taken away; in inner experiences, this formal factor of intuition is Time.[53]

Experience is empirical cognition, but cognition (dependent as it is on judgments) requires reflection *(reflexio),* and consequently consciousness of activity[54] in arranging the multitude of ideas according to a rule of unity,[55] that is, a concept; and, finally, it requires thought as such (which makes it different from sense perception). On this account consciousness is divided into the discursive (which, being logical, must take the lead because it provides the rule) and intuitive consciousness. Discursive consciousness (the pure apperception of its mental activity) is simple. The "I" of reflection contains no manifold within itself, and is always one and the same in every judgment, because it contains merely the formal part of consciousness. On the other hand, inner experience contains the material of itself as well as a manifold of the [142] empirical, inner perception, that is, the "I" of apprehension (hence an empirical apperception).

I, as a thinking being and as a being endowed with senses, am one and the same subject.[56] However, as an object of inner empirical intuition, so far as I am inwardly affected by temporal sensations (simultaneous or successive), I cognize myself only as I appear to myself, not as a thing-in-itself.[57] Such cognition depends on a temporal condition which is no concept of the understanding (hence not mere spontaneity), and hence is a condition in regard to which my faculty of ideas is passive. It is a condition that belongs to receptivity. Therefore, through inner experience I always know myself only as I appear to myself. This axiom has frequently been distorted to read: It only *seems* to me *(mihi videri)* that I have definite ideas and sensations, and that, indeed, I only appear to exist. This illusion is the basis of erroneous judgment emanating from subjective causes falsely treated as objective. Appearance, however, is no judgment, but merely empirical intuition which, through reflection and concept of the understanding resulting therefrom, becomes inner experience and consequently truth.

The cause of these errors lies in the fact that the terms *inner sense* and *apperception* are generally considered synonymous by psychologists, although inner sense should designate only psychological (applied) consciousness, while apperception should designate logical (pure) consciousness. From this it is evident that the only perception we have of ourselves by means of the inner sense is of how we appear to ourselves, because apprehension *(apprehensio)* of impressions of the inner sense presupposes a formal condition of the inner perception of a subject. The condition is Time, which certainly is not a concept of the understanding. It is merely a subjective condition by which inner sensations are given to us in consequence of the nature of the human soul. Thus it is not without our power to know what an object is in itself.

This note does not really belong to anthropology. In anthropology, experiences are appearances united according to the laws (rules) of the understanding, and no question is asked concerning the manner of representing things as they are apart from their relation to the senses[58] (as   [143]   they are in themselves). This investigation belongs to metaphysics which has to do with the possibility of knowledge a priori. Nevertheless, it was necessary to go back as far as we did just to avoid the mistakes of the speculative mind with regard to this question. On the whole, knowledge of man through inner experience, according to which he judges others, is of great importance and perhaps even more difficult to achieve than the ability to judge others correctly, in that the one who investigates his inner consciousness easily carries many things into his own self-consciousness instead of simply observing what is there. On this account it is advisable and even necessary to begin with observed phenomena within oneself before proceeding to make exact statements concerning man's nature, that is, before proceeding to the study of inner experience.

APOLOGY FOR SENSIBILITY

§ 8.   UNDERSTANDING is highly esteemed by everyone. Its very definition as the higher cognitive faculty only goes to show that whoever ventures to praise it would be sent away with the same ridicule earned by an orator praising virtue: *Stulte! quis unquam vituperavit.*[59] Sensibility, on the other hand, is in bad repute. We say uncomplimentary things, such as   (1) that it confuses the power of imagination;   (2) that it boasts, and is like a sovereign mistress, stubborn and hard to subdue, whereas it ought to be only the handmaid of the understanding;   (3) that it is even deceptive, so that we cannot be sufficiently on our guard where it is concerned.[60] Yet sensibility is not without praise, especially among poets and people of good taste. They highly esteem the figurative representation of ideas not only as a gain, but because in this way concepts need not be analyzed into their constituent parts with painstaking care to express the full meaning of a thought or the emphasis (the force) of speech and the self-evidence (the clarity in consciousness) of sensibility. They declare that understanding without adornment is a deficiency.* We

---

*   Since we are speaking here only of the cognitive faculty, and, therefore, of ideas (not of the feeling of pleasure or displeasure), sensibility will mean nothing more than sense perception (empirical perception [MS: sense-*perception*—Ed.]) in distinction to concepts (pertaining to thoughts) as well as pure perception (pertaining to the perception of Space and Time).

do not need panegyrists here, but only someone to act as a defender of sensibility against the accuser.

[144]   The passive element in sensibility, which we cannot ignore, is really the cause of all the difficulties we ascribe to it. The inner perfection of man consists in having the power to use all his faculties, a power to subject their use to his own free volition. For this, it is necessary that the understanding should rule without weakening sensibility (which in itself is like a mob of people since it does not think) because without sensibility no material would be provided for the use of the law-giving understanding.

Justification of Sensibility Against the First Indictment

§ 9.   *The senses do not confuse.* We cannot say of a person who grasps, but has not yet ordered, a given manifold, that he confuses it. Perceptions of the senses (empirical ideas with consciousness) can only be called inner phenomena. Only the understanding, which joins perceptions and combines them under a rule of thought, by introducing order into the manifold, establishes them as empirical cognition, that is, experience. The understanding is, therefore, neglecting its duty if it judges rashly, without having arranged sense impressions according to concepts, and then later complains of their state of confusion, which it blames on man's sensual nature. This reproach applies equally to the unfounded complaint concerning the confusion of outer as well as inner perceptions through sensibility.

Sense perceptions certainly precede perceptions of the understanding and display themselves en masse. Yet the harvest [*Ertrag*] is more abundant when the understanding with its order and intellectual form is added. The same is true when, for example, the understanding brings into consciousness significant expressions for the

concept, emphatic perceptions for the feeling, and interesting[61] perceptions for the determination of the will.
The riches, which rhetoric and poetry place before the
understanding all at once   [145] (en masse) often embarrass the understanding if it tries to clarify and explain
all the acts of reflection which it performs, even
obscurely, in such a process.[62] Sensibility, however, is
not to blame. On the contrary, it is to be esteemed for
having presented abundant material to the understanding, in comparison with which its abstract concepts are
often very paltry indeed.

Justification of Sensibility Against
the Second Indictment

§ 10.   *The senses do not control the understanding.* They,
          on the contrary, offer themselves to the un-
derstanding only for the sake of being put to work in its
service. That the senses do not wish to have their significance misunderstood, a significance which belongs to
them specifically in what we call the common sense of
human intelligence *(sensus communis),* is a fact that cannot
be interpreted as an arrogant intention to dominate the
understanding. There are judgments which, in view of
the fact that they are not brought formally to the tribunal[63] of the understanding for final decision, appear to
be dictated directly by sense. They are embodied in
so-called mottoes or oracular outbursts (such as those to
whose utterance Socrates ascribed his own genius). It is
thereby supposed that our first judgment about that
which is wise and just to do on a particular occasion is
generally the correct one and that pondering over it will
only lead to something artificial. These judgments, however, do not actually come from the senses; instead, they
proceed from real, though obscure, deliberations of the
understanding. The senses make no claim in this respect;
they are like the common people, though not like the
rabble *(ignobile vulgus),* who are happily willing to subor-

dinate themselves to their superior, the understanding, as long as they are listened to. However, if certain judgments and insights are regarded as proceeding directly from the inner sense, without the mediation of understanding, and if these are further regarded as governing themselves so that sensations are passed off as judgments, we have nothing but that fanaticism which is akin to insanity.

[146]   Justification of Sensibility Against the Third Indictment

§ 11.[64]   *The senses do not deceive.* This statement is the rejection of the most important, as well as, strictly speaking, the emptiest reproach which can be directed against the senses; not because they do not judge correctly, but because they do not judge at all. For this reason error must always be charged to the understanding. Sensible appearances *(species, apparentia),* however, turn to the understanding, if not for justification, at least for vindication. Thus man often mistakes the subjective for the objective. (He thinks a distant tower is round if he sees no corners on it. He believes the sea to be higher than its shore [*altum mare*] when the distant[65] water meets the eye through rays of light more sharply bent. The full moon seems to be farther away and therefore larger when he sees it ascend at the horizon through a hazy atmosphere than when it is high in the heavens, although he catches sight of it from the same visual angle.)[66] Thus man takes appearance for experience. In this way man errs, not through any shortcoming of his senses, but through a failure of his understanding.

Logic charges sensibility with the flaw that cognition, as it is advanced by logic, is associated with shallowness (individuality and limitation to the particular), whereas understanding which tends toward the universal, and therefore has to accommodate itself with abstrac-

tions, is associated with denseness. The aesthetic treatment, whose first claim is popularity, follows a course on
which both fallacies can be avoided.

ON THE POTENTIALITY OF THE
COGNITIVE FACULTY

§ 12.[67]   THE preceding section, which dealt with the
            faculty of appearance, concentrated on as-
pects which no man can control. It leads us to a discussion
of the concepts of the easy [leicht] and the difficult
[schwer], which literally signify in German only material
conditions and powers. But in Latin (leve et grave),[68] by an
exact analogy, they should signify   [147] that which can
be done (facile) and that which, relatively speaking, cannot be done (difficile). What is scarcely possible of being
done is regarded as subjectively impracticable[69] by a
creature who doubts whether he has the necessary ability
to perform in certain situations and relationships.
    Facility in doing something (promptitudo) must not
be confused with readiness in such actions (habitus).
Facility signifies a certain degree of mechanical ability,
the "I can if I want to" indicating a subjective possibility.
Readiness signifies subjective-practical necessity,[70] that
is, habit, which signifies a positive degree of the will
acquired through the oft-repeated use of one's faculty, "I
want to because duty asks me to." We cannot explain
virtue by saying that it is readiness for free and lawful
actions, because virtue would then be a mere mechanism
of applying power. Virtue, on the contrary, is moral
strength in pursuit of one's duty,[71] a duty which should
never be a matter of habit, but should always proceed,
fresh and original, from one's mode of thought.
    The easy is contrasted with the difficult, but many
times it is contrasted with the burdensome as well. Whatever requires for its accomplishment a great deal less

power of application than a subject has at his command is regarded by him as easy. What is easier than going through the formalities of social visits, of congratulations, and of condolences? But what is more demanding for a busy man? They are friendship's vexations (drudgeries) from which everyone heartily wishes to be free. And yet everyone has scruples against violating such social customs.

What vexations there are in the external customs which are thought to belong to religion, but which in reality are related to ecclesiastical form! The merits of piety have been set up in such a way that the ritual is of no use at all except for the simple submission of the believers to ceremonies and observances, expiations and mortifications (the more the better). But such compulsory services, which are mechanically easy (because no vicious inclination is thus sacrificed), must be found morally very difficult and burdensome to the rational man. When, therefore, the great moral[72] teacher said, "My commandments are not difficult,"[73] he did not mean that they require only limited exercise of strength in order to be fulfilled. As a matter of fact, as commandments which require pure dispositions of the heart, they are the hardest that can be given. Yet, for   [148] a rational man, they are nevertheless infinitely easier to keep than the commandments involving activity which accomplishes nothing *(gratis anhelare, multa agendo nihil agere),*[74] like those upon which Judaism is built. Even the mechanically easy feels like lifting hundredweights to the rational man when he sees that all the energy spent is wasted.

To make the difficult easy is meritorious. To depict what is difficult as easy, although one is not able to accomplish it himself, is deception. There is no merit in doing what is easy. Methods and machines, and among these the division of labor among various craftsmen, make many things easy which would be hard to do with one's hands without other tools.

To point out difficulties before one gives the order

to go ahead with the task (as for example, in metaphysical investigations) may have the effect of a deterrent, but it is better than concealing the difficulties. He who regards everything he wants to do as easy is reckless; he who performs everything he does with ease is adept; while he whose work shows signs of great labor is awkward. The social exchange of ideas (conversation) is merely a game wherein everything has to be easy and has to appear easy. Ceremonious (stiff) conversation, for example, the pompous "good-bye" when one makes a departure after a banquet, should be abolished as something antiquated.

According to the difference in temperament, the mental disposition of people differs when they are faced with a business undertaking. Some begin with difficulties and fears (the melancholic), while others (the sanguine) are at once inspired by the hope and assumed easiness of completing the job.

But what shall we say of the vainglorious boaster, whose claim is not founded on mere temperament—"What man wants to do, he can do"? This is just a high-sounding tautology. What he wants to do upon the command of his morally commanding reason is exactly what he ought to do. Consequently, it is what he can do (since reason would not command him to do the impossible). Yet, a few years ago, there were such fools who extolled this high-sounding tautology even in a physical sense, announcing themselves as world-assailants, but this breed has long since disappeared.

Habit (consuetudo) finally makes the endurance of evil easy (which, under the name of patience, is falsely honored as a virtue), because sensations of the same type, when continued without alteration for a long time, draw our attention away from the senses so that we are scarcely conscious of them at all.   [149] On the other hand, habit also makes the consciousness and the remembrance of good that has been received more difficult, which then gradually leads to ingratitude (a real vice).[75]

Customary habit (assuetudo), however, is a physical

and inner compulsion to proceed farther in the very same way in which we have been traveling. Acquired habit deprives good actions of their moral value because it undermines mental freedom and, moreover, it leads to thoughtless repetitions of the same acts (monotony), and thus becomes ridiculous. Customary expletives (clichés used merely to stuff the emptiness of thoughts) make the listener apprehensive that he will have to hear these favorite expressions over and over, and they make the orator into a talking-machine. The reason for being disgusted with someone's acquired habits lies in the fact that the animal here predominates over the man, so that instinctively, according to the rule of acquired habit, that person is categorized as another nature, a nonhuman nature, so that he runs the risk of falling into the same class with the beast. Nevertheless, certain continued practices may be started intentionally and kept up when Nature refuses help to the free will; for example, to become accustomed in old age to the time of eating and sleeping, or to the quality and quantity of food, or sleep, thus making it gradually mechanical. But this is the exception to the rule, and it occurs only in a case of necessity. Generally, all acquired habits are objectionable.

ON THE ARTIFICIAL GAMES PLAYED WITH SENSORY PERCEPTIONS

§ 13.[76] DELUSION *(praestigiae),* to which the understanding is subjected by sense perception, may be either natural or artificial; it is either illusion *(illusio)* or deception *(fraus).* The delusion whereby we are forced to accept as real, by the evidence of our eyes, something which we declare to be impossible through the use of our understanding, is called optical delusion *(praestigiae).*

Illusion is that visual error which persists although

we know at the same time that the supposed object is not
real. This caprice   [150] of the mind is very agreeable to
the senses and is amusing when, for example, we look at
the perspective drawings of the interior of a temple, or as
Raphael Mengs[77] says about the painting from the school
of the Peripatetics (I think he refers to Correggio): "If we
look at them long enough, the people seem to walk"; or,
we are tempted to try to mount the painted steps through
the half-open door in Amsterdam's town hall.

Deception of the senses exists when the appearance
vanishes as soon as we know the nature of the object. It is
the same with all kinds of sleight of hand. Clothing whose
color attractively sets off one's complexion constitutes an
illusion, while makeup is a deception; we are misled by
the former and mocked by the latter. Thus it happens
that we do not like statues of men or animals which have
been painted in natural colors, because we are constantly[78] deceived into treating them as living, whenever
we come upon them unexpectedly.

Fascination (*fascinatio*) in an otherwise sound mental state is a delusion of the senses about which it is said
that the senses are not dealing with natural things. The
senses seem to contradict each other because the judgment that an object (or a characteristic of it) exists is
irresistibly changed after closer attention to the judgment that the object does not exist (or if, then in a
different shape). It is like a bird that flits against a mirror
in which he sees himself, sometimes thinking that the
reflection is another bird, sometimes that it is not. Such
games, in which men do not trust their own senses, occur
especially in those who are intensely dominated by passion. There is the case of the lover who (according to
Helvétius)[79] saw his beloved in the arms of another. The
beloved, who plainly deceived him, was able to say: "You
faithless one, you do not love me any more. You believe
what you see, instead of what I tell you!" More insolent,
at least more injurious, has been the deception practiced
by ventriloquists, gassnerists, mesmerists, and other pre-

tended necromancers.[80] In olden times ignorant women who pretended to do something supernatural were believed to be witches; and even in this century belief in witchcraft has not been fully rooted out.* It seems that the feeling of wonder at [151] something unprecedented has in itself much that is alluring to weak minds. This is not because new prospects are suddenly opened to him, but because the weak person is seduced by them into escaping from the tiresome work of understanding and into making others as ignorant as himself.[81]

ON THE ADMISSIBLE MORAL PERCEPTION

§ 14.[82] COLLECTIVELY, the more civilized men are, the more they are actors. They assume the appearance of attachment, of esteem for others, of modesty, and of disinterestedness, without ever deceiving anyone, because everyone understands that nothing sincere is meant. Persons are familiar with this, and it is even a good thing that this is so in this world, for when men play these roles, virtues are gradually established, whose appearance had up until now only been affected. These virtues ultimately will become part of the actor's disposition. To deceive the deceiver in ourselves, or the tendency to deceive, is a fresh return to obedience under the

* In this very century a Protestant clergyman testifying in Scotland as a witness in such a case, said to the judge: "Your Honor, I assure you on my priestly word that this woman is a witch." The judge replied: "And I assure you on my judicial word that you are no magician yourself." The word *Hexe* (witch) has now become a German word. It derives from the first words of the Mass formula used at the Consecration of the Host which the faithful behold with bodily eyes as a small disc of bread. After the formula has been pronounced, however, the faithful must look upon the bread with spiritual eyes as the body of a man. The words *hoc est* have been associated with the word *corpus;* thus *hoc est corpus* was changed to *hocus-pocus.* I suppose this resulted from pious reticence at saying and profaning the actual words, just as the superstitious are accustomed to do in the face of supernatural objects, in order to avoid sacrilege. [The etymology of *Hexe* (witch) today is assumed to derive from *Hag* (fence, hedge, little forest). Therefore *Hexe* is a demonic woman inhabiting such an area—Ed.]

law of virtue. It is not a deception, but rather a blame-less[83] deluding of ourselves.

There is a disgust of one's own existence, which arises from the emptiness of mind toward the sensations for which the mind continually strives, that is caused by boredom. One grows weary of inactivity, that is, the weariness of all occupation that could be called work, and which could drive away that disgust because it is as-sociated with hardship, a highly contrary feeling, whose original cause is none other than a natural inclination toward being at ease (rest without preceding fatigue). This inclination, however, is deceptive even with regard to the purpose which [152] the human reason ordains for man, namely, self-contentment, when he does noth-ing at all (when he vegetates without purpose), because he assumes that he can do nothing evil in this state. This inclination toward further self-deception (which can be achieved by concentrating one's attention on the fine arts or, more effectively, through social activities) is called passing the time *(tempus fallere)*. Here, indeed, the ex-pression signifies the intention, which is really an inclina-tion to self-deception through lazy inactivity, when the mind amuses itself by dallying with the fine arts, or when at least a mental cultivation is effected by a peaceful effort, which is pointless in itself; otherwise it would be called killing time. Force accomplishes nothing in the struggle against sensuality in the inclinations; instead we must outwit these inclinations, and, as Swift says, in order to save the ship,[84] we must fling an empty tub to a whale, so that he can play with it.

Nature has wisely implanted in man the propen-sity[85] to easy self-deception in order to save, or at least lead man to, virtue. Good and honorable formal behavior is an external appearance which instills respect in others (an appearance which does not demean). Womankind is not at all satisfied when the male sex does not appear to admire her charms. Modesty *(pudicitia),* however, is self-constraint which conceals passion;[86] nevertheless, as an illusion it is beneficial, for it creates the necessary distance between the sexes so that we do not degrade the one as a mere instrument of pleasure for the other. In general, everything that we call decency (*decorum*) is of the same sort; it is just a beautiful illusion.

Politeness (*politesse*)[87] is an appearance of affability which instills affection. Bowing and scraping (compliments) and all courtly gallantry, together with the warmest verbal assurances of friendship, are not always completely truthful. "My dear friends," says Aristotle, "there is no friend."[88] But these demonstrations of politeness do not deceive because everyone knows how they should be taken, especially because signs of well-wishing and respect, though originally empty, gradually lead to genuine dispositions of this sort.

Every human virtue in circulation is small change; only a child takes it for real gold. Nevertheless, it is better to circulate pocket pieces than nothing at all. In the end, they can be converted into   [153] genuine gold coin, though at a considerable discount. To pass them off as nothing but counters which have no value, to say with the sarcastic Swift[89] that "Honesty [is] a pair of Shoes worn out in the Dirt," and so forth, or to slander even a Socrates (as the preacher Hofstede[90] did in his attack on Marmontel's *Belisar*), for the sake of preventing anyone from believing in virtue, all this is high treason perpetrated upon humanity. Even the appearance of the good in others must have value for us, because in the long run something serious can come from such a play with pretenses[91] which gain respect even if they do not deserve to. Only the illusion of the good inside ourselves must be wiped out, and the veil, with which self-love conceals our moral infirmity, must be torn away. The appearance is deceptive if one pretends that one's guilt can be erased, simply cast off, by doing something that is without moral value, or one can convince oneself of being in no way in the wrong. Good examples of repentance of sins at the end of life are represented as actual improvement, or willful transgression is represented as human weakness.[92]

ON THE FIVE SENSES[93]

§ 15.[94]   SENSIBILITY in the cognitive faculty
(the faculty of intuitive ideas) is twofold:
sense and imagination. Sense is the faculty of intuition in
the presence of an object. Imagination is intuition without the presence of the object. The senses, however, are
in turn divided into outer and inner (sensus internus). The
outer sense is where the human body is affected by
physical things. The inner sense is where the human body
is affected by the mind. It should be noticed that this
inner sense, as a bare faculty of perception (of the empirical intuition), must be regarded as differing from the
feeling of pleasure and pain, that is, from the susceptibility of the subject to be determined through certain ideas
for the conservation or rejection of the condition of
these ideas, which might be called the interior sense
(sensus interior). An idea that comes through the senses,
and of which one is conscious as it arises, is specifically
called sensation, when at the same time the perception
centers our attention on the state of the subject.

§ 16.[95]   To begin with, we can divide the senses of
physical sensation into those of   [154] the
sensation of vitality (sensus vagus), and those of organic
sensation (sensus fixus), and, since they are met with only
where there are nerves, into those which affect the whole
system of nerves, and those which affect only those
nerves which belong to a certain member of the body.
The sensations of warmth and cold, even those which are
aroused by the mind (for example, through quickly rising
hope or fear), belong to the vital sense. The shudder
which seizes men even at the idea of something sublime,
and the terror, with which nurses' tales drive children to

bed late at night, belong to the latter type. They penetrate the body to the center of life.[96]

The organic senses, however, so far as they relate to
external sensation, we can conveniently reckon as five,
no more and no less.

Three of them are more objective than subjective,
that is, they contribute, as empirical intuition, more to
the cognition of the exterior object, than they arouse the
consciousness of the affected organ. Two, however, are
more subjective than objective, that is, the idea obtained
from them is more an idea of enjoyment, rather than the
cognition of the external object. Consequently, we can
easily agree with others in respect to the three objective
senses. But with respect to the other two, the manner in
which the subject responds can be quite different from
whatever the external empirical perception and designation of the object might have been.

The senses of the first class are (1) touch (tactus),
(2) sight (visus), (3) hearing (auditus). Of the latter class
are (A) taste (gustus), (B) smell (olfactus). All together
they are senses of organic sensation which correspond in
number to the inlets from the outside, provided by nature so that the creature is able to distinguish between
objects.

On the Sense of Touch

§ 17.[97] THE sense of touch lies in the fingertips and
their nerve endings (papillae), and enables us
to discover the form of a solid body by means of contact
with its surface. Nature seems to have endowed man
alone with this organ, so that he is enabled to form a
concept of a body by touching it on all sides. The anten-
nae of insects [155] seem merely to show the presence
of an object; they are not designed to explore its form.
This sense is also the only one of immediate external
perception; therefore, it is the most important and the
most reliably instructive of all senses. Nevertheless, it is

also the clumsiest because the matter whose surface is to
inform us about the shape of the object has to be solid.
(In respect to the vital sensation, we are not now concerned with whether or not the surface is hard or soft,
much less whether or not it feels warm or cold.) Without
this sense organ we would be unable to develop a concept
of any bodily form, and it is to the perceptions of this
sense that the other two senses of the first class[98] must
originally be referred in order to produce empirical
knowledge.

On Hearing

§ 18.[99] THE sense of hearing is one of the senses
of merely indirect perception. Through the
air which surrounds us, and by means of it, a distant
object is perceived to a large extent. Through this
medium, which is set in motion by the mouth, the organ
of speech, people are most easily and completely able to
share their thoughts and feelings with others. This is
particularly true when the sounds intended to be heard
by others are clearly articulated and systematically combined with the understanding into language. The form of
an object is not given through hearing, and sounds of
speech do not lead to a direct idea of what the form is.
Because sounds are nothing in themselves or at any rate
not objects, but merely signs of inner feelings, they are
the best means of expressing concepts. Persons born
deaf, who must therefore remain speechless, can never
arrive at anything more than an analogue of reason.
    Music, as a regular play of auditory sensations, is, so
to speak, a language of mere sensations (devoid of any
concepts). The sense of vitality is not only inspired inde-
scribably and diversely by music, but it is also
strengthened. The sounds are tones, and they are for
hearing what colors are for sight. Music is a communication of feelings in the distance to all present within the

surrounding space, and it is a social pleasure which is not diminished by the fact that many people participate in it.

[156]   On the Sense of Sight

§ 19.[100]   SIGHT is a sense of indirect perception appearing to a certain organ (the eyes) sensitive to agitated matter, namely light, which is not, like sound, just a wavelike disturbance of a fluid element[101] that spreads itself on all sides in surrounding space. Rather, light is an emanation by which the locus of an object in space is determined, and by means of which the structure of the universe becomes known to us to such an immeasurable extent that, especially in the case of the fixed stars, when we compare their distance with our terrestrial standards, we become fatigued with the long row of figures. We have almost more cause to be astonished at the delicate sensitivity of the eye in perceiving such weakened impressions than at the magnitude of the object (the structure of the universe), especially when we look at the universe in detail with the help of the microscope, for example, when we examine infusoria. The sense of sight, while not more indispensable than the sense of hearing, is, nevertheless, the noblest, since, among all the senses, it is farthest removed from the sense of touch, which is the most limited condition of perception. Not only does sight have the greatest radius of perception in space, but it also receives its sense organ as being least involved (because otherwise it would not be mere sight). Consequently, it comes nearer to being a pure intuition (the immediate idea of a given object without admixture of evident sensation).

These three outer senses lead the subject through reflection to cognition of the object as something outside ourselves. When the sensation, however, becomes so strong that the awareness of the activity of the organ becomes stronger than the awareness of the relation to an

external object, then outer perceptions are changed into
inner perceptions. To notice smoothness or roughness in
what we touch is quite different from inquiring about the
shape of an external body. The same holds true when
someone speaks so loud that it hurts the ears, so to speak;
or, when someone blinks his eyes while stepping from a
dark room into the bright sunshine. The latter will be
blind for a few moments because of the strong   [157] and
sudden light; the former will be deaf because of the
shrieking voice. Both persons are unable to attain a concept of the object because of the intensity of the sense
impression; their attention centers only on the subjective
idea, namely, the modification of the organ.

On the Senses of Taste and Smell

§ 20.[102]   THE senses of taste and smell are both more
subjective than objective. The sense of taste
is activated when the organ of the tongue, the gullet, and
the palate come into touch with an external object. The
sense of smell is activated by drawing in air which is
mixed with alien vapors; the body itself from which the
vapors emanate may be distant from the sensory organ.[103] Both senses are closely related, and he who is
deficient in the sense of smell is likewise weak in taste.
Neither of the two senses can lead by itself to the cognition of the object without the help of one of the other
senses; for example,[104] one can say that both are affected
by salts (stable and volatile) of which one must be broken
up by liquefaction in the mouth, the other by air which
has to penetrate the organ, in order to allow its specific
sensation to reach it.

General Remarks Concerning the External Senses

§ 21.[105]   WE may divide the sensations of the external senses into those of mechanical and
those of chemical operation. To the mechanical belong

the three higher senses, to the chemical the two lower senses. The first three senses are those of perception (of the surface), while the other two are senses of pleasure (of innermost sensation). Therefore it happens that nausea, a stimulus to rid oneself of food the quickest way through the gullet by vomiting, is given to man as such a strong vital[106] sensation, since such an internal feeling can be dangerous to the animal.

However, there is also a pleasure of the intellect, consisting in the communication of thought. But when it is forced upon us, the mind finds it repugnant[107] and it ceases to be nutritive as food for the intellect. (A good example of this is the constant repetition of amusing or witty quips, which can become indigestible through sameness.) Thus the natural instinct   [158] to be free of it is by analogy called nausea, although it belongs to the inner sense.

Smell is, so to speak, taste at a distance, and other people are forced to share a scent whether they want to or not. Hence, by interfering with individual freedom, smell is less sociable than taste; when confronted with many dishes and bottles, one can choose that which suits his pleasure without forcing others to participate in that pleasure. Filth seems to awaken nausea less through what is repulsive to eye and tongue than through the stench associated with it. Internal penetration (into the lungs) through smell is even more intimate than through the absorptive vessels of mouth or gullet.

The more strongly the senses themselves feel affected by the intensity of the inflow which comes to them, the less information they provide. On the other hand, if they are expected to yield a great deal of information, they must be affected moderately. In the strongest light we see (distinguish) nothing; and a stentorian, forced voice stupefies (suppresses thought).

The more susceptible to impressions the vital sense (that is, the more delicate and sensitive), the more unfortunate is the man.[108] The more susceptible man is toward the organic sense (the more sensitive), and, on the other hand, the more callous he is toward the vital sense, the more fortunate he is. I say more fortunate, certainly not morally better, for he has the feeling of his own well-being more under control. The capacity for sensation derived from the subject's own power *(sensibilitas sthenica)* may be called delicate sensitivity; that coming from the subject's weakness which cannot adequately withstand the penetration of sense impressions into consciousness, that is, attending to sense impressions against one's will, can be called tender-hearted submission *(sensibilitas asthenica).*[109]

Questions

§ 22.[110]   To which organic sense do we owe the least and which seems to be the most dispensable? The sense of smell. It does not pay us to cultivate it or to refine it in order to gain enjoyment; this sense can pick up more objects of aversion than of pleasure (especially in crowded places) and, besides, the pleasure coming from the sense of smell cannot be other than fleeting and transitory. Yet as a negative condition of well-being, this sense is not unimportant, as, for example, when it warns us not to   [159] breathe noxious air (such as vapor from a stove, or the stench from a swamp or from dead animals), or keeps us from eating rotten food. The second pleasure-sense, the sense of taste, is of similar importance; it has, however, the specific advantage of furthering companionship in eating, something the sense of smell does not do; moreover, taste is superior because by anticipation it judges the benefit of food beforehand, at the very gate of entrance to the alimentary canal. The benefit of food is closely linked with a rather certain prediction of pleasure as long as luxury and indulgence have not overrefined the sense. In the case of people who are ill, the appetite, which is usually of benefit to them and something of a medicine, fails in its function. Smell of food is, so to speak, a foretaste, and to the hungry man it is an invitation to enjoy his favorite food, while the satisfied man is repelled by the same smell.

Is there anything vicarious in the senses, that is, can one sense be used as a substitute for another? There may be. One can evoke by gestures the usual speech from a deaf person, granted that he has once been able to hear. In this, the eyes serve [in place of ears]. The same thing may happen through observing the movements of his teacher's lips, indeed by feeling the movements of the lips of the other person, and this [of course] can occur in darkness [where not sight, but touch, is the substitute for hearing]. If the person is born deaf, however, the sense of seeing the movements of another's organs of speech must convert the sounds, which his teacher has coaxed from him, into a feeling of the movements of his own speech muscles. But he will never attain real concepts, since the signs necessary to him are not capable of universality. The deficiency of a musical ear which can perceive sounds but not tones, or of the person who can speak but not sing, is a handicap hard to explain. There are also people who can see well but who are unable to distinguish colors, people to whom all objects appear like copper engravings.

Which deficiency or loss of sense is more serious, that of hearing or sight? When it is inborn, deficiency of hearing is the least reparable, but if the deficiency only comes later after the use of the eyes is cultivated through observation of gestures, or more directly through reading of script,   [160] then such a loss can be somewhat compensated for by sight, especially if the sufferer is well-to-do. An old man who has become deaf misses this means of social communication very much. We see many blind people who are talkative, companionable, and happy at the table; but it is hard to find someone who has lost his hearing behaving in company other than bored, mistrusting, and dissatisfied. He sees in the faces of his table-companions all kinds of expressions of affection, or at least of interest; he tires himself out trying in vain to understand their meaning; he is condemned to loneliness in the midst of others.

§ 23.[111]   THERE is in the last two senses (which are more subjective than objective) a suscepti-bility to certain objects of external sensations which are merely subjective and operate upon the organs of smell-ing and tasting by a stimulus which is neither smell nor taste. The stimulus is felt like the influence of certain stable salts that incite the organs to specific evacuations. Consequently, these objects are not really enjoyed;[112] nor are they absorbed thoroughly by the organs. They only come into contact with the organs and then they are quickly discarded. They can be used without satiation all day long (except during the time of eating and sleeping). The material most commonly used for this sensation is tobacco, be it in snuffing, or in placing it in the mouth between the cheek and the gums to stimulate the flow of saliva, or in smoking it through pipes, just as Spanish ladies in Lima smoke a lighted cigar. Instead of tobacco the Malayans make use of the areca nut rolled up in a betel leaf *(betel areca),* with the same effect. Apart from any consideration of medical benefit or injury, which may result from the secretion of fluid in the organs of both senses, this craving *(pica)* is, as a mere excitation of the sense-feeling, an oft-repeated stimulus recollecting attention to one's own state of mind, which would other-wise lull to sleep or become boring through sameness and monotony. Instead, those means of stimula-tion   [161] always intensify the feeling of the senses as the doses are administered. This kind of familiarity of a man with himself takes the place of fellowship, because in place of conversation it fills an emptiness of time not with conversation but with continuous newly excited and quickly vanishing sensations that have to be renewed as stimuli time and again.

ON THE INNER SENSE[113]

§ 24.[114] THE inner sense is not pure apperception, a consciousness of what man does, since that belongs to the faculty of thinking. The inner sense is rather a consciousness of what man experiences, as far as he is affected by his own play of thought. It is subject to inner perception, and consequently based on the relation between ideas within time (whether they are simultaneous or successive). The perceptions of the inner sense and the inner experience (veridical or apparent) resulting from the combination of the perceptions cannot be considered as merely anthropological. If they were, it would be a matter of learning whether or not man has a soul (as a special incorporeal substance). Rather, the perceptions of the inner sense are psychological, whereby we believe that we perceive such a sense within ourselves. The mind, which is represented as a mere faculty of feeling and thinking, is regarded as a substance especially resident in man. There is but one inner sense then, because we do not have various organs of inner sensation, and because we might say that the soul is the organ of the inner sense of which it is said that it is subject to delusions which consist in one's taking internal phenomena either for external phenomena, that is, taking imagination for sensation, or even for inspiration[115] prompted by another Being, which is not an object of external sense. Illusion is then fanaticism or visionariness, and both are deceptions of the inner sense. In both instances there is mental illness, which lies in the inclination to accept the play of ideas of the inner sense as empirical knowledge, although it is only fiction,[116] or to deceive ourselves by intuitions which are formed in accordance with such fictions (day dreaming). Such a way of thinking often deludes itself with a pretended frame of mind, possibly because it is thought to be wholesome and superior to the lowliness of sense ideas. Accordingly, that which man has

purposely introduced into his mind he considers as
something that must previously have   [162] been there,
and he believes that he has only uncovered something in
the depths of his soul, which in reality he has forced upon
himself.

This is the way it has been with the fanatical and
inflammatory inner sensations of Bourignon[117] or with
the fanatical and frightening ones of Pascal.[118] This ill
humor of the mind cannot be conveniently removed by
rational ideas (for indeed, what can they do against supposed intuitions?). The inclination to retire into oneself,
together with the consequent delusions of the inner
sense, can only be brought into order if man is returned
to the external world, into the order of the things which
present themselves to external senses.

ON THE CAUSES OF INCREASING
OR DECREASING SENSORY PERCEPTIONS
ACCORDING TO DEGREE[119]

§ 25.[120]   SENSES are increased in degree by means
of 1) contrast,   2) novelty,   3) change,
4) intensification.[121]

a.   Contrast

Contrast [Abstechung] is the juxtaposition, commanding our attention, of mutually opposite sense ideas
under one and the same concept. It is distinguished from
contradiction which consists in the uniting of mutually
clashing notions. A well-cultivated piece of land in a
sandy desert sets off the idea of the cultivation by mere
contrast, like the so-called paradisaical region in the area
of Damascus in Syria. The tranquil, simple, and contented life of a man in the country, a house with a
thatched roof, where you find taste and comfort within,

heightens the perception and we gladly dwell on it because the senses are thereby strengthened, especially if it is contrasted with the din and the glamour of a court, or even of a large city. On the other hand, there is poverty and pride, the splendid adornment of a lady glittering with diamonds, though her linen is soiled; or, as once with a Polish magnate, extravagantly laden tables along with countless waiters in crude footwear. These things do not stand in contrast, but in contradiction [163] in which one sense idea weakens the other because it tries to unite opposites in one and the same concept, which is impossible. One can also make a comical contrast and portray an apparent contradiction in the tone of truth,[122] or something seemingly contemptible can be portrayed in the language of praise in order to make the absurdity more apparent, as Fielding[123] parodies great men in *Jonathan Wild,* or as Blumauer[124] in his travesty parodies Virgil. Also, for example, a writer parodies a heartrending novel like *Clarissa*[125] lightly and with profit, and thus strengthens the senses by freeing them from the conflict which false and harmful concepts have instilled into them.

b. *Novelty*

Through the new, to which also belongs the rare and the hidden, attention is enlivened. What is new stands for an acquisition whereby the sense ideas acquire more power. The everyday routine or the habitual extinguishes the sense idea's strength. However, this does not apply to the discovery, the contact with, or the public exhibition of a work of antiquity, whereby something is rediscovered which was expected to have been destroyed by the force of time during the natural run of things. The senses of the expert are heightened to their utmost attention when he is able to sit upon a piece of masonry of an old Roman theatre (in Verona or Nîmes), or to hold in his hands a piece of household goods of that nation,

brought to light many centuries later from the lava of old
Herculaneum, or when he can show a coin dating from
the time of the Macedonian kings, or a cameo of an
ancient sculpture, and so forth. The inclination to acquire
knowledge merely because of its novelty, rarity, and
inaccessibility is called curiosity. This inclination, despite
the fact that it only plays with ideas and is otherwise
without interest in their object, is not to be criticized
except when it engages in spying on what really is of
interest to others alone. As to the bare sense impression
each morning, through the mere novelty of the sensations it brings, makes all ideas of the senses (as long as
they are not diseased in any way) clearer and livelier than
they generally are toward evening.

[164]   c.   *Change*

Monotony (complete uniformity of sensations) ultimately leads to atony of sensations (lack of attention to
one's condition), so that sense perception is weakened.
Variation freshens sensation just as a sermon read in the
same tone, whether it be shouted out or delivered with
measured yet uniform voice, puts the whole congrega-
tion to sleep. Labor and rest, city and country life, social
discourse and mere play, entertainment in solitude, now
with prose, now with poetry, sometimes with philosophy, and sometimes with mathematics, all these changes
of activity strengthen the mind. The same power of vitality is at work here that arouses the awareness of sensation; but the various organs of the power of vitality
relieve each other in their activity. Thus it is easier to
bear one's weight a limited time in walking, where first
one muscle (of the leg) and then another is at rest, than it
is to remain standing rigid in the same place where one
muscle must work without relief. Therefore travel is so
alluring; it is only regrettable that for idle people it leaves
behind a void (atony) as the consequence of the
monotony of their domestic life.

Nature has so ordered it that even grief creeps in unbidden between pleasant and sensuously agreeable sensations, and thus makes life interesting. But to mix in grief intentionally, for the sake of variation, is absurd, just as it is absurd to hurt oneself, or to have oneself awakened, just to enjoy falling asleep again. Another example of this is Fielding's novel *(The Foundling)* to which an editor, after the author's death, for the sake of variety appended a final part, a wedding (which concludes the story), in order to introduce the element of jealousy. Making a situation worse does not add to the interest which the senses take in it, not even in a tragedy. The end is not open to variation.[126]

d.   *The Increase of Quality Toward Perfection*

A continuous sequence of purposively arranged[127] successive sense ideas, which are different in degree, has, if each of the following ideas is stronger than its predecessor, the attribute of   [165] extreme tension *(intensio);* to approach this extreme is inspiring, while transgressing it is exhausting *(remissio).* However, at a point between the two conditions lies the perfection *(maximum)* of the sensation, which is followed by insensibility and, consequently, lifelessness.

If you want to keep your faculty of the senses alive, you must not begin with strong sensations (because they make us insensitive to subsequent sensations), but rather deny them to yourself and restrain yourself at the very beginning in order to be able gradually to escalate later. The orator in the pulpit begins by way of introduction with a cold instruction of the understanding, which points to the consideration of the concept of duty; then he introduces a moral interest into the interpretation of his text; and then he concludes in the application with an appeal to all motives of the human soul through the sensations which can give emphasis to that particular interest.

Young man! Deny yourself satisfaction[128] (of amusement, of debauchery, of love, etc.), not with the Stoical intention of complete abstinence, but with the refined Epicurean intention of having in view an ever-growing pleasure. This stinginess with the cash of your vital urge makes you definitely richer through the postponement of pleasure, even if you should, for the most part, renounce the indulgence of it until the end of your life. The awareness of having pleasure under your control is, like everything idealistic, more fruitful and more abundant than everything that satisfies the sense through indulgence because it is thereby simultaneously consumed and consequently lost from the aggregate of totality.

ON THE DECREASING, WEAKENING, AND ENTIRE LOSS OF THE FACULTY OF THE SENSES

§ 26.[129] THE faculty of the senses may be either weakened, decreased, or entirely lost. We have such corresponding conditions as drunkenness, sleep, unconsciousness, apparent death (asphyxia), and actual death.

Drunkenness is the unnatural condition of inability to order one's sense ideas according to the laws of experience, as long as the condition is the effect of excessive indulgence in drink.[130]

By verbal definition, sleep is a condition in which   [166] a healthy person is unable to be aware of ideas through external senses. However, to find an explanation of this remains for the physiologists who, if they are able, may explain this exhaustion, which is also a gathering of strength for renewed external sense perception (whereby man considers himself as newborn in the world, and whereby probably a third of our life-span passes unaware and unregretted).[131]

The unnatural condition of numbed sense organs, resulting in a lesser degree of self-awareness than would normally be the case, is an analogue of drunkenness; therefore you might say that one suddenly aroused from sleep is drunk with sleep, because he does not have full control over his awareness. But even when awake, a cessation of the play of sense perceptions can occur when a sudden attack of embarrassment, while trying to decide what to do in an unforeseen situation, results in the stopping of the orderly and ordinary use of one's reflective faculty. In such a case we say, he has lost his composure; he is beside himself (with joy or terror); he is perplexed, nonplussed, and puzzled; he has lost his Tramontano,[132]* and so forth, this condition is to be considered as a sudden falling asleep for the collecting of one's sense impressions. Suddenly affected by strong emotions (of terror, anger, and, indeed, joy) man is, so to speak, beside himself (in an ecstasy when he believes that he is seized by an intuition which is not of the senses), and he has no power over himself; and he is momentarily paralyzed in the use of external senses.

§ 27.[133]   UNCONSCIOUSNESS which usually follows dizziness (a quickly revolving change of many dissimilar sensations beyond comprehension) is a foretaste of death.[134] The complete suspension of all sensation is called asphyxia, or apparent death, which, as far as we can judge externally, may be distinguished from actual death (as in persons drowned, hanged, or suffocated) by its potential return to life.

Nobody can experience his own death (since it requires life   [167] in order to experience); he can only observe it in others. Whether death is painful cannot be judged from the rattling in the throat or the convulsions of the dying person, this seems rather to be a mere

---

* Tramontano, or Tramontana, is the name of the North Star; and *perdere la tramontana* means losing the North Star (as the sailor's guiding star), and figuratively losing one's bearings, being at a loss.

mechanical reaction of the vital power, and perhaps it is a gentle sensation of the gradual release from all suffering. The natural fear of death, entertained even by the most unhappy, or the most wise, is therefore not a fear of dying, but rather, as Montaigne[135] rightly puts it, a fear of having died (that is, of being dead). This is a thought the victim of death expects to entertain after dying, because he thinks of his corpse as himself, though it no longer is, and he thinks of it as lying in a dismal grave, or somewhere else. This deception cannot be removed because it is inherent in the nature of thinking as a way of speaking to oneself and of oneself. The thought, I am not, cannot exist at all; because if I am not, then it cannot occur to me that I am not.[136] I may indeed say that I am not well, and so forth, and negate similar predicates of myself (as happens with all *verba*); but to negate the subject itself when speaking in the first person (thereby destroying itself) is a contradiction.

On Imagination[137]

§ 28.[138]   THE imagination (*facultas imaginandi*), as a faculty of perception without the presence of the object, is either productive, that is, a faculty of the original representation of the object (*exhibitio originaria*), which consequently precedes experience, or it is reproductive, that is, a faculty of the derived representation (*exhibitio derivativa*), which recalls to mind a previous empirical perception. Pure perception of Space and Time belongs to the productive faculty; all the others presuppose empirical perception which, if it is linked with the concept of the object, thus becoming empirical cognition, is called experience. Imagination, as far as it involuntarily produces images, is called fantasy. He who is accustomed to consider these images as (inner or outer) experiences, is a visionary. To become the victim of the involuntary play of one's imagination during sleep (a healthy state) is called dreaming.

Imagination is, in other words, either poetical (pro-

ductive), or merely recollective (reproductive). The productive faculty   [168], however, is nevertheless not creative, because it does not have the power to produce a
sense impression which has never before occurred to our
senses. One can always identify the material which gave
rise to that impression. To one who has never seen red
among the seven colors, we can never explain the sensation of the color red. To one who is born blind, we cannot
make any colors intelligible, least of all a secondary color
such as green, which is derived by mixing two primary
colors, yellow and blue. The imagination, however,
would not have the slightest idea of this color unless one
had seen both colors mixed.

This holds true for each one of the five senses; that
is, the sensations produced by the five senses in their
synthesis cannot be made through the faculty of imagination, but must be drawn originally from the faculty of the
senses. There have been people who could no more than
distinguish between black and white; and for them, although they could see well, the visible world must have
appeared to be engraved on copperplate. And there are
more people than one would suppose who have a good, if
not extremely sensitive, sense of hearing, though, unfortunately, they do not have a musical ear. Their sense of
tone does not permit them to imitate sounds (to sing),
nor does it distinguish mere noise from sound. The same
may apply to the sensations of smell and of taste; they,
too, may be lacking the sensitivity for many a pleasurable
sensation offered by objects; and we may believe that we
understand each other while our sensations may differ
from those of others, not only in degree, but, radically,
also in kind. There are people who lack the sense of smell
entirely; they regard the sensation of drawing pure air
through the nose as the sensation of smell, and consequently they cannot understand any explanation which
tries to describe the sensation of smell to them. But
where the sense of smell is lacking, there is also a lack of
taste. It is futile to explain and describe taste to someone

who does not have this sense. But hunger and its satisfaction (satiation)[139] is something quite different from taste.

Therefore, however great an artist the imagination may be, even if it be a sorceress, it still is not creative, but must gather the material for its images from the senses. But as stated above   [169], the images are not so universally communicable as the concepts of the understanding. We sometimes speak (though only figuratively) of the sensitivity of perception of the imagination as a sense. We say the person has no sense for something; though in not grasping communicated ideas and combining them in thought there is an inability not of sense, but partly of the understanding. He himself speaks without thinking, and therefore others do not understand him; he speaks no sense *(non-sense)*.[140] This is a deficiency that must be distinguished from what is devoid of sense, where thoughts are paired in such a way that another person does not know what to make of it.

The fact that the word "sense" (but only in the singular) is used so often as a synonym for "thought" should indicate that it is of a higher level than that of thinking. Consequently, we have expressions which say that something contains a rich or profound sense (hence the word maxim),[141] and sound human understanding is also called common sense, and is placed on the highest level, although this expression really denotes only the lowest level of the cognitive faculty. All this is based upon the fact that the imagination, which supplies the content of understanding, that is, content to its concepts for the sake of knowledge, seems to give a reality to its invented notions because of the analogy between them and real perceptions.

§ 29.[142]   INTOXICATING food or drink are material means to excite or soothe[143] the imagination.* Some of the food and drink   [170] weaken, as

---

* I do not concern myself here with what is not instrumental to a purpose, but which is rather a natural consequence of a condition into which

poisons, one's vitality (certain mushrooms, wild rose-mary, acanthus, Peruvian chicha, South Sea Islanders' ava, and opium); others strengthen the powers of vitality, or at least arouse them (like fermented beverages, wine and beer, or distilled beverages like brandy); but all of them are unnatural and artificial. He who indulges in them in such excess that he is for a time unable to arrange his sense perceptions according to the laws of experi-ence,[144] is said to be drunk or intoxicated,[145] and getting oneself into such a condition voluntarily or intentionally is described as getting drunk. All these methods, how-ever, are meant to serve the purpose of making man forget the burden which seems to be an integral part of life itself. Such a widespread inclination and its influence on the use of the understanding deserve special con-sideration in a pragmatic anthropology.

All stultifying drunkenness, such as comes from opium or brandy, that is, drunkenness which does not encourage sociability or the exchange of thought, has something shameful about it. Wine and beer provide intoxication for social purposes; wine has simply a stimulating effect, while beer is more nourishing and satisfying like food. There is, however, a characteristic difference. The beer-drinking bout is associated with taciturn fantasies, and frequently with impolite behavior,

---

someone has been placed and whereby his imagination alone disconcerts him. Such instances are dizziness caused by looking down from the edge of something high (possibly also by looking from a narrow bridge without a railing), or seasickness. The board on which a timid man steps would, if it were resting on the ground, cause no fear; however, if it is placed across a deep precipice as a bridge, then the thought of the mere possibility of tripping is so powerful that the person attempting to cross over is really in danger. Seasickness (which I myself experienced on a trip from Pillau to Königsberg, if it is permissible to refer to it as a sea voyage), affected me with nausea and, as I think I have observed, was brought about merely by my eyes, because the rolling of the ship, as seen from the cabin, allowed me to see sometimes the bay, and sometimes the heights of Balga, so that the recurrent falling after the rising of the ship provoked, by means of the imagination, an antiperistaltic movement in the muscles of my stomach.

whereas a wine-party is merry, boisterous, and teeming with wit.

Excessive[146] social drinking that leads to the befogging of the senses is by no means becoming to a man, not only with respect to the company with whom he enjoys himself, but also from the standpoint of self-esteem, particularly when a man leaves the company staggering, or at least with an unsure step, or merely babbling. But much can be said for tempering our judgment at such an indiscretion, since the border line of self-control can be so easily overlooked and overstepped. It must be remembered that the host desires that the guest depart from the house entirely satisfied *(ut conviva satur)*[147] with his hospitality.

Freedom from care, along with heedlessness caused by intoxication, is a deceptive feeling or increased vitality. In such a state the intoxicated man is not aware of the obstacles of life, even though his nature requires him to overcome them constantly (in which also exists his well-being), and he is happy in his weakness[148] in view of the fact that Nature is actually working in him to renew his conscious life   [171] by gradually rebuilding his strength. Women, clergymen, and Jews[149] ordinarily do not become drunk, at least they carefully avoid all appearance of it, because they are weak in civic life and must restrain themselves (for which sobriety is required). Their external value depends simply on other people's belief in their chastity, piety, and their separatistic character.[150] Because, as far as the Jews are concerned, all separatists, that is, such as submit not only to a general law of the state, but also to a particular law (of their own sect), are, as foreign elements and as pretended elected ones, particularly exposed to the attention of the community and to harsh criticism. Hence they cannot relax their self-attention because intoxication, which removes heedfulness, is to them scandalous.

A Stoic admirer of Cato said: "his virtue was strengthened by wine" *(virtus eius incaluit mero);*[151] and a modern German says about the Teutons: "They formed their councils (to wage war) at a drinking-bout, so that the decisions would be passionate; and, when they were sober, they reconsidered their decisions, so that they might not be wanting in intelligence."[152]

Drink loosens the tongue *(in vino disertus)*.[153] But it also opens the heart wide, and it is a vehicle instrumental to a moral quality, that is, openheartedness. Restraining one's thoughts[154] is an oppressive state for a sincere person, and merry drinkers do not readily tolerate an overly reserved drinker because he is an observer who notices the faults of others while he keeps his own under control. Also Hume says: "I hate a drinking companion who never forgets. The follies of the last debauch must be buried in eternal oblivion, in order to give full scope to the follies of the next."[155] Good-naturedness is presupposed when this license is granted to a man to cross the boundary line of sobriety for a short time, for the sake of sociability. Half a century ago a fraudulent policy was used by the Nordic courts when they sent delegates who could drink much without getting drunk themselves; they made others drunk in order to extract information from them or to persuade them. This practice, however, has disappeared along with the crudity of the customs of those times; to issue a warning against this corruption would be superfluous in view of the morally improved conditions of the present day.

There is also a question whether the temperament or the character of a person can be investigated when the person gets drunk. I do not think so.   [172] A new fluid has been mixed with the fluid which flows in his veins; the nerves are stimulated in a different manner so that the natural temperature is no longer clearly revealed, but is replaced by another. Consequently, one person who gets drunk is amorous, another becomes vainglorious, a third becomes quarrelsome, a fourth (especially when drinking beer) is tenderhearted, or sanctimonious, or silent altogether. But when they have all slept off their stupor, and when they have been reminded of their talk during the past evening, they all laugh at the strange or ill humor of their senses.

§ 30.[156]   ORIGINALITY (nonimitative production) of the imagination is called genius when it harmonizes with notions. If originality does not harmonize with notions, then it is called fanaticism. It is noteworthy that we cannot imagine another suitable form for a rational being than the form of man. Every other form would represent only a symbol of a certain human quality, for example, the serpent as the image of malicious cunning, but it would not represent the rational being itself. Therefore our imagination populates all other planets with nothing but human forms although it is probable that they may be formed very differently because of the diversity of soil which supports and nourishes them and because of the variety of the elements of which they are composed. All other forms which we might give them are caricatures.*

When the lack of a sense (for example, sight) is inborn, then the handicapped person will try to compensate for the missing sense with another sense, and the productive faculty of the imagination will be used to a high degree. He will try to explore the forms of external bodies through the sense of touch, and, where this sense does not suffice on account of magnitude (for example, of a house), he tries to grasp the spaciousness through still another sense, possibly through hearing, that is, through the echo of a voice in the room. If finally, however, a successful operation allows the organ   [173] to

---

*   Therefore the Trinity, an old man, a young man, and a bird (the dove), must be understood not as actual forms which resemble their objects, but rather as mere symbols. Pictorial expressions of the descent from heaven and the ascension to heaven are just such symbolic expressions. We cannot proceed in any other way; we have to anthropomorphize if we want to provide our notions of rational being with illustration. It is, however, unfortunate and childish if, as a consequence, the symbolic representation becomes the notion for the object as such.

receive a sensation, then he must first of all learn to see and hear, that is, he has to associate his notions with the perceptions received from the objects.

Concepts of objects often induce us to give them a form of our own making (created by the productive faculty of imagination). When one reads or hears of the life and deeds of a man who is great by virtue of his talent, merit, or rank, then one is generally misled in ascribing considerable stature to him in the imagination, whereas one ascribes a paltry, flexible stature to someone who is described as having a sensitive and gentle character. Not only the peasant, but also someone fairly well acquainted with the ways of the world, feels strange when the hero, whose appearance had been judged by the deeds sung of him, presents himself as a little fellow, and when the sensitive and gentle Hume presents himself as a square-built fellow. Therefore we must not raise our hopes too high in anticipation of anything, because the imagination naturally inclines toward the highest expectation, for actuality is always more limited than the idea that serves as a pattern for realization.

It is not advisable to praise a person too highly in advance when we wish to introduce him to others for the first time; it might rather be a malicious trick on the part of a rogue to make a person seem ridiculous. The imagination raises the idea of what is anticipated so high that the victim can only suffer. This is just what happens when a book, a drama, or anything else belonging to the gracious life is announced with exaggerated praise; when we do come to know it, it can only be disappointing to us. Merely having read a good drama weakens the impression when we see it enacted. But if what was praised in advance turns out to be just the opposite of what we were led to anticipate, then the object portrayed, provided it is otherwise innocuous, arouses the greatest laughter.[157]

Variable forms, which of themselves really have no meaning that might excite attention, when set in motion, like the flickering of an open fire or the twisting and babbling of a brook flowing over stones, fill the imagination with a host of ideas of an entirely   [174] different sort (from that of sight), namely, to play in the mind and to be absorbed in meditation. Even music, for one who does not listen as a connoisseur, can throw a poet or a philosopher into a mood in which, depending on his vocation or avocation, he can capture thoughts as well as master them; yet if he were sitting alone in his room, he would not be able to grasp them so readily. The reason for this phenomenon seems to be the following: when, through a manifold that of itself can excite no attention, the sense is distracted by some other object that strikes it more forcibly, thinking is not only facilitated but also enlivened in so far as it needs a more concentrated and enduring faculty of imagination to give substance to its ideas. The English *Spectator*[158] reports the tale of a barrister who, when pleading, was in the habit of taking a thread from his pocket which he incessantly twisted and unwound on his finger. Then one day, when his opponent, a rogue, secretly removed the thread from his pocket, the barrister was completely at a loss and spoke nothing but nonsense. Therefore one says, "He has lost the thread of his discourse."[159] The sense which is concentrated on one sensation (because of acquired habit) does not react to other sensations, and therefore is not diverted; but the faculty of imagination in this way may be better maintained in its regular course.

ON THE SENSORY PRODUCTIVE FACULTY WITH ALL ITS BRANCHES

§ 31.[160]   THERE are three distinct varieties of the sensory productive faculty. These are the pictorial perception in space *(imaginatio plastica)*, the associative perception in time *(imaginatio associans)*, and the sensory productive faculty of affinity based on the shared lineage of ideas from each other *(affinitas)*.[161]

a.   On the Pictorial Sensory Productive Faculty

Before the artist can depict a corporeal form (palpably, so to speak), he must have prepared it in his imagination. This   [175] form is an invention which, when involuntary (as perhaps in a dream), is called fantasy and is not to be associated with the artist; but if it is voluntary, it is called composition or discovery. If the artist bases his work on images resembling objects of nature, his productions are called natural.[162] But if he bases his work on images which cannot have any existence in experience, then the created products (like the palace of the Prince Palagonia in Sicily)[163] are called fantastic, unnatural, or caricatures. Such flashes of imagination are like[164] daydreams (*velut aegri somnia vanae finguntur species*).[165] We play with the imagination frequently and gladly, but (as fantasy) the imagination just as often plays with us, sometimes very inconveniently.

The play of fantasy in a sleeping person is called a dream, which occurs even in a healthy condition. On the other hand, dreaming betrays a morbid state when it happens during waking hours. Sleep, as detachment from every faculty of external perception and, especially, from voluntary motions, seems to be required by all animals, and even by plants (by the analogy of plants to animals) for the recovery of forces spent during waking hours. But the same thing seems also to be the case with dreaming: the vitality would be extinguished if it were not always kept active in sleep by means of dreams, and the deepest sleep would bring death along with it. When we say that we have had a good sleep without dreaming, we are indeed saying nothing more than that we remember no dreams upon awakening. In view of the rapid changes of the imagination, this could happen just as well in waking hours when we are gazing steadily at a fixed point in a state of distraction. If the person is asked what he is thinking at this moment, the reply will be: "I have been thinking nothing at all." If upon awakening there were not many gaps in our memory (caused by inattention to interconnecting perceptions), and if the next night we would begin to dream just where we had left off the night before, then I do not know whether we would not imagine that we were living in two different worlds. Dreaming is a wise provision of Nature for exciting vitality through emotions which have been caused by involuntarily invented events, while muscular movements, depending on volition, are in the meantime suspended.   [176] But we must not take the content of dreams to be revelations from an invisible world.

b. On the Associative Sensory Productive Faculty

The law of association is that empirical perceptions, which frequently follow one another, create an acquired habit in the mind, so that when one perception is engendered, the associated one also arises.[166] It is futile to demand[167] a physiological explanation of this phenomenon. We may use whatever[168] serves as an hypothesis (which itself is again a fabrication), like Descartes' hypothesis of his so-called material ideas of the mind.[169] At least any such explanation would not be pragmatic, that is, we cannot use it for any technical purpose, for we have no knowledge of the brain, nor of the sections of the brain in which the traces of impressions derived from perceptions might harmonize sympathetically with each other, so far as the parts are in at least indirect contact.

This association often extends very far, and the imagination frequently runs from hundreds into thousands so rapidly that it seems we have completely skipped certain links in the chain of perceptions, although we are merely not conscious of them.[170] Consequently, more often than not, we must ask ourselves: "Where am I? From what point did I begin my conversation? How did I arrive at this conclusion?"*

c.   On the Sensory Productive Faculty of Affinity

By affinity I understand the union established by the derivation of the manifold from a single foundation. What interrupts and destroys social   [177] conversation is the jumping from a given subject to one of a quite different sort. In this case the empirical association of perceptions is only subjective; that is, one person associates perceptions differently from another, and such association is misleading and, with respect to form, a kind of nonsense. Only when a subject has been exhausted and there is a short pause, can one introduce another subject of interest. Irregular, roaming imagination confuses the mind through the changing reference to different perceptions that are linked to nothing objective, so that he who departs from a company of this sort feels as though he has been dreaming. There must always be a theme according to which the manifold is ordered, not only with silent thinking, but with the sharing of thoughts; and, consequently, the understanding must also be at work at the same time. Nevertheless, here the play of the imagination follows the rules of sensibility, which provides the material whose association is achieved without consciousness of the rule, consonant with the understanding but not derived from it.

The word affinity (*affinitas*) here reminds one of a catalytic interaction found in chemistry, an interaction analogous to an intellectual combination, which links two elements specifically distinct from each other, but inti-

---

*   He who enters upon a social discourse must, therefore, begin with what is present and near at hand, and thus gradually lead to what is more remote as long as it can be of any interest. Thus, a good and common subject is the bad weather for a person who walks from the street into a group assembled for mutual conversation. If, upon entering a room, one begins to speak of the latest news from Turkey currently appearing in the papers, then the imagination of others would be struck too forcibly, since they would not understand what has led him to speak of it. The mind demands a certain order in the communication of thoughts, and much depends on the general circumstances and the opening statement, not only in conversation, but also in a sermon.

mately affecting each other and striving for unity with each other, whereby the combination creates a third entity that has properties which can only be brought about by the union of two heterogeneous elements.

Despite their dissimilarity, understanding and sensibility by themselves form a close union for bringing about our cognition, as though one were begotten by the other, or as though both had a common origin, which is impossible; at least we cannot conceive how things so dissimilar could have sprung from one and the same source.*

§ 32.[171]   [178]   THE imagination is not so creative as one would like to believe. We cannot think of any other form that would be suitable for a rational being than the form of a human being. For this reason the sculptor or painter always depicts a man when he represents an angel or a god. Every other figure seems to have members which, according to his idea, do not befit the structure of a rational being (like wings, talons, hooves). On the other hand, he can make things as large as he wishes.

Deception caused by the strength of the human imagination often goes so far that one believes he sees and feels, as outside himself, something that exists only in his head. Therefore, the person who looks into an abyss is overcome by dizziness even though he has a broad surface around him to prevent his falling, or perhaps even leans against a strong railing. Strange is the fear of certain mentally sick people that they will have an

---

*   The first two kinds of composition of perceptions could be called mathematical (of enlargement), but the third would be called dynamic (of production), whereby an entirely new entity arises (somewhat like a chemical compound). The play of powers in inanimate Nature, as well as in the animate, in the soul as well as in the body, is based on separating and uniting the dissimilar. We reach cognition of the play of powers by experiencing the effects; the ultimate cause and the most basic ingredients into which their substance can be analyzed, cannot be found by us. What is the reason for the fact that all known organic beings are propagated through the union of the

inner impulse willfully to cast themselves down from a high place. The sight of others enjoying loathsome things (for example, when the Tunguses suck out and gulp down the mucus from their children's noses) causes the witness to vomit, just as if such a pleasure were forced on him.

The homesickness of the Swiss (and, as I have it from the lips of an experienced general, also of the Westphalians and the Pomeranians from certain areas), which befalls them when they are transferred to other lands, is the result of a longing that is aroused by the recollection of a carefree life and neighborly company in their youth, a longing for the places where they enjoyed the very simple pleasures of life. Later, when they visit these places, they they find their anticipation dampened and even their homesickness [179] cured. They think that everything has drastically changed, but it is that they cannot bring back their youth. It is remarkable that such homesickness befalls peasants of a penniless province, where there are strong family ties, and it strikes them more deeply than it does those who are busy earning money and who take for their motto: *Patria ubi bene.*[172]

If we have heard that this or that person is a bad man, we believe we can read malice in his face. Here invention mingles with the experience of a single sensation, especially when emotion and passion are added. According to Helvétius,[173] a lady looked through a telescope and saw in the moon the shadows of two lovers; the clergyman, who subsequently made the observation, said: "Not exactly, Madam; they are two belfries of a cathedral."

One can add to all this the sympathetic workings of

---

two sexes (which we call male and female)? We cannot very well assume that the Creator was merely amusing himself out of eccentricity and just making on this earth-globe [MS, Cassirer: globe—Ed.] an arrangement that pleased him. Rather, it seems impossible that organic creatures can originate from the matter of this earth in any other way than through the existence of the two sexes established for this purpose. In what obscurity does the human reason lose itself when it seeks to establish the reason for our lineage, or when it only tries to make a guess at it?

the imagination. The sight of a person in a convulsive or epileptic attack incites us to similar convulsive movements. The same is true when someone yawns, and we are induced to yawn with him. The physician Michaelis[174] reports the case of a soldier in the army in North America, who fell into a violent delirium, and two or three bystanders were suddenly thrown into the same frenzy upon seeing him, although it was just a passing attack. It is not advisable, therefore, for neurotic people (hypochondriacs) to visit madhouses just for the sake of curiosity. For the most part, they shun them of their own accord because they fear for their saneness. We also find that when someone explains something emotional to vivacious people, especially something that may have occurred to him[175] causing anger, their attention is so aroused that they make faces and involuntarily engage in a play of features appropriate to the emotion. We might also have noticed that on occasion married people gradually acquire[176] similarity of features, and it is explained that this is due to the fact that they were married on account of the similarity *(similis simili gaudet).*[177] But this is false. For Nature instead strives by the instinct of the sexes for the diversity of the subjects so that they fall in love with each other and develop all the variety which Nature has implanted in them. Instead, it is the intimacy and the inclination with which they often look into each other's eyes when they are close to each other in solitary conversations that produces sympathetic [180] and similar countenances which, upon becoming fixed, finally pass into permanent features.

Finally, the inclination to tell harmless lies can be referred to the unintentional play of the productive imagination, something which may be called fantasy. This inclination is invariably to be met with in children, now and then in adults who are otherwise well-disposed, and at times it is almost a hereditary disease. Events and pretended adventures, that are narrated, issue from the imagination like a descending avalanche of snow, although the person telling the tale has nothing to gain except to be interesting. Such a case is Shakespeare's Sir John Falstaff[178] who made two buckram-clad men into five men before he had completed his tale.

§ 33.[179] IMAGINATION is richer and more fertile with ideas than sense is, and the imagination becomes, if coupled with passion, more lively when the object is absent than when it is present. This is evident when something happens which calls the idea of an object to mind which for a time seemed to be extinguished by distracting influences. Once a German prince,[180] a rugged warrior, though a nobleman, took a journey to Italy to banish from his mind his love for a peasant girl on his estate. But, upon his return, the first glimpse of her dwelling awakened his imagination so much more intensely than continuous association would have done that he yielded to his resolution without further delay, which, fortunately, was what was expected. This malady, the result of an inventive imagination, is incurable except through marriage, which reflects truth (*eripitur persona, manet res*— LUCRETIUS).[181]

The inventive imagination causes a kind of association with ourselves, which, though it may be merely phenomena of the inner sense, is nevertheless analogous to the outer sense. The night enlivens it and raises it above its real values, just as the moon in the evening cuts a great figure in the heavens, though on a bright day it merely looks like an insignificant little cloud. Imagination flourishes in one who works intellectually in the stillness of the night, or who quarrels with an imaginary opponent, or builds castles in the air as he walks about his chamber. But everything that then seemed important loses its significance in the morning after a night's sleep. Yet in the course of time this bad habit [181] causes a weakening of mental powers. Therefore, the taming of one's imagination, by going to sleep early in order to rise early, is a very useful rule for the psychological diet.

Certain females, however, and hypochondriacs (who commonly have their ailment for just this reason) prefer the opposite type of conduct. Why are ghost stories, which are welcomed late at night, distasteful to us and not appropriate for conversation as soon as we arise in the morning? At that time we ask instead: "What has been happening in the house and in the world?" or else we continue our work of the preceding day. The reason for this is that what is in itself nothing but play is suitable for the relaxation of powers expended during the day, but what is business is suitable for a man strengthened as well as reborn, as it were, through a good night's rest.

The faults (*vitia*) of the imagination are that its inventions are either unbridled or unruly (*effrenis aut perversa*). The unruly invention is the worst kind. Unbridled inventions can find their place in a possible world (that of fable), but unruly inventions cannot find their place in any world because they are self-contradictory. A fault of the first type, that is, of unbridled imagination, is illustrated by the Arabs who look with horror at the hewn forms of men and animals frequently encountered in the Libyan Desert, Ras-Sem.[182] They consider them to be real men turned into stone by a curse. It is, however, a contradiction when the same Arabs say that these statues of animals, on the day of the general resurrection, will snarl at the sculptor with the reproach that, though he made them, he was unable to give them souls. Unbridled fantasy can still be checked (like the fantasy of that poet[183] who was asked by Cardinal Este on the occasion of the presentation of a book dedicated to him, "Maestro Ariosto, where the devil did you get all this rubbish?"). Unbridled fantasy has an embarrassment of riches, but unruly fantasy approaches madness where it has won control over the man so that the unfortunate fellow cannot regulate the course of his ideas.

Furthermore, a political artist, just as well as an aesthetic artist, can guide and rule the world (*mundus vult decipi*)[184] by imagination if he knows how to make a false show of reality, for example, of freedom of a people (like that in the English Parliament), or of rank and equality (as in the French Convention), which consist in mere formalities. [182] Nevertheless, it is better to have for yourself only the appearance of possessing this gift that ennobles humanity than to feel yourself simply bereft of it.

OF THE FACULTY OF VISUALIZING THE PAST AND THE FUTURE BY MEANS OF THE IMAGINATION

§ 34.[185] THE faculty of visualizing the past intentionally is the faculty of memory; and the faculty of visualizing something as future is the faculty of foreseeing. So far as they are sensible, both are based upon the association of ideas of the past and future condition of the subject with the present; and although they are not themselves perceptions, yet as a linking-together of perceptions in time, they serve to connect in a coherent experience what is no more with what does not yet exist, by means of what is present. They are called the faculty of memory and the faculty of divination, of respicience and prospicience (if the use of such terms may be allowed), where one is conscious of one's ideas as those which could be encountered in past or future situations.

a.   Of Memory

Memory differs from the merely reproductive imagination in that it is able to reproduce the former ideas voluntarily, for the mind is not a mere play of imagination. Fantasy, that is, the creative imagination, must not be interwoven with it, because then the memory would be unreliable. To grasp something in memory, to reflect on it easily, and to retain it for long, these constitute the formal perfections of memory. But these properties are seldom found together. If someone believes he has something in his memory but cannot bring it into consciousness, he says he cannot recall it (not to be able to recall means much the same as declaring oneself senseless). The effort to recall, if one should strive to do so, is mentally fatiguing, and one does well to distract oneself for a while by other thoughts, and then from time to [183] time look back to the object for a moment. Then one ordinarily catches one of the associated ideas which will bring it back.

To grasp something in the memory methodically *(memoriae mandare)* is called memorizing (not *studying,* as the common man says of the preacher who merely learns by heart the sermon that he intends to deliver). Memorizing may be mechanical, ingenious, or judicious. The first depends simply on frequent and literal repetition, for example, in learning the multiplication table, when learners must go through a whole sequence of numbers following each other in the usual order, for the sake of reaching what is desired. For instance, when the beginner is asked: "How much are three times seven?" he begins with three times three, and continues until he reaches twenty-one; but if you ask him: "How much are seven times three?" he will not immediately remember, but must reverse the numbers, so as to place them in the usual order. If what is memorized is a sacred formula in which no expression is to be altered, but which must be reeled off correctly, then people with even the best memory are afraid to depend on it (in fact this fear itself could make them err). Therefore, they consider it necessary to read it off, as the most experienced preachers do, because the least alteration of words would be ridiculous.

Ingenious memorizing is a method of imprinting certain ideas on the memory by association with correlative ideas, which of themselves (as far as understanding is concerned) have no relationship with each other, for example, sounds of a language which are supposed to correspond to images that are wholly dissimilar. In this case, in order to fix something in the memory more easily, we encumber ourselves with still more correlative associations. Consequently, as a procedure of the unruly imagination,[186] the pairing of two ideas which cannot go together, under one and the same concept, is absurd. At the same time, it is also a contradiction between the means and the intention, since one tries to ease the burden on the memory, but the means chosen to do so make the burden heavier by unnecessarily loading it with associations of quite disparate ideas.* The observation that wags seldom have a reliable memory [184] *(ingeniosis non admodum fida est memoria)*[187] is explained by this phenomenon.

Judicious memorizing is nothing but using a table for the classification of a system of thought (for example, that of Linnaeus)[188] wherein, if one should have forgotten anything, he can duly recover it by enumerating the links which he has retained; or else by remembering the sections of a once visibly arranged whole (for example, the provinces of a country on a map, which lie to the north, to the west, etc.), for here we need understanding, and understanding is reciprocally helpful to the imagination. Most of all, the judicious use of the topic, that is, a framework for general concepts, called commonplaces,[189] facilitates remembering through class division, as when we distribute books on properly labeled shelves.

There is no mnemonic art *(ars mnemonica)* for general learning. Among the special tricks of this kind are

---

* The picture book, like the pictorial Bible, or indeed one of the illustrated compendiums of law, is a visual treasure chest for the childish teacher, so that he can make his pupils still more childish than they were before. As an example for such a manner of teaching, the titles of the compendium of law contain the most appropriate words *"de heredibus suis et legitimis"* [we have learned from our heritage, and only the legitimate heritage—Ed.]. The word *heritage* has been concretized by a box with a padlock, the word *our* by a sow, and the word *legitimate* by the two tablets of Moses.

aphorisms in verse *(versus memoriales)*, where the rhythm
has a regular stress that helps the mechanism of memory.
One must not speak disdainfully of the prodigies of
memory, Pico della Mirandola,[190] Scaliger,[191] Angelo
Politian,[192] Magliabechi,[193] and others, those polyhisto-
rians who carry material[194] for the sciences in their heads
that would load a hundred camels with books. We must
not scorn them even though they do not possess the
faculty of judgment suitable for sifting all this knowledge
for practical use. It is meritorious enough to have produced raw material abundantly, even though other heads
must employ themselves later in order to process it with
judgment *(tantum scimus, quantum memoria tenemus)*.[195]
One of the ancients said: "The art of writing has ruined
memory (and made it partly superfluous)."[196] There is
some truth in this sentence, since the common man
usually has better control of the many things that are
thrust upon him, and can devote his attention to one
thing after another and, when he has time, to think about
it, because in so doing memory is mechanical,   [185] and
there is no subtlety involved. On the other hand, the
learned man, whose mind holds many different thoughts
at once, is likely to be distracted from his obligations or
domestic affairs, because he has not paid sufficient attention to them. But, to be sure, the pocket notebook is a
great convenience in which to write everything stored in
our head and to find it easily and exactly. The art of
writing always remains a splendid art, because, even if it
is not used to impart knowledge to others, it will still
substitute for the most extensive and reliable memory,
and can compensate for the lack of it.

A greater evil is forgetfulness *(obliviositas)*, where
the head, no matter how often it is filled, always remains
as empty as a barrel with holes in it. This reproach is
sometimes undeserved, as in the case of old people who
can easily recall events of earlier years although they
constantly fail in reference to more recent events.
Forgetfulness is often caused by habitual distraction,

which particularly affects ladies who read novels. In this type of reading the lady aims only at entertaining herself for the moment. She knows that what she is reading is only fiction, and she has complete freedom in letting her imagination run its own course, something which is naturally distracting and which makes for habitual absent-mindedness (lack of attention to the present). The inevitable result is a weakening of memory. This practice of killing time and making oneself useless to the world, while later complaining of the brevity of life, is one of the deadliest attacks on the memory, aside from the fantastic frame of mind which also results from it.

b.   On the Faculty of Foreseeing (*praevisio*)

§ 35.[197]   To possess this faculty is of greater interest than anything else because it is the condition of all possible practice and all possible purposes to which man relates the use of his powers. All desire contains (doubtful or certain) anticipation of what is possible [186] through foresight. Recalling the past (remembering) occurs only with the intention of making it possible to foresee the future; we look about us from the standpoint of the present in order to determine something, or to be prepared for something.

Empirical foreseeing is the anticipation of similar cases (*exspectatio casuum similium*) and requires no knowledge of causes and effects, but only the remembering of observed events, as they usually follow upon each other. Repeated experiences help to develop skill in empirical anticipation. What the wind and weather will be is of interest to the navigator and to the farmer. But in this respect we do not reach much farther than the so-called Farmer's Almanac, whose predictions are praised when they come true, and are forgotten if they do not materialize; thus predictions always receive a certain amount of credit. We could almost believe that Providence has intentionally interwoven the capriciousness of all sorts of weather so inscrutably that it is not easy for men to make necessary arrangements for every occasion, but rather they need to use their understanding in order to be prepared for whatever might happen.

Living carelessly (without foresight and care) does not give much credit to a man's understanding; it is like the Carib[198] who sells his sleeping-mat in the morning, and in the evening is perplexed because he does not know where he will sleep during the night. But as long as no offense against morality is incurred, we may consider him who is hardened to all sorts of events as a happier man than the one who takes all the joy out of living by looking only on the bleak side of life. Among all the prospects which man can have, the most comforting is, on the basis of his present moral condition, to look forward to something permanent and to further progress toward a still better prospect. On the other hand, if he courageously decides from now on to enter upon a new and better way of life, he must often say to himself: "Nothing good will come of it anyway. I have frequently (because of procrastination) given this promise, but I have always broken it under the pretext of making an exception just this once." Thus the expectation of similar cases makes the prospect rather bleak.

However, when what may hover over us depends upon fate, rather than upon the use of our free will, looking into [187] the future is either presentiment, that is, foreboding[199] (praesensio)* or expectation (praesagitio). Presentiment likewise signifies an occult sense for what is not yet present. Expectation signifies a consciousness of the future through reflection upon the law of the sequence of events (the law of causality).

* There has recently been a desire to distinguish between the words *ahnen* and *ahnden,* but *ahnen* is not a German word, therefore, we have to consider only the latter. *Ahnden* is equivalent to "keep something in mind." Used with the dative it means that something presents itself vaguely to my mind. Used with the accusative it means to remember someone's deed with malicious intention (that is, to punish). It is always the same notion only used in different ways.

We readily see that all presentiment is a chimera; for how can we be aware of what does not exist? If there are judgments arising from obscure concepts of such a causal relation, then they are not presentiments. On the contrary, we can develop concepts which lead to a causal relation, and we can explain how a causal relation belongs to judgment so conceived. Presentiments, for the most part, are of the fearful sort. Anxiety, which has physical causes, takes the lead with vagueness as to what the object of fear is. Yet there are also gay and bold presentiments of enthusiasts who scent the imminent revelation of a mystery even though the human being has not been given such a receptivity of the senses, and the epoptae[200] believe that they see the unveiling of what they are expecting in mystical intuition. The second sight of the Scottish Highlanders also belongs to this type of marvel. It is a vision wherein some among them believe they see a man tied to a mast, the news of whose death they claim to have received before the mail could have reached them.

c.   On the Gift of Divination *(facultas divinatrix)*

§ 36.[201]   PREDICTING, fortune-telling, and prophesying can be distinguished as: the first is foreseeing according to the laws of experience (therefore it is natural); the second is contrary to the well-known laws of Nature (therefore unnatural); the third, however, is inspired by a cause that is distinct from Nature (therefore supernatural), or at least so considered. This ability [188] seems to originate from the influence of a god and is also properly called the faculty of divination (whereas every shrewd guess about the future is improperly called divination also).

To say about someone that he is able to foretell this or that fate may indicate a wholly natural skill. But of one who pretends to a supernatural insight we must say that he is a specious soothsayer, like the gypsies of Hindu descent, who call fortune-telling from the palm of the hand reading the planets; or[202] like the astrologers, treasure hunters, and the alchemists, who all were outshone in Greek antiquity by Pythia [priestess of the Delphic oracle], and in our day by the ragged Siberian Shaman. The soothsayings of the auspices and haruspices of the Romans did not purport to discover what is hidden in the course of the world's events so much as to discover the will of the gods to whom they had joined themselves in accordance with their regligion. But how the poets came to consider themselves also as inspired (or possessed), and as speaking the truth (*vates*), and how they could claim to have during their poetical impulses (*furor poeticus*) any intuition, can only be explained by the fact that the poet, unlike the prose-orator who prepares his ordered speech well in advance and with plenty of leisure, has to snatch the favorable moment of his inner mood as it comes over him with its lively and powerful imagery and feeling, while he behaves as if he were only passive. An old saying explains this by claiming that genius is mixed with a certain amount of madness. The belief in oracular utterances is also based on this observation when passages from the works of famous poets (who are believed to have been inspired) are chosen at random (*sortes Virgilianae*);[203] or when a means similar to the treasure-chest of the more modern Pietists is used to uncover the hidden will of heaven; or when the interpretation of the Sibylline Books is concerned, which, it is said, should have foretold for the Romans the destiny of their state. Alas, they lost parts of[204] them because of their misapplied niggardliness.

All prophecies which foretell an inevitable fate of a nation, that is to befall the nation by its own fault and, consequently, which is to be brought about by its own free will, have in themselves (besides the fact that such knowledge is useless since it cannot be avoided) the absurdity that in this unconditional fate (*decretum*   [189] *absolutum)* there is thought to be a mechanism of freedom, the concept of which is self-contradictory.

The ultimate of absurdity, or of fraud, in soothsaying may be that a madman has been considered a seer (of invisible things), as if[205] a spirit spoke in him which acted as a substitute for the soul, already long departed from the body. And so the mentally ill (and epileptic as well) passed for an *Energumen* (one possessed), and he was called a *Mantis* by the Greeks if the possessing demon was considered a good spirit. The interpreter of the *Mantis,* however, was called a prophet. All foolishness must be exploited so that we can take possession of the future, the foreseeing of which interests us greatly, by skipping all the steps that might lead us there by means of the understanding through experience. *O, curas hominum!*[206]

Moreover, there is no science of soothsaying so certain and so far-reaching as astronomy, which foretells the revolutions of the heavenly bodies, even to infinity. This, however, could not curtail a mysticism which instead of making the numbers of historical epochs dependent upon certain events, as reason requires, wanted, on the contrary, to make events dependent upon certain sacred[207] numbers, thereby turning chronology itself, so necessary a condition of all history, into a fable.

ON INVOLUNTARY INVENTION IN A SOUND MENTAL STATE, THAT IS, ON DREAMS

§ 37.[208]   THE investigation of the natural constitution of sleep, dreams, and somnambulism (under which we may include talking aloud during sleep) lies outside the field of a pragmatic anthropology, because we are unable to deduct from these phenomena any rules[209] of conduct in the state of dreaming, since rules are valid only for people who are awake and do not wish to dream, or[210] who want to sleep without being disturbed by dreams.[211] The Greek emperor who condemned to death a man who related to his friends a dream in which he had killed the emperor, under the pretext that "the man would not have had such a dream unless he were planning it in his waking hours," is   [190] guilty of a judgment both cruel and contrary to experience. "When we are awake, we enjoy a common world; but, when we are asleep, every man enjoys his own world." Dreaming seems to belong so necessarily to sleeping that sleeping and dying would be just the same thing, if the dream were not added as a natural, though involuntary, agitation of the inner vital organs by means of the imagination. Thus I remember well that, as a boy, when I went to sleep tired from playing, I would suddenly awaken at the moment of falling asleep, because of a dream that I had fallen into the water, being turned around and around, and was on the point of sinking, and I would quickly awaken only to fall asleep again more peacefully. This was probably caused by the reduction of the breathing activity of the chest muscles, which is completely dependent on the autonomic system, and consequently, with the reduction of breathing, the action of the heart is impeded so that the imagination of the dream tries to restore the rate of breathing again.[212] Here is where the beneficient effect of dreams, in spite of the so-called nightmare *(incubus)*, comes in. Without the dreadful imagination of a specter oppressing us and the exercise of all muscular power to get into another position, the stopping of the flow of our life's blood would quickly end our existence. For that very reason Nature seems to have arranged that the majority of dreams contain difficulties and perilous situations, because such ideas excite the powers of the soul more than when everything goes along as we wish and will. We frequently dream that we cannot rise to our feet, or that we have lost our way, or that we have become confused in delivering a sermon, or that before a large audience in a moment of forgetfulness we have put on a nightcap instead of a wig, or that we can fly through the air at will; or we awaken laughing merrily without knowing why. How it happens that we are placed in a dream in the long distant past, and speak with those long dead, and why we are tempted to treat it as a dream, although we see ourselves forced to hold imagination as reality, will always remain unexplained. Yet we can take it as certain that there can be no sleep without a dream, and whoever believes he has not dreamed, simply cannot recall his dream.

[191] On the Faculty of Designation (*facultas signatrix*)

§ 38.[213] THE faculty of understanding the present as a means of connecting the conception of what is foreseen with that of the past is the faculty of designation. The action of the mind in effecting this connection is designation (*signatio*), which is also called signalizing, of which the highest degree is called attribution.

Forms of objects (as perceived), as far as they serve only as means of perception through notions, are symbols; and any cognition through symbols is called symbolic or figurative (*speciosa*). Characters are not yet symbols, because they also can be mediate (indirect) signs which mean nothing by themselves, but mean something by joining with perceptions and then lead through them to notions. Therefore, symbolic cognition must not be opposed to intuitive but to discursive cognition.[214] In the discursive cognition, the sign (character) accompanies the notion only as a watchman (*custos*) in order to reproduce the notion when an occasion arises. Symbolic cognition is therefore not opposed to the intuitive cognition (through sense perception), but rather it is opposed to the intellectual cognition (through notions). Symbols are merely instruments of the understanding; but they are only indirect instruments by analogy to certain perceptions to which the notion of the symbol can be applied, so that the notion can be provided with meaning through the presentation of an object.

He who can express himself only in symbols has only a few notions of understanding. What is so often admired as a lively performance,[215] which savages (and sometimes would-be wise men among primitive people) manifest in their speech, is nothing but a deficiency of notions, and therefore a lack of words to express them. For example, when the American savage says, "Let us bury the hatchet," he means, "Let us make peace." As a matter of fact, the old songs, from Homer to Ossian, or from Orpheus to the Prophets, owe their eloquence merely to the lack of means for expressing their concepts.

To claim that the actual phenomena of the world, which present themselves to the senses, are merely a symbol of an intelligible world hidden in the background (as Swedenborg does),[216] is fanaticism. However, in the exhibition of concepts (called ideas) which belong [192] to that morality which is the essence of all religion and which consequently come from pure reason, we must distinguish the outer shell, useful and necessary for a time, from the thing itself, the symbolic from the intellectual (public worship from religion)—this is enlightenment. If this is not done an Ideal (of pure practical reason) would be replaced by an idol and the final purpose would be unsuccessful. It is not to be disputed that all peoples on the earth have begun by making such a substitution and that, when it is a matter of what their teachers themselves really intended in composing their sacred writings, we must not interpret them symbolically but, rather, literally; to twist their words would be unfair. However, when it is not a matter of the veracity of the teacher, but rather essentially of the truth of the doctrine, then we can and ought to interpret the writings as only a symbolic type of representation through which established forms and customs are to accompany those practical ideas, because otherwise the intellectual meaning, which constitutes the final purpose, would be lost.[217]

§ 39.[218]   WE can divide signs into voluntary (artificial), natural, and miraculous signs.[219]

A.   To the first type belong *1*) signs of gesticulation (imitative, which are also partly natural); *2*) characters (letters, which are signs for sounds); *3*) tone signs (notes); *4*) signs agreed upon between individuals, for the purposes of communication (ciphers); *5*) class signs of free men honored with hereditary superiority (coats of arms); *6*) signs of service, in prescribed costume (uniforms and livery); *7*) badges of honor, for service (ribbons awarded by orders); *8*) signs of dishonor (brandings and so forth). To this type also belong the literary signs of pause, question or emotion, and astonishment (signs of punctuation) in written material.[220]

All language is a signification of thought; the supreme way of indicating thought is by language, the greatest instrument for understanding ourselves and others. Thinking is speaking to ourselves. (The Indians of Tahiti call it "the language inside the body.") Consequently, there is also hearing ourselves inwardly (by means of the reproductive imagination). To the man born deaf, speaking is a feeling of play of lips, tongue, and jaw; and it is hardly possible to imagine that he does more when speaking than carry on a play with physical[221] feelings, without thinking or having real concepts.   [193] Yet even those who can speak and hear do not always understand either themselves or others. This is to be attributed to the lack of the power of designation, or to its faulty use (when signs are taken for things, and vice versa), and to the fact that men, especially where reason is concerned, who speak the same language are miles apart in regard to concepts. This is manifest only by chance, when each person is dealing with his own concepts.

B.   Concerning the natural signs, the relation of signs to things signified is, depending on the time, either demonstrative, or remonstrative, or prognostic.

The pulse signifies to the physician the presence of a feverish condition in the patient, just as smoke signifies fire. Reagents reveal to the chemist elements concealed in water, just as the weathercock reveals the wind, and so forth. However, whether blushing betrays consciousness of guilt, or rather a delicate sense of honor, or just a response to the imputation of something of which one would have to be ashamed, is quite uncertain in particular instances.

Burial mounds and tombs are signs of remembrance of the dead, just as pyramids are perpetual reminders of the former great power of a king. The layers of shells in districts situated far from the sea, the holes of the Pholades in the high Alps, or volcanic residue [in places] where fire no longer bursts forth from the earth, signify to us the ancient condition of the world and provide the basis for an archeology of nature, though, to be sure, they are not so plainly visible as the scars of a wounded warrior. The ruins of Palmyra, Balbek, and Persepolis are telling monuments of the state of art in ancient nations,[222] as well as sad indications[223] of the change of all things.

Prognostic signs are the most interesting of all, because the present is but a moment in the series of changes, and human desire leads us to ponder the presently only for the sake of future consequences (*ob futura consequentia*), thus making us especially attentive to these signs. In regard to future events in the world, the surest prognosis is in astronomy.[224] But it is childish and fantastic when heavenly configurations, conjunctions, and altered positions of plants are represented (in the *Astrologia Judiciaria*) as allegorical signs in the heavens of impending human[225] destinies.

[194]   Natural, prognostic signs of an impending illness or convalescence, or (like the *facies Hippocratica*) of imminent death, are phenomena which, based upon long and frequent experience, serve the physician as a guide in administering his cure even after [226] the discovery of the relation between cause and effect. The same holds true for the so-called critical days.[227] Yet[228] the auguries and haruspices, set up by the Romans for political purposes, were a superstition sanctioned by the government in order to direct the people in perilous times.

C.   Among the miraculous signs (events in which the nature of things reverses itself), apart from those of which we do not yet make anything (monstrosities among men and animals), there are signs and wonders in the sky—comets, balls of light shooting through the high atmosphere, northern lights, solar and lunar eclipses. It is especially when several such signs coincide, and are accompanied by war, pestilence, and so forth, that they are thought by the great terrified populace to herald the imminent doomsday and the end of the world.

Appendix

The marvelous play of the human imagination is worth mentioning. It involves the confusing of signs for things, so that an inner reality is posited for signs as if things had to conform to them. Since the course of the moon in its four phases (new moon, first quarter, full moon, and last quarter) cannot be divided in whole numbers more exactly than into twenty-eight days (and the zodiac of the Arabians is divided into twenty-eight houses of the moon), of which one-fourth makes seven days, the number seven has thereby acquired a mystical importance. Consequently the creation of the world had also to comply with this observation, particularly when there were to be (according to the Ptolemaic system) seven planets, seven[229] tones in a scale, seven primary colors in the rainbow, and seven metals. Hence climacteric years also came into existence[230] (seven times seven, and, nine also being a mystical number for the people of India, seven times nine, as well as nine times nine), upon the conclusion of which human life is supposed to be in greatest danger. The seventy prophetic weeks[231] (that is, 490 years) also constitute in Judeo-Christian chronology not only the divisions of the most important events (between God's call   [195] to Abraham and the birth of Christ), but they determine quite exactly the limit of life, so to speak a priori, as if chronology did not have to be guided by history, but, vice versa, that history had to be guided by chronology.

There are other instances, also, in which it is habitual to make things depend upon numbers. When a physician, to whom a patient sends the fee by a servant, unwraps the paper and finds therein eleven ducats, he becomes suspicious that the servant may have stolen one, for why should there not be a full dozen? At an auction the person who buys a set of porcelain will bid less when there is not a full dozen. If there should be thirteen plates, the only value he would place on the thirteenth would be that, should one be broken, he still would have the full dozen. But if one does not invite a dozen guests, what reason can there be for giving preeminence to this precise number? In his will a man bequeathed to his cousin eleven silver spoons and added: "Why I do not bequeath him the twelfth, he himself will know best" (the dissolute young man at his table had secretly stuck a spoon in his pocket, and the old man had noticed it, but did not care to shame him.[232] Upon reading the will one could easily guess what the meaning of the testator was, though only from the preconceived judgment that nothing but a dozen would be a full number. The twelve signs of the zodiac (a number which seems to be considered analogous to the twelve jurors in England) have also acquired such a mystical meaning. In Italy, Germany, and in other places perhaps,[233] a table of thirteen guests is taken as ominous because it is supposed that one of them, whosoever it may be, will die in the same year;[234] just as at a table of twelve jurors, the thirteenth, who finds himself among them, can be no other than the defendant who will be judged. (I have found myself at such a table where the lady of the house upon sitting down noticed this supposedly evil state of affairs and quietly ordered her son who was numbered among us to eat in another room, so that the gaiety might not be disturbed.) The mere magnitude of a number, when there are enough of the things it denotes, arouses our astonishment by the fact that it does not, in counting, complete a round number according to the decadic system (which in itself is quite arbitrary). The emperor   [196] of China reportedly has a fleet of 9,999 ships, and one secretly asks oneself, why not one more? Although the answer might be: "Because this number of ships is sufficient for his needs." In reality, however, the question does not address itself to the needs, but rather to the implication of numerical mysticism. It is still worse,[235] although not unusual, when anyone, who has brought his fortune to 90,000 thalers by means of fraud and stinginess, cannot rest until he has the full 100,000, even though he does not use it. Achieving this goal, he probably deserves the gallows, even though he does not get it.

To what childishness does man descend in his ripe old age, when he allows himself to be held by the leash of sensuousness! Let us now see how much better or worse he fares when he pursues his course in the light of understanding.

ON THE FACULTY OF COGNITION
AS FAR AS IT IS BASED
ON UNDERSTANDING

§ 40.[236]   UNDERSTANDING as the faculty of thinking (representing something by means of
concepts), is called the higher cognitive faculty (as distinguished from sensuousness, which is the lower), because
the faculty of perceptions (pure or empirical) contains
nothing but the particulars of objects, whereas the faculty of concepts contains the universals of the ideas of the
objects, that is, the rule to which the multitude of sensuous perceptions must be subordinated, so that unity in
the cognition of the object can be achieved. Certainly
understanding is of higher rank than sensibility.[237] Irrational animals can get along with sensibility alone following their implanted instincts, like a nation without a head
of state. However, a head of state without a nation (like
understanding without sensibility) has no power at all.
Between the two, moreover, there is no actual dispute
about rank, though one is considered higher and the
other lower.

The word understanding is, however, also taken in a
particular sense if it is subordinated to understanding in a
general sense as one member of classification, together
with two other faculties; and then   [197] the higher cognitive faculty (materially, that is, considered not by itself,
but rather in relation to the cognition of objects), consists
of understanding, judgment, and Reason. Let us now
observe how one man differs from another in this mental
faculty, or how his customary use or misuse is distinguished, first in a healthy mind, and then also in mental
illness.

ANTHROPOLOGICAL COMPARISON OF THE THREE HIGHER COGNITIVE FACULTIES WITH EACH OTHER[238]

§ 41.[239] THE correct[240] understanding excels not only through abundance of concepts but also through the proper concepts for the cognition of an object; consequently, it leads to the apprehension of truth through ability and skill. Many a man has a lot of concepts in his head, which altogether tend toward similarity with what one wants to hear from him; but when it comes to the object and its determination, the concepts miss the mark. Such a man may have concepts of vast scope, and may even be a man of adroit concepts. Correct understanding, which is sufficient for concepts of general cognition, is said to be sound understanding (sufficient for all needs). Such an understanding says, with the sergeant of the cavalry in Juvenal: *Quod sapio satis est mihi, non ego curo—esse quod Arcesilas aerumnosique Solones.*[241] It goes without saying that Nature's gift of a precise and correct understanding will know to limit itself in regard to the range of knowledge expected of it, and that the man endowed with such understanding will use it modestly.[242]

§ 42.[243] IF the word understanding means the faculty of cognition of rules (and this is done through concepts), so that the understanding encompasses the entire higher cognitive faculty, then the rules are not to be understood as those by which Nature guides man in his behavior, as occurs in animals which are motivated by natural instinct; but, rather, as only such rules which man himself makes.[244] What man merely learns, and thus entrusts to his memory, he performs only mechanically (in accordance with the laws of reproductive imagination) and he does it without the use of his under-standing. A servant, who has to pay a compliment merely in order to comply with established form, needs no un-derstanding, that is, he does not have to think for himself. But when the master is away and domestic affairs are his own responsibility [198] then many rules of behavior have to be observed which cannot be literally prescribed.

Correct understanding, expert judgment, and well-founded reason comprise the whole scope of the intellec-tual cognitive faculty, especially when this faculty is also judged as an ability for the promotion of the practical, that is, of certain ends and purposes.

Correct understanding is sound understanding as long as it maintains the properness of concepts necessary for the purpose for which they are used. By joining sufficiency *(sufficientia)* and exactitude *(praecisio),* we ar-rive at properness, which constitutes the quality of the concept. Properness contains neither more nor less than the object demands *(conceptus rem adaequans).*[245] Con-sequently, a correct understanding is the first and foremost of all the intellectual faculties because it satis-fies[246] its end with the least means.

Craftiness, the use of the head for intrigue, is often mistaken for great, though misused, understanding; but it is only a way of thinking[247] of very narrow-minded people, and is quite different from cleverness though it does have a semblance to it. One can deceive a person only once, a fact that is very disadvantageous to the subsequent plans of the crafty man.

The domestic or civil servant under orders needs only to have understanding. The officer, to whom only a general rule is prescribed, and who is then left on his own, needs judgment to decide for himself what should be done in a given case. The general, who must consider potential future cases and who must think out rules on his own, must have Reason. The talents necessary for such different uses are very distinct. "Many a man shines in the second rank, who would be invisible in the first." *(Tel brille au second rang qui s'éclipse au premier.)*[248]

Quibbling is not the same thing as having understanding. And to draw up maxims only for show, as Christina of Sweden did, maxims against which her conduct stood in opposition, cannot be called reasonable. This asks for an answer like the one the Duke of Rochester gave to the English King Charles II, when the king met him in deep meditation. The King asked, "Why are you thinking so deeply?" Answer: "I am composing your Majesty's epitaph." King: "How does it run?" Answer: "Here lies   [199] King Charles II, who said many wise things in his life but never did anything wise."[249]

To be silent in company, and only occasionally to make a very general judgment, looks like being reasonable, just as a certain degree of rudeness is passed off as (old-fashioned German) frankness.

By instruction natural understanding can also be enriched with many concepts, and it can be provided with rules. But the second intellectual faculty of distinguishing whether something is under the rule or not, which is the faculty of judgment *(judicium),* cannot be taught, but only exercised. Consequently, the growth of the second faculty engenders maturity, and increasing understanding, which comes only with the passage of time. It is also easy to see that this could not be otherwise, because instruction communicates the rules. Therefore, if there were any doctrines concerning judgment, then there would have to be general rules by which we may distinguish whether or not something agrees with the rule. Such a process would ask questions *ad infinitum.* The nature, then, of the understanding is that it does not come for years, that it is based upon one's own long experience; and whose judgment the French[250] Republic seeks in the assembly of the so-called Elders.

This faculty, which concerns itself only with what is feasible, what is fitting, and what is proper (for technical,[251] aesthetic, and practical judgment), is not as brilliant as those faculties which are generative.[252] It only accompanies sound understanding, and links understanding with Reason.

§ 43.[253]   IF understanding is the faculty of rules, and judgment is the faculty of discovering the particular, so far as it is an instance of this rule, reason, then, is the faculty of deriving the particular from the universal, and of representing the particular according to principles and as necessary. One can also explain reason by referring to the capacity of judging and acting (in a practical sense) according to fundamental principles. Man needs reason for every moral (and consequently also religious) judgment, he cannot build on dogmas and established customs. Ideas are concepts of reason, which cannot be represented adequately by any object within the realm of experience. They are   [200] neither perceptions (like those of Space and Time) nor feelings (such as eudaemonic desires), both of which belong to sensibility. Ideas are, instead, concepts of perfection which we may always approach but never completely attain.

Pedantic reasoning (without sound Reason) is a use of reason which misses its final purpose, partly from inability, and partly from a mistake concerning the point of view. To rave with reason is to proceed according to principles in the form of one's thoughts,[254] but as to matter and[255] scope, the means just run opposite to one's intentions.

Subordinates must not try to guide themselves by pedantic reasoning because the principle which should be employed must often be concealed from them, or at least remain unknown to them.[256] But the general or commanding officer must have reason, because instructions cannot be given him for every case that might arise.[257] Yet to require that a so-called layman (*laicus*) should not use his own reason in religious matters, particularly since religion is to be appreciated as moral, but instead follow the appointed clergyman *(clericus)* and thus someone else's reason, is an unjust demand because as to morals every man must account for all his doings. The clergyman will not and even cannot assume such a responsibility.

In cases like these however, men are inclined to seek more security for their own person so that they neglect completely their own use of reason and submit passively and obediently to precepts laid down by holy men. People do this not so much by feeling inept with regard to insight (for the essence of all religion is morality, which becomes evident to every person rather soon), but, rather, they do it out of craftiness, partly in order to push the blame upon someone else when a mistake has been made, and partly, and more particularly, to escape gracefully from anything that is essential (like a change of mind), which is much more difficult to perform than the ritual of worship.

Wisdom, as the Idea of a perfect[258] and practical use of reason, is an expectation which may be too ambitious to require of human beings. Even someone else cannot infuse wisdom into a person to the least degree; on the contrary, it must grow out of a man's own self. The guidelines for achieving wisdom consist of three leading maxims: *1*) Think for yourself; *2*) (in communication with other people) Put yourself in the place of the other person; *3*) Always think by remaining faithful to your own self.[259]

[201] The age at which man reaches the full use of his reason can be fixed, in respect to his skill (the capacity to fulfill a certain purpose), somewhere in his twentieth year; in respect to his cleverness (in using other men for his own purposes), in the fortieth; and finally, in respect to wisdom, somewhere in the sixtieth year. In this last period wisdom is more negative, it is inclined to see all the follies of the first two periods; and at this point we can say: "It is too bad to have to die now, when we have learned for the first time how we could[260] have lived

properly." But such judgment is rather uncommon in this period because as the attachment to life becomes stronger the more the value of life decreases in both action and enjoyment.

§ 44.[261]   JUST as the faculty of discovering the particular for the universal (the rule) is called judgment, so the faculty of discovering the universal for the particular is called intelligence *(ingenium)*. Judgment concentrates on detecting the differences within the manifold as to partial identities; intelligence concentrates on marking the identity within the manifold as to partial differences. The superior talent of both lies in noticing either the smallest similarity or dissimilarity. The faculty to do this is acuteness *(acumen),* and observations of this sort are called subtleties, which, if they do not advance knowledge, are either called[262] empty sophistries or conceited prattlings *(vanae argutationes)* even though the understanding has not been used in an untrue but, nevertheless, useless way. Acuteness is, consequently, bound not only to the faculty of judgment, but applies to intelligence as well. In the first case it is considered valuable more for the sake of exactitude *(cognitio exacta),* while in the second instance it is on account of the fertility of the good mind. Therefore, intelligence is said to be blooming, and, just as Nature seems to be more at play with her blossoms, but tending to business with her fruits, so the talent encountered in the intelligence is ranked lower in influence (in respect to the aims of Reason) than the faculty of judgment. Common and sound understanding lays claim neither to intelligence nor to acuteness, both furnish a kind of luxury of mind, whereas common, sound understanding limits itself to what is truly needed.

[202] ON THE SOUL'S WEAKNESSES AND ILLNESSES WITH RESPECT TO ITS COGNITIVE FACULTY

a. General Division

§ 45.[263]   THE defects of the faculty of cognition are either mental weaknesses or mental illnesses. The illnesses of the soul with regard to the cognitive faculty can be listed under two main types. The one is melancholia (hypochondria) and the other is mental disorder (mania). A melancholic man is well aware that the train of his thought does not move properly, but he has not sufficient control over himself to direct, restrain, or control the course of his thought. Unjustified joy and grief whimsically change in such a person like the weather which one has to accept as it comes. Mental disorder indicates a voluntary[264] stream of thoughts which follows its own (subjective) law. The subjective law runs contrary to the (objective) law which is in agreement with the rules of experience.

With regard to sense perception, mental disturbance is either irrationality or insanity. As to perversity of judgment and reason, it is known as delirium or imbecility. If a person habitually fails (by daydreaming) to compare his imagination with the laws of experience, he is a visionary (a whimsical person). If he does so because of emotional excitement, he is an enthusiast. Unexpected fits of the stricken person are called attacks of fancy *(raptus)*.

The simpleton, the imprudent, the stupid, the coxcomb, the fool, and the buffoon are all different from the mentally disordered. They differ not merely in degree but in the distinctive quality of mental discord. Despite their failings these people do not belong in a madhouse. A madhouse is a place where people, not withstanding maturity and age, must be controlled even as to their most trifling affairs of life by someone else's reason. Insanity accompanied by emotional excitement is called madness. It is often present from the beginning, but it may also spring up unexpectedly like poetic inspiration[265] *(furor poeticus)*, and in such cases it may border on genius. When such an attack of a facile but uncontrolled flood of ideas [203] affects reason, it is called fanaticism. Brooding over one and the same idea, to which there is no possible solution, like the loss of a spouse who cannot be called back to life, is stupid foolishness. Such a person tries to find peace in the pain. Superstition is more comparable to insanity, and fanaticism, to delirium. The mental derangement of the fanatic is often called (in mild terms) exaltation, but it might also be called eccentricity.

The wild talk of persons in fever, or an attack of fury, akin to epilepsy, which may occasionally be brought on sympathetically by powerful imagination when someone is confronted merely with the blank, staring gaze of a madman (for this reason people with unsteady nerves are advised not to extend their curiosity to the cells where these unfortunates are kept), are not to be taken for insanity because of their temporary nature. But what is called a quirk (which is not a mental sickness, because we usually mean by mental sickness a sad melancholic derangement of the inner sense) is mostly a certain person's conceit which borders on insanity. Such a person's demand that others, upon comparison with him, should despise themselves, is a desire which runs counter to its own purpose (like that of a crazy man). By raising such a claim, he excites these people to check his vanity in every possible way, so that they are eager to tease him, and to expose him to ridicule because of his offensive foolishness. Milder is the expression of a whim *(marotte)* which someone entertains. It is supposed to be a popular fad that never meets the approval of intelligent people. For example, the gift of presentiment, inspirations similar to those of the genius of Socrates, and qualities purported to be grounded in experience but really based on such unaccountable influences as sympathy, antipathy, and idiosyncracy *(qualitates occultae)* are all chirping like a cricket in the person's head; but no one else can hear them. The mildest of all deviations across the borderline of sound understanding is the hobbyhorse. It reflects a fondness for the occupation with objects of the imagination, with which the understanding only plays for amusement. Rather than involving oneself with serious business, the hobbyhorse provides something like busy idleness. For old folks, retiring people, and the well-to-do who are returning again to the carefree life of childhood, this frame of mind is not only a health-bringing excitement which keeps one's vitality alive, but it is also something charming and at the same time, something to chuckle about, yet in such a way that [204] the one laughed about can join in laughing happily with the others. However, with youths and busy people such hobby-riding also serves as recreation; and scoffers, who denounce these harmless little follies with pedantic seriousness, deserve Sterne's reprimand: "Let everybody ride his own hobbyhorse up and down the streets of the city, *as long as he does not make you sit behind him.*"[266]

b. On Mental Weaknesses in the Cognitive Faculty

§ 46.[267]   HE who lacks intelligence is a dull person *(obtusum caput)*. He may, by the way, have a good head in matters of understanding and reason. But we must not demand of him that he play the poet, as happened in the case of Clavius, whose schoolmaster wanted to apprentice him to a blacksmith because he could not make verses. Clavius became a great mathematician as soon as he got hold of a book of mathematics. A mind of slow apprehension is therefore not necessarily a weak mind. The one who is alert with abstractions is not always profound, he is more often very superficial.

Lack of judgment without intelligence is stupidity

(stupiditas). But the same lack of judgment accompanied by intelligence is silliness. He who exhibits judgment in business is clever. If, in addition, he has intelligence as well, he is called wise.[268] The jester, as well as the sophist, who only conceitedly exhibit these characteristics, are disgusting fellows. Through failures one becomes intelligent; but the one who has trained himself in this subject so that he can make others wise through their own failures, has used his intelligence. Ignorance is not stupidity. Consider the reply of a certain lady to the question of an academician: "Do the horses eat at night too?" She replied: "How can such a learned man be so stupid?" Ignorance is usually evidence of a good understanding as long as a person knows how to ask good questions (in order to learn either from nature or from another person).

Simple is he who cannot grasp much through his understanding, but he is not stupid unless he grasps it incorrectly. Honest but stupid (as some improperly describe Pomeranian servants) is a false and highly reprehensible aphorism. It is false because honesty (which is respect for duty based upon principles) is practical reason.   [205] It is highly reprehensible because it presupposes that everyone would deceive if only he felt skillful enough to do so; and that everyone who does not deceive merely displays his own inability. Hence the proverbs: "He has not invented gunpowder"; "He will not betray his country"; "He is no wizard," speak of misanthropic principles which say, that, assuming the good will in men whom we know, we still cannot be sure. We can only be sure when we know of their inability. Thus, Hume says, the Grand Sultan does not entrust his harem to the virtue of those who are said to guard the harem, but rather to the guards' inability (as black eunuchs).[269] Being very limited (narrow-minded) as to the range of one's concepts does not constitute stupidity, but what matters is the quality of the concepts (that is, the fundamental principles). That people allow themselves to be engaged in treasure seeking, alchemy, and trading in lotteries, is not to be attributed to their stupidity, but to their evil intent in wanting to get rich at the expense of others without a proportionate effort of their own. Craftiness, cunning, slyness *(versutia, astutia)* is the art of deceiving others. The question is: Whether the deceiver must be wiser than the one who is easily deceived, and whether the latter is the stupid one? The sincere man who readily trusts (believes, and gives credit), is sometimes, but very unjustly, called a fool because he is an easy catch for rogues; as the proverb says: "When the fool goes to market, the merchants rejoice." It is true and wise that I should never again trust the one who has once deceived me, because he is corrupt as to his fundamental principles. However, never to trust any other man, just because one man has deceived me, is misanthropy. The deceiver is really the fool. But what if one great deception has enabled a man to place himself in such a position that he no longer needs another person and the person's confidence? In that case the character under which he appears may completely change, but only in that, instead of being laughed at as a deceived deceiver, the unfortunate fellow is spat upon, and there is not even a permanent advantage in that.*

* The Palestinians, living among us, or at least the greatest number of them, have through their usurious spirit since their exile received the not-unfounded reputation of deceivers. It seems strange to think of a nation of deceivers; but it is just as strange to think of a nation made up of nothing but merchants, which are united for the most part by an old superstition that is recognized by the government [206] under which they live. They do not seek any civil honor, but rather wish to compensate their loss by profitably outwitting the very people among whom they find protection, and even to make profit from their own kind. It cannot be otherwise with a whole nation of merchants, who are nonproductive members of society (for example, the Jews in Poland). Their condition, sanctioned by ancient precepts and recognized even by us (who share certain holy books with them, and among whom they live), cannot be altered by us without serious consequences, even though they have made the saying "buyer be aware" the supreme principle of morality in their dealings with us. In place of the futile project of moralizing about this nation with regard to the matter of deception and honor, I prefer to outline my own conjecture of the origin of this peculiar condition (that is, of a nation composed of nothing but merchants). In the

§ 47.[270] [206] DISTRACTION (*distractio*) is the state of diverting attention (*abstractio*) from certain ruling ideas by means of shifting to other dissimilar ideas. If the distraction is intentional, it is called dissipation; if it is involuntary it is absentmindedness (*absentia*).

One of the mental weaknesses is to be attached, through reproductive imagination, to an idea to which one has given great or lasting attention, and from which one is not able to get away, that is, one is not able to set the course of imagination free again. [207] If this evil is habitual and directed to one and the same object, it may possibly result in insanity. To be distracted in society is impolite, and often laughable as well. Women are ordinarily not subject to this impulse, unless they devote themselves to learning. A servant who looks distracted

---

most ancient times riches were brought [MS: to Asia (Minor)—Ed.] by trade with India, and from thence by land to the western shores of the Mediterranean Sea, and to parts of Phoenicia (to which Palestine belongs). Indeed, wealth had been able to make its way to many other places, for example, to Palmyra, to Tyre in ancient times, to Sidon, and by means of a trip over the sea, to Eziongeber and Eloth [cities on the Red Sea—Trans.], as well as from the Arabian coast to Thebes, and thence across Egypt to the Syrian coast; but, Palestine, with its capital Jerusalem was very well-situated for caravan trade. Probably the phenomenon of the former [MS: unique—Ed.] riches of Solomon was due to the location of Palestine; and even up to Roman times the surrounding country was full of merchants. Because they had far-reaching commercial relations with people of their own language and religion, these merchants, after the destruction of their city, were able to migrate gradually into far-distant lands (in Europe) taking language and religion with them, maintaining their connection with each other, and finding security in whatever countries they went to because of their profitable bargaining. Therefore, we may suppose that their dispersion throughout the world, with their unity in religion and language, must not be attributed to a *curse* that had been inflicted upon this people. On the contrary, the dispersion must be considered as a *blessing,* especially since the wealth of the Jews, if we think of them as individuals, apparently exceeds per capita that of any other nation at the present time. [MS: last two sentences are slightly different, "therefore the greatest disaster of the state turned into the greatest luck of its citizens. It is to be assumed that the riches in *money* of this widely-scattered people would exceed the riches of any other nation of the same number, if all their riches would be added up (about which Morris Langallerie has made a proposal). Provided that riches mean happiness—Ed.]

while waiting on table is usually thinking of something evil, either he is plotting something or he thinks about the possible consequences.

To distract oneself[271] is to relax one's involuntary reproductive imagination in order to check the flow of afterthoughts in one's head as, for example, the clergyman does when he has delivered his memorized sermon. This is a necessary and partially artificial way of taking care of one's mental well being. A continual reflection on one and the same subject leaves you with reverberations, so to speak (like the repetitive theme of dance music which is still hummed by those who are returning home from a fête; or, like children who incessantly repeat the selfsame bon mot of their liking, especially when it has a rhythmic sound). Such an echo molests the mind, and the only way to get rid of it is by distraction and by focusing the attention upon some other object, for example, reading the newspapers. Recovering control of oneself *(collectio animi)* in order to be ready for each new task furthers mental health by restoring the balance between one's powers of the soul. The most wholesome means of recovering control is social conversation on various subjects, similar to playing. Such conversation must not change from one subject to another by violating the natural relationship of ideas, for then the state of mental distraction would break up the company because everything is confused and the unity of conversation is entirely lacking. Furthermore, the mind would find itself disturbed and in need of new distraction in order to restore balance again.

One can see from this that there is an (uncommon) art which helps maintain mental regimentation, whereby a busy man may distract himself in order to collect his powers. But when one has collected one's thoughts, that is, when one has set them in readiness, so that they may be used as desired, then one cannot call a person distracted [208] who is purposely immersed in his own thought. On an inappropriate occasion or when he is turning to another conversation, so that he cannot pay enough attention to the ongoing conversation, such a person can only be blamed for absentmindedness, something which is improper on social occasions. Thus it is an unusual art, to be able to distract oneself without ever appearing distracted. If distraction is habitual, it gives the person who is afflicted with this evil the appearance of a dreamer, and it makes him useless for society because, without checking his imagination by reason, he blindly follows the free play of his imagination. The reading of novels, in addition to causing many other mental discords, has also the consequence that it makes distraction habitual. Although through the depiction of characters, who actually can be found among men (even if with some exaggeration), thoughts are given the coherence of a true story which always has to be presented in a certain systematic way, the mind nevertheless is at the same time free enough to invent digressions (still other fictional occurrences) during the reading. On this account the train of thought becomes fragmentary, so that one lets ideas of one and the same object become scattered *(sparsim)* instead of conjoining *(conjunctim)* them in the mind according to the unity of the understanding. The teacher from the pulpit or in the academic lecture-hall, the prosecutor or the attorney who has to demonstrate mental composure in free speaking (on the spur of the moment) or at least in conversation, must each pay attention to three things. First, he must concentrate on what he is now saying, in order to represent it clearly; second, he must look back to what he has said; and third, he must look forward to what he intends to say. If he fails to give consideration to any of these three, and if he fails to arrange them in this order, then he will certainly be distracting both himself and his listeners or readers. An otherwise good mind cannot disregard these rules without being called confused.

§ 48.[272]   A generally sound understanding (with-
               out any mental weakness) can also be
accompanied by weaknesses with regard to its exercise.
Such weaknesses entail either a delay until the growth to
proper maturity or they even necessitate one's being
represented by someone else in matters of a civil nature.
An otherwise healthy person's (natural or legal) inability
to use his own understanding in civil affairs is taken care
of by tutelage. If the inability is based upon immaturity of
age, it is called minority (being under age), if it is based
upon legal   [209] arrangements, in respect to civil affairs,
it may then be called legal or civil tutelage.

     Children are naturally minors and their parents are
their natural guardians. The wife, whatever her age, is
declared to be a minor in civil matters, and the husband is
her natural custodian. If she lives with him, but keeps her
estate for herself, then another person is the custodian.
Although the wife, by the nature of her sex, has a glib
enough tongue to represent herself and her husband
when it comes to speaking, even in a court of law (concerning what is mine and thine), she could be declared to
be more than of age according to the letter. But just as
women are not expected to be drafted because of their
sex, so women cannot defend their rights personally. In
order to take care of their civil affairs they must employ a
representative. Such legal tutelage, in respect to public
transactions, makes women even more powerful as to
domestic welfare, because the rights of the weaker sex
apply here, which the masculine sex by his nature feels
called upon to honor and defend.

     Yet to make oneself behave like a minor, degrading
as it may be, is, nevertheless, very comfortable. Naturally
it has not escaped leaders who are known to utilize the
docility of the masses (because they hardly unite on their
own). The leaders have also recognized that letting the
masses think on their own without guidance by others is
dangerous, even lethal. Heads of state call themselves

fathers of the country because they know better how to make their subjects happy than the subjects themselves understand. But the people are condemned to permanent tutelage in respect to their own best welfare. When Adam Smith[273] improperly says that rulers were, without exception, the greatest spendthrifts of all, he is strongly refuted by the (wise!) sumptuary laws passed in many countries.

The clergy holds the layman firmly and continually in tutelage. The people have no voice and no judgment as to the way which leads them to the kingdom of heaven. People are not to use their own eyes to get there; they will be led, and even though Holy Scriptures are placed in their hands so that they may see with their own eyes, they are at once warned by their guardians   [210] not to discover therein anything other than what the guardians certify to be contained in them. The mechanical management of men under the regimen of others is everywhere the surest means of maintaining lawful order.

Learned men usually allow themselves to be kept in a state of tutelage by their wives as far as domestic arrangements are concerned. When a servant shrieked that there was a fire in one of the rooms, a learned man, buried in books, answered, "You know, things of that sort are my wife's affair." Finally, a spendthrift, who has already reached majority according to the law, can bring upon himself a reversion to civil minority if, after[274] legally attaining majority, he shows a deficiency in intelligence as to the management of his estate, which classifies him as a child or an imbecile. Judgment, about this, however, lies outside the field of anthropology.

§ 49.   DULL[275] (hebes), like an untempered knife or hatchet, is he to whom nothing can be taught; he is unfit for learning. The person who has only the skill of imitation is a copycat; but he who can be the author of intellectual and artistic productions is a man who has a head. Quite different from this is simplicity (as opposed to artificiality),[276] of which some say, "Perfect art again becomes Nature," and in which one succeeds only late in life. Simplicity is a faculty of arriving at the same end through sparing one's means, that is, arriving by the most direct way. The person who possesses this gift (a wise man) is, by virtue of his simplicity, not at all simplistic.

The man who cannot get used to business is stupid because he has no power of judgment.

A fool is he who sacrifices things of value to purposes which are of no value; for example, he sacrifices domestic bliss to splendor outside of his house. When foolishness is offensive, it is buffoonery. We may call someone foolish without insulting him; in fact, he may call himself foolish; but to become the object of rogues (according to Pope) and be called a fool cannot be taken by anyone with equanimity.* Haughtiness is foolishness, primarily because it is stupid to expect   [211] of others that they should regard themselves lowly in comparison with myself. As a consequence they would always play tricks on me to defeat my purposes so that the laughs would be on me. But such an imputation would also imply insult, and insult produces well-deserved hate. The word fool applied to a woman does not have the same harsh meaning as the word fool applied to a man, because a man does not feel that he can be insulted by the conceited presumption of a woman. And so foolishness appears to apply solely to the notion of male haughtiness. If we call a man who injures himself (temporarily or perpetually) a fool, and consequently add hate to our contempt of him, though he has not injured us directly, then we must consider his foolishness as an offense to human-

---

* If one replies to someone's joke: "You can't be serious," it is a mild way of saying, "You are jesting," or "You are not judicious." A judicious man is a correct and practical, but artless judge. Nature alone can make a man judicious, experience can make a judicious man wise, that is, it can enable him in the artful use of the understanding.

ity in general and hence as an offense directed against someone else. Whoever acts contrary to his own legitimate interest is also at times called a fool, even though he injures only himself. Arouet, Voltaire's father, said to someone who congratulated him upon his famous sons, "I have two fools for sons; the first is a fool in prose, the other in verse." (One had thrust himself into Jansenism and was persecuted; the other had to make amends in the Bastille for his satirical poems.) In general, a madman values things too highly, whereas a fool values himself more highly than he should if he were sensible.

Labeling a person a dandy or a fop is based upon the concept of impudence as foolishness. The dandy is a young fool; the fop is an old one; both are misled by rogues or pranksters. The dandy draws our pity; the fop, however, draws bitter contempt. A witty German philosopher and poet illustrated the French epithets *fat* and *sot* (under the generic name *fou*) by the following example. "The dandy," he said, "is a young German on the way to Paris. The fop is the very same person having just returned from Paris."[277]

Complete mental weakness [212] which either does not suffice for even animal activities (as among the Cretins of Valais) or which is just sufficient for a mere mechanical imitation of external actions which animals can perform (such as sawing, digging, and so forth) is called idiocy. This should not be called sickness of soul, but rather lack of soul instead.

c.   On Mental Ailments

§ 50.[278]   THE major division, as already mentioned above,[279] is the division into melancholia (hypochondria) and mental disorder (mania).[280] The name of the former[281] is derived as analogous to being startled by the chirping noise of a house-cricket in the quiet of the night. The noise disturbs the peace of mind necessary for sleep. The illness of the hypochondriac is such that certain inner, bodily sensations do not only disclose an actually existent illness inside the body, but they can also cause an illness because human nature, by virtue of a peculiar quality lacking in animals, can strengthen or sustain a feeling by centering attention on certain local impressions.[282] On the other hand, either intentional abstraction, or abstraction caused by other distracting occupations, may weaken the symptoms and, if such abstraction becomes habitual, the illness may disappear altogether.* In such a way hypochondria, considered as melancholia, becomes the cause for taking imaginary physical ills for something actual. The patient is well aware that these are imaginings, but from time to time he is unable to break loose from them. Or, conversely, from a genuine physical discomfort (like intestinal pressure caused from having eaten flatulent food), hypochondria will produce imaginings of all sorts of external events and concerns about one's intestinal tract.[283] They will disappear completely as soon as digestion has been completed and flatulence has ceased. The hypochondriac is a capricious fellow (a visionary) of the most pitiful sort, obstinately unable to come to grips with his imaginings, always running to the physician, who has no end of trouble with him and who can only quiet the patient in the same way in which he   [213] quiets a child (that is, with pills containing bread crumbs instead of remedies). Moreover, when this patient, who despite his perpetual ailments never really falls ill, consults medical books, he becomes completely insufferable because now he believes that he feels in his body all the discomforts which he has read about in the books. Extraordinary gaiety, in the form of lively wit and happy laughter, serves as a symptom of this sick imagination to which the

---

*   I have remarked in another writing that averting attention from certain painful sensations, and concentrating on some other object voluntarily grasped in thought can ward off the painful sensations so completely that they are unable to break out into an illness. ["Another writing" refers to *Von der Macht des Gemüths*—Trans.]

patient feels occasionally subjected; thus falling victim to the ever-changing sport of his moods. Anxious fear, childish in character, of the thought of death nourishes this sickness. But whoever does not tend to overlook these thoughts with manly courage will never enjoy life properly.

Still, on this side of the border of mental disorder is the sudden change of moods[284] *(raptus)*, an unexpected leap from one subject to a totally different one without apparent motivation. Occasionally the change precedes every disturbance as an indication; but frequently the mind is already so disorganized that such attacks of irregularity become the rule. Suicide is often just the result of a *raptus*. Because he who, in the violence of emotion, has slit his throat will soon after patiently allow it to be sewn up again.

Melancholy *(melancholia)* can also be a mere delusion of misery which the low-spirited self-tormentor (inclined toward feeling wretched) creates for himself. In itself it is not yet a mental disorder, but may easily lead to it. In other respects it is a mistaken but frequently used expression to speak of a melancholy mathematician (for example, Professor Hausen)[285] when one means only a profoundly thoughtful person.

§ 51.[286]   THE delirious talk (delirium) of a person waking in a feverous state is a physical illness and requires medical attention. Only the delirious person, in whom the physician perceives no signs of such a sickness, is called crazy, for which the word deranged is but a mild term. Therefore, if someone has intentionally caused an accident, the question arises, whether any or how much blame should be attached to such an afflicted person. Above all it has to be determined first whether he was crazy at that moment or not. For the solution of this question the court of justice cannot refer him to the medical faculty but must refer him to the philosophical faculty (because of the incompetence of the court regarding this question). The question of whether the accused at the time of his act was in full possession of his natural faculty of understanding [214] and judgment is a wholly psychological question; and although physical derangement of the spirit perchance might now and then be the cause of an unnatural transgression of the moral law (which dwells in everybody), physicians and physiologists are generally still not advanced enough to see deeply into the mechanisms inside a human being in order to determine whether the attack caused the atrocity, or whether it could have been predicted (without anatomy of the body). Moreover, concerning the question whether the mental condition of the agent was one of derangement or of a fixed purpose held with a sound understanding, forensic medicine *(medicina forensis),* is meddling with alien business which the judge knows nothing about. He must at least refer it to another faculty as something not belonging to his competence.*

§ 52.[287]   IT is difficult to bring systematic classification to what is essential and incurable disorder. Moreover, it is of little use to occupy oneself with it because all methods of cure must be fruitless and fall short of their aim since the powers of the subject cannot cooperate (as is the case with bodily ailments) and yet the goal can only be attained through that person's own use of the understanding. Even though it can be only indirectly pragmatic and tell you what not to do, anthropol-

---

* Thus such a judge declared a woman insane who in despair murdered a child because she had been sentenced to the house of correction. Consequently she was exempt from the death penalty. The judge argued that he who draws real conclusions from false premises is insane. The woman concerned had concluded that the sentence to serve in the house of correction was an indelible loss of honor, more severe than death itself (which is quite false). So she came to the conclusion that she had earned death for herself. The person was declared insane; and, as such she is exempted from the death penalty. On the basis of this argument it might easily be possible that all criminals be declared insane persons whom we should pity and cure, but never punish. [The text follows the A and similar B₃ versions. The "for herself" was added in B—Ed.]

ogy requires at least an attempt at a general outline of this most profound degradation of humanity which seems to originate from Nature. Derangement may be classified as tumultuous, methodical, and systematic.

1.   Madness *(amentia)* is the inability to bring ideas into mere coherence necessary for the possibility of experience. Because   [215] of their garrulity, women in the madhouses are chiefly subject to this illness. Their vivid imagination adds so many digressions to what they are saying that no one can grasp what they are really trying to say. This first kind of derangement is tumultuous.

2.   Insanity *(dementia)* is that disturbance of the mind, wherein everything which the insane person relates, is in accord with the possibility of an experience, and indeed with the formal laws of thought; but, because of falsely inventive imagination, self-concocted ideas are treated as if they were perceptions. Those who believe they are everywhere surrounded by enemies, and those who regard all glances, words, and otherwise indifferent actions of others as directed against them personally and as traps set for them belong to this category. These people, in their unfortunate madness, are often so acute at interpreting as directed against them what others do inadvertently, that, if the data were only true, we would be obliged to pay the highest respect to their understanding. I have seen nobody who has ever been healed of this illness (because to be mad with reason is a peculiar sort of predisposition). However, they are not to be counted among the asylum fools, because, being concerned only with themselves, they direct their supposed craftiness only to their own welfare, without putting anyone else in danger. Consequently they do not need to be locked up for the sake of safety. This second kind of derangement is methodical.

3.   Delirium *(insania)* is disordered faculty of judgment in which the mind is deceived by analogies, which are being confused with concepts of similar things, so that the imagination offers dissimilar objects as similar and universal ones in a process resembling that of the understanding. Mental patients of this type are usually very cheerful; they write insipid verse and take pleasure in the richness of what, in their opinion, is such an extensive realm of analogous concepts. The delirious person of this type cannot be cured because he is creative and entertaining through diversity, like poetry in general. This third kind of derangement is methodical, but fragmentary only.

4.   Lunacy *(vesania)* is the sickness of a disordered reason. The patient disregards all the facts of experience and aspires to principles which can be entirely exempted from the test of experience. Such a patient fancies that he comprehends the incomprehensible,   [216] and that such things as the invention of a method for squaring the circle, perpetual motion, the unveiling of the transcendental forces of Nature, and the comprehension of the mystery of the Trinity are all within his power. He is the quietest of all hospital patients; and, because of his self-contained speculation, he is the farthest removed from a state of frenzy. With complete self-sufficiency, he closes his eyes to all the difficulties of investigation. This fourth type of derangement could be labeled systematic.

There is in this last type of mental disturbance not merely disorder and departure from the laws which govern reason, but also positive unreason, that is, a different rule, a totally dissimilar standpoint into which the soul is transported, so to speak. From such a perspective the soul looks at all objects in another way; and from the *sensorio communi,*[288] which is required for unity of life (of the animal), it finds itself transported to a faraway place[289] (hence the word derangement or displacement). A mountainous landscape sketched from a bird's-eye perspective permits a completely different judgment of the region than a sketch made from the perspective of level ground. The soul does not really feel, or see itself in another location (for it cannot perceive itself in relation to its position in space without being contradictory, because it would otherwise look at itself as the object[290] of its outer sense, when in itself it is capable of being an object of its inner sense only); however, in this way we explain the so-called mental dislocation as well as we possibly can. It is astonishing, however, that the faculties of the unsettled mind still arrange themselves into a system, and that Nature even strives to bring a principle of unity into unreason, so that the thinking faculty does not remain idle, even though it is employed, not objectively in the true cognition of things, but only subjectively for the continuation of animal functions.

But then the attempt to observe oneself by physical means, in a condition approaching derangement into which one has voluntarily placed oneself in order to observe better even what is involuntary, shows enough reason for the investigation of the causes of phenomena. However, to conduct experiments on the mind, and even to make it ill to a certain degree for the purpose of observing it and then to investigate its nature on the basis of findings which may have presented themselves, is dangerous. Thus, for example, after taking a specific dose of napellus   [217] (a poisonous root), Helmont[291] claims to have perceived a sensation, as if he were doing his thinking in his stomach! Another physician increased his doses of camphor little by little until it seemed to him as if everything in the street were topsy-turvy. Many have experimented on themselves with opium for so long that they fell into a state of mental debility whenever they gave up further use of this means of artificial stimulation of thought. An artificially induced derangement could easily become a genuine one.

Related Remarks

§ 53.[292] THE germ of derangement develops together with the germ of reproduction, and is thus hereditary. It is dangerous to marry into families where even a single such creature has been produced. If there should have been even one deranged child in the mother's family (although the mother herself is free from the evil), regardless of how many children a married couple may have free of this evil inheritance due, for example, to their taking after their father and his parents or grandparents, then sometime in this marriage there will appear a child taking after the maternal line (as one can also tell from the resemblance of features) and be born with an inherited mental disorder.

People often think that they can name the accidental causes of this malady, so that it may appear not inherited but rather acquired, and that[293] the unfortunate one were to blame for it. "Love made him crazy," people say of one; while of another they say, "Pride made him crazy," and of a third person they say, "He has studied too hard." Falling in love with a person of high social standing and to expect from that person the folly of marriage is not the cause but the result of derangement; and as far as pride is concerned, an insignificant person's demand that others bow and scrape before him, and the insinuation that others challenge his position presupposes mental derangement without which he would not have dared to make such demands in the first place.

But, as to studying too hard,* there is no need to warn young people. With regard to studying, youth needs [218] spurs, rather than reins. Even the strongest

---

* It is an ordinary thing to see a merchant overextend himself and dissipate his powers in vast schemes. Anxious parents, however, have nothing to fear from overtaxing the industriousness of young people (as long as their minds are otherwise sound). [218] A student is protected by Nature from such overloading with knowledge by finding subjects distasteful, over which he only broods and breaks his head to no avail.

and most persistent effort on this score can only weary
the mind, so that a man becomes averse to knowledge;
but such an effort cannot put the mind out of sorts, unless
it was already confused from the beginning and therefore
took delight in mystical books and revelations transcend-
ing ordinary human understanding. Also in this area
belongs the inclination to devote oneself to the reading
of books which have received a certain holy unction,
merely for the sake of the printed word and without
concern for the moral import. To describe this, a certain
author has hit upon the expression, "He is scripture-
crazy."

I have doubts whether there is a distinction between
general lunacy *(delirium generale)* and that which is fixed
upon a definite object *(delirium circa objectum)*. Unreason
(which is something positive and not just a lack of reason)
is like reason, a mere form to which objects can be
adapted; and both reason and unreason, therefore, concern themselves with the general. However, what first
comes into the mind at the (usually sudden) outbreak of a
crazy disposition (the accidentally encountered subject
matter about which the person will rave later) will be
from then on the insane person's chief concern, since it
is, because of the novelty of the impression, more firmly
fixed in his mind than anything else occurring afterward.

One also says of a person in whose head something
has gone wrong: "He has crossed the line," just as if a
man, who crosses the equator for the first time were in
danger of losing his understanding.[294] But this is only
misunderstanding. It only means to say that the dandy
who, suddenly and without taking any great pains, hopes
to get rich by taking a trip to India, draws up his plan, like
a fool, from the beginning. While he pursues his scheme,
the incipient folly grows and, upon his return, even if
fortune has been kind to him, it shows itself fully grown.

The one who talks aloud to himself and the one who
is caught gesticulating to himself in his room, falls under
the suspicion that something is not right in his head.

[219] This is especially the case if he believes that he is blessed or haunted and in conversation and in relation with higher beings. However, it is not the case when he does not consider or does not even wish himself to be chosen for such revelations, while conceding that other holy men might be capable of supersensory intuition.

The only general characteristic of insanity is the loss of a sense for ideas that are common to all *(sensus communis)*, and its replacement with a sense for ideas peculiar to ourselves *(sensus privatus);* for example, in broad daylight a man sees a light burning on a table, which, however, another person standing next to him does not see; or he hears a voice which no one else hears. It is a subjectively necessary touchstone of the correctness of our judgment and, consequently, of the soundness of our understanding that we relate our understanding to the understanding of others, and not merely isolate ourselves within our own experiences, and make public quasi judgments which are merely based on our own private ideas. Therefore, the prohibition of books only on the basis of theoretical opinions is an insult to mankind (especially when they have no influence on legal matters). In this way we are deprived not of the only but still of the greatest and most useful means of correcting our own thoughts. We are used to making public statements in order to see whether they also agree with the understanding of others. Otherwise, something merely subjective (for example, habit or inclination) would easily be taken for something objective. It is in just this that illusion consists, something which is said to be deceptive, or rather something whereby one is misled into self-deception in the application of a rule. He who does not bother about this touchstone, but gets it into his head to acknowledge his own private opinion as already valid without regard for, or even against, common opinion, has submitted to a play of thoughts in which he proceeds and judges in a world not shared with other people, but rather (as in a dream) he sees himself in his own little world. Sometimes it is only the terminology, with which an otherwise clearheaded man wishes to communicate his perceptions to others, that does not seem to accord with the principle of common sense. Such a person usually sticks to his opinion, like Harrington,[295] the gifted author of *Oceana,* who had the whim that his transpiration (effluvia) jumped from his skin in the form of flies. However, this could well have been electrical effects on a body overcharged with this matter, an experience which somebody [220] claims to have had before. Harrington perhaps desired to point out only the similarity to a feeling of jumping off, rather than actually seeing these flies.

Derangement accompanied by raging *(rabies),* that is, an affection of anger (toward a real or imaginary object) which renders one insensitive to all external stimuli, is only one variety of mental imbalance. It often seems to look more frightening than it is in its consequences and it is, like a paroxysm in an acute illness, not so much rooted in the mind as rather caused by material factors. It can often be removed by a physician with a dose of medicine.[296]

ON THE TALENTS OF THE COGNITIVE FACULTY

§ 54.[297]   BY talent (natural gift) we understand that quality of the cognitive faculty which depends not on education but on the natural ability of the subject. These talents are productive intelligence *(ingenium strictus sive materialiter dictum),* sagacity,[298] and originality of thought (genius).

Intelligence is either comparative *(ingenium comparans),* or argumentative *(ingenium argutans).* Intelligence unites (assimilates) heterogeneous ideas, which often, according to the law of the imagination (that is, association), lie apart from each other. It is a peculiar faculty of classifying, which belongs to the understanding (as the faculty of recognizing the general) in so far as the understanding attributes objects to a certain class. Intelligence subsequently requires the application of the power of judgment in order to determine the particular and the general, and to use the thinking faculty for the purpose of gaining knowledge. To be intelligent (in reading or writing) is something that cannot be learned through the mechanism of schooling and its discipline. Rather, it belongs, as a distinct talent, to the liberality of disposition in the mutual exchange of ideas *(veniam damus petimusque vicissim)*.[299] Intelligence is a characteristic of the understanding which is hard to explain. It is like a favor given to you which contrasts with the strictness of judgment *(judicium discretivum)* in the application of the general to the particular (that is, of the concepts of class to those of the species), which not only hampers the faculty of assimilation, but also the inclination to use this faculty.[300]

[221] ON THE SPECIFIC DIFFERENCES
    BETWEEN THE COMPARATIVE AND
    THE ARGUMENTATIVE INTELLIGENCE

a. On Productive Intelligence

§ 55.[301] IT is pleasing, generally accepted, and encouraging to find similarities amidst dissimilar objects; and so the intelligence provides material for the understanding to make its knowledge more general. On the other hand, though judgment, which qualifies concepts and contributes more to their correction than to their extension, is indeed praised and recommended, it is nevertheless sober, exacting, and, as regards freedom of thought, restricting; and just for this reason it is unpopular. The activity of the comparative intelligence is rather like play; while that of the judgment is more like business. Intelligence is primarily a flower of youth, judgment a ripe fruit of old age. He who unites both to a high degree in a product of the mind is perspicacious (perspicax).

Intelligence[302] snatches at sudden ideas; judgment strives toward insight. Deliberation is a burgomaster's virtue (to protect and govern the city by given laws, under the superior command of the castle). In the other hand, Buffon,[303] the great author of a system of nature, was considered bold (hardi) by his fellow-citizens for ignoring the deliberations of judgment, even though his daring enterprise appears rather lacking in modesty (frivolity). Intelligence usually prefers the appetizer, whereas judgment usually prefers the main course. The hunt for witty remarks (bons mots), such as the Abbé Trublet's[304] richly exemplifies, the kind that stretches intelligence upon the rack, makes shallow minds or turns a conscientious man away in disgust. Intelligence is inventive when it comes to fashions, that is, assumed rules of behavior, which are pleasing only because of their novelty, and which must be exchanged, before they become customary, for other forms which are just as transitory.

Intelligence in punning is stale; while needless subtlety (micrology) of judgment is pedantic. Humorous intelligence arises from directing the head to appreciate paradoxes, in which the (sly) knave peers from behind the naïve sound of simplicity in order to subject somebody (or even his own opinion) to laughter.   [222] Heaping the very opposite of what is worthy of applause with obvious praise (persiflage) and making the contemptible through contrast even more contemptible is very rousing through the surprise at the unexpected, for example, as Swift's "Art of Sinking in Poetry,"[305] or Butler's Hudibras.[306] Such a type of intelligence, however, is always just a pastime and light bantering (like Voltaire's). On the other hand, the person who clothes true and important principles in a disguise (like Young in his satires),[307] can well be called a heavy hundredweight as to intelligence, because this is a serious occupation which calls forth more admiration than amusement.

A proverb *(proverbium)* is not properly called a witty remark (bon mot), because it is a commonly accepted form of expressing a thought, which is to be propagated by imitation, even though it may well have been a witticism in the mouth of the first speaker. Speaking in proverbial clichés is therefore the speech of the populace and indicates complete loss of intelligence in the relation with the refined world.

Profundity is certainly not an affair of cleverness.[308] But so far as cleverness, through the figurative element which it adds to thoughts, can be a vehicle or a garment for reason, and its management of morally practical ideas, it can be thought of as profound cleverness (in contrast to the superficial one). For example, take one of those so-called wonderful aphorisms of Samuel Johnson about women, which is quoted in Waller's biography: "Doubtless he praised many women whom he would have hesitated to marry, and perhaps he married one he would have been ashamed to praise."[309] Here the whole element of wonder resides in the play of antithesis; but reason gains nothing by it. But whenever reason encountered controversial questions, his friend Boswell could not entice from Johnson any of those oracular utterances which he sought so incessantly, not even one which would have revealed a trace of wit. Everything he uttered about the religious sceptic, about the rights of the government, or even about human freedom, came out with a heavy coarseness because of his natural disposition and the pampering by his flatterers. This coarseness was called rudeness* by his admirers, and it indicated his

---

* Boswell relates that when a certain lord in his presence expressed his sorrow that Johnson had not had a finer education, Baretti said, "No, no, my lord, you could have done with him whatever you wanted, he would always have been a bear." "True, but would he not have been a *dancing bear?*" the lord asked. A third person, one of his friends, thought to soften this by saying, *"He has nothing of the bear but his skin."* [See James Boswell, *Life of Samuel Johnson,* ed. Crocker (New York, 1867) 1. 252—Trans.]

great[310] [223] inability to combine cleverness and thought in a profound way. Also, men of influence, who paid no attention to his friends who recommended him as an extraordinarily qualified member for parliament, seem to have valued his talent highly. Intelligence, sufficient for the composition of a dictionary of a language, is not adequate for the inspiration and entertainment of ideas and reason necessary for the understanding of important matters. Modesty comes naturally to the mind of anyone who sees himself called to it, and mistrust comes to his own talents when he does not want to judge for himself, but rather take the judgments of others (preferably unnoticed) into consideration. Johnson never possessed these characteristics.

b.   On Sagacity, or the Gift of Investigation

§ 56.[311]   To discover something (that lies hidden either in ourselves or somewhere else) requires in many instances the special talent of knowing how to search effectively. Discovery requires a natural gift of preliminary judgment (*judicium praevium*) as to where the truth may indeed be found; it requires the ability to hit upon the clues, and to use the least appearance of relevancy, in order to find or construct, what one is seeking. The logic of schoolmen teaches us nothing about this gift. But Bacon of Verulam gave us in his *Organum*[312] a brilliant example of method as to how the hidden characteristics of Nature could be exposed by means of experiment. But even this example fails to provide instruction according to any definite rules as to how one should search successfully. One must always first make some supposition (begin with a hypothesis) and proceed from there. All this has to occur according to principles, certain modes of procedure. How to find these procedures is the crucial problem. Venturing forth blindly, and trusting upon one's good luck until one stumbles over a stone and finds a piece of ore, and subsequently the lode as well, is indeed bad advice for investigation. Nevertheless, there are people of talent, [224] who, so to speak, with the divining rod in hand track down the treasures of knowledge, without ever having learned to do so; and no wonder, when they cannot teach others, they merely demonstrate how they do it, because it is a gift of Nature.

c. On Originality of the Cognitive Faculty or Genius

§ 57.[313]   To invent something is entirely different from discovering something. The thing that one discovers is assumed as already existing, only it had not yet been recognized; for example, America existed before Columbus. But what one invents, such as gunpowder, was not known before the artist* made it. But both, invention and discovery, can be of value. However, one may find something he was not looking for at all (like the gold assayer who found phosphorus), and then there is no merit in it whatsoever. The talent for invention is called genius.[314] But this name is attributed only to an artist, consequently to one who knows how to make something, not to him who merely stores information and knows about many things. It is also not attributed to an artist who merely imitates, but it is attributed to one who has been inspired to create something original in his work; finally, it is attributed to this artist only when his creation is exemplary, that is, when it is worthy to be imitated[315] as an example *(exemplar)*. Therefore, human genius is "the exemplary originality of man's talent" with regard to this or that type of artistic product. We also call a talented mind a genius; then this word is to mean not merely a person's gift of Nature, but the person himself

---

*   Long before the time of the monk Schwartz, gunpowder was used in the siege of Algeciras, and its invention seems to belong to the Chinese. But it may be, however, that some German who obtained this powder analyzed its contents (for example, by washing out the saltpeter in lye, by rinsing away the carbon, and by burning the sulphur), and thus discovered it, although he did not invent it.

as well. To be a genius in many departments is to be a vast genius (like Leonardo da Vinci).

The proper field for a genius is the imagination, because imagination is creative, and just because it is less subject to the coercion of rules than other faculties, it is more capable of originality.   [225] Because it always requires a student to imitate something, the mechanism of instruction is indeed detrimental to the budding of a genius as far as originality is concerned. However, every art requires certain mechanical and basic rules like the conformity of the product with the underlying idea, that is, truth in the presentation of the object one has in mind. This is something that must be learned through the discipline of schooling, and it is always a function of the art of imitation. But to set the imagination free from this constraint also, and to allow the inborn talent, even though it is contrary to its Nature, to proceed without rules and ramble about, would result perhaps in original nonsense, which[316] would surely not be exemplary, and hence could not be counted as genius.

Spirit[317] is the animating principle in a person. In the French language spirit and wit share the same term, that is, esprit; but this is different in German. We say that a speech, a handwriting, a lady in society, and so forth, are beautiful, but without spirit. The supply of wit does not count here because we may become disgusted with it, since its effect leaves nothing worthwhile behind. If all these above-mentioned things and persons are to be called spirited, then they must arouse our interest by means of ideas. Spirit sets the imagination into motion and it provides such faculties with a large field of operation. Therefore, how about using the German term "inborn spirit" [eigenthümlicher Geist] to express the French word génie? Our nation permits itself to be told that the French have in their own language a word which we do not have in ours. We are told to borrow from them, whereas they in turn have borrowed the word genius from Latin, which means nothing else but inborn spirit.

The cause, however, why this exemplary originality of talent is known by this mystical name, is that the man who has genius cannot explain to himself its outbursts nor how he arrived at a skill which he never tried to learn. Invisibility (of a cause regarding an effect) is a subordinate notion of spirit (a genius which has been associated with the talented from birth) whose inspiration it simply follows, so to speak. The mental powers, however, must operate harmoniously with the help of the imagination; otherwise they would not inspire but would disturb each other; the harmonizing must arise from the nature of the subject;[318]   [226] wherefore we can say that genius can also be described as the talent "by which Nature gives rules to art."

§ 58.[319]   FOR the present we may leave uninvestigated the question of whether the world on the whole is particularly served by great geniuses, because they often take new roads and open up new vistas; or whether mechanical minds, even if they are not epoch-making, with their common and slowly advancing understanding on the crutches of experience, have contributed most for the growth of the arts and sciences (because, even if no one is stimulated to admire them, it is true that they also cause no confusion). However, a certain type of them, men of genius as they are called (though they might better be called apes of genius), have rallied together under the banner bearing the words "minds extraordinarily endowed by Nature," and have declared that both painstaking study and research are amateurish and that they have laid hold of the spirit of all science in one grasp, although they pretend to administer it in small doses, concentrated and powerful. This type, like that of the quack and charlatan, is very detrimental to progress in scientific and ethical education when he, like the professional or dictator, dogmatizes from the chair of wisdom in the tone of conviction on matters of religion, politics, and morals, and thus knows how to conceal the paltriness of his mind. What else is there to do than to laugh, and patiently pursue one's course with industry, orderliness, and clarity, without even giving such an impostor a second look?

§ 59.[320]   ACCORDING to the disparity of the national character and soil, into which it was born, genius also appears to have different original seeds within itself and seems to develop them in different ways. In the Germans, it usually reveals itself more in the roots; in the Italians, more in the leafage; in the French, more in the blossom; and in the English, more in the fruit.

The generalistic mind (interested in all the different kinds of knowledge) is still distinguished from the genius, who is understood as the inventive mind. The generalistic mind can be inventive about what can be learned; in fact he is a person who possesses historical knowledge of what has been done in all scientific fields; he is called a polyhistorian, like Julius Caesar Scaliger.[321] But the genius is a man not only of wide range of mind but also of intensive intellectual greatness, who is epoch-making in everything he undertakes (like Newton and Leibniz).[322] A subordinate, but still not common, type of genius is the architectonic mind that understands the methodical interrelations of all sciences and sees how they support each other.   [227] However, there is also something like gigantic erudition which is often cyclopean, because it lacks one eye, the eye of true philosophy which puts the understanding to the purposeful use of this vast collection of historical knowledge equal to the load of a hundred camels.

Purely natural minds (*élèves de la nature, autodidacti*) may often be taken for geniuses because they have thought out for themselves many a thing that they could have learned from someone else; and thus they are geniuses in something which in itself should not attract a genius' attention; just as there are many in Switzerland who are inventors as far as the mechanical arts are concerned. But precocious wonder children *(ingenium praecox)*, of an ephemeral nature, like Heinecke[323] in Lübeck, or Baratier[324] in Halle, are a deviation from the rules of Nature, they are rarities for a naturalist's showcase. Their very early maturity is a source of attention, but often also cause enough for repentance on the part of those who promoted them in the rudiments of learning.

Since the full employment of the cognitive faculty for its own advancement, even in theoretical knowledge, ultimately stands in need of Reason, which provides the rules without which it cannot be advanced, we can comprehend the demand which Reason makes on cognition as three questions which are directed at the three cognitive faculties: What do I intend to do? (asks the understanding);* What is of importance? (asks the judgment); What is the result? (asks the Reason).

The ability to answer all three questions varies according to the ability of minds. The first question requires only a clear mind to understand itself; and this natural talent is quite common after some education, particularly if one draws attention to this ability. To answer the second question properly is a greater rarity, because all sorts of ways are open to analyze the concept in question and to propose an apparent solution of the problem. What is the only   [228] exactly appropriate answer to a question (for example, in lawsuits, or at the outset of certain plans of action designed for an identical purpose)? There is a certain talent which can make the correct choice for a given instance *(judicium discretivum)*. Such a talent is much desired but also very seldom at hand. The lawyer who continues citing many facts which are supposed to support his assertions, makes the decision more difficult for the judge, since he himself is in the dark. But if the lawyer, after developing his argument, knows how to hit upon the point (for there is only one

---

* Intention is here to be understood only in the theoretical sense: What do I intend to maintain as *true?*

point) of primary importance, then the matter is settled shortly, and the verdict of reason follows by itself.

The understanding is positive and dispels the darkness of ignorance; judgment is more negative so that errors can be avoided which result from the dim light in which objects appear. Reason reduces the potential for errors (prejudices) and thereby safeguards the understanding through the universality of principles. Booklearning may increase knowledge, but it does not expand the concept and insight unless reason intervenes. Booklearning, however, is still different from subtilizing, the plainly experimental use of reason which does not employ any law of reason. If the question is whether or not I should believe in ghosts, I could subtilize about their possibility in divers ways; but reason prohibits the superstitious assumption of their possibility without a principle of explanation firmly based on the laws of experience.

By means of the great differences between minds as to the way they look at exactly the same objects, and at each other, by means of the friction between them and the connections between them as well as the separations, Nature produces, for analysts and thinkers, a drama of endless variety that is worth seeing. For the class of thinkers the following maxims (which have already been mentioned as conducive to wisdom)[325] may be laid down as immutable laws: 1) think independently; 2) (in communication with people) put yourself in thought into the place of the other person; 3) always think in harmony with your own self.

The first principle is negative (*nullius addictus jurare in verba magistri*),[326] it is the principle of freedom from restraint; the second principle is positive, it is that of the Liberals who accommodate themselves to the concepts of others; [229] the third is the principle of a consistent (in the sense of logically correct) way of thinking. Anthropology can exhibit examples of each of these three principles, and even more examples of their opposites.

The mightiest revolution coming from inside of man is "his departure from his self-incurred tutelage." Instead of letting others think for him, while he was merely imitating or allowing himself to be guided by others, he now dares to proceed, though still shakily, with his own feet upon the ground of experience.

Second Book[1]

On the Feeling of Pleasure and Displeasure

CLASSIFICATION: *1)* Sensuous pleasure, *2)* intellectual pleasure. The first is either conceived   A. by sensation (gratification), or   B. by the imagination (taste); the second (that is, the intellectual pleasure) is conceived either *a.* by representable concepts or *b.* by ideas. The opposite, displeasure, is also conceived in the same way.

ON SENSUOUS PLEASURE

A.   On the Feeling for the Pleasant, or On Sensuous Pleasure in the Sensation of an Object

§ 60.[2]   GRATIFICATION is a pleasure of sensation, and whatever amuses a sense is said to be pleasant. Pain is displeasure of sensation and whatever produces it is unpleasant. They are opposed to each other, not like gain and deficiency (+ or 0), but like gain and loss (+ and −), that is, one is not contrasted with the other merely as an opposite *(contradictorie, sive logice oppositum)*,[3] but rather as a counterpart *(contrarie sive realiter oppositum)*.[4] The expressions for what pleases or displeases, and for what lies in between, the indifferent, are too broad, because they may also refer to the intellectual, wherein they would not coincide with gratification and pain.

It is possible to explain these feelings also by the effect which the sensation of our physical condition has on the mind. [231] Whatever incites me directly (through my senses) to abandon (to depart from) my condition is unpleasant to me, it gives me pain; and whatever drives me to maintain (to remain in) my condition is pleasant to me, it gratifies me. But we are incessantly moved by the stream of time, and the change of sensations resultant from it. Even if the abandonment of one instant, and the occurring of another, is one and the same act (of change), it is, nevertheless, in our thought and in our awareness of change, a temporal sequence conforming to the relation of cause and effect. Now the question arises whether the awareness of leaving the present state, or the prospect of entering a future state, awakens in us the sensation of gratification. In the first instance the gratification is nothing more than ending the pain and therefore something negative; whereas in the second instance the presentiment of pleasantness, that is an expected intensification of the state of pleasure, would be something positive. It can, however, already be conjectured, that the former will take place in any case since time drags us from the present to the future (not the other way round), and that we are compelled at first to depart from the present, without any certainty into which other state we shall enter. We are only certain that it will be a different one which in itself can be the cause of a pleasant feeling.

Gratification is the feeling of advancement; pain is that of a hindrance of life. But the life (of the animal) is, as physicians have also noticed, a continuing play of the antagonism between these two feelings.

Therefore pain must precede every gratification; pain always comes first. What else but a quick death from joy would follow a steady advancement of vitality, which cannot be increased beyond a certain point anyway?

Also, no gratification can immediately follow another; but between one and another there must occur pain. Actually small checks on our vital power, with interspersed advancements, constitute the state of health which we erroneously take for a continuously felt condition of well-being, since it always consists only of erratic sequences of pleasant feelings (constantly interspersed with pain). Pain is the incentive to activity, and, above all, in activity we feel that we are alive; without such a good, inertia would set in.

[232] Pain, which disappears slowly (like the gradual recovery from an illness or the slow reacquisition of lost capital), is not followed by strong gratification, because the transition is not noticed. I subscribe with full conviction to these maxims of Count Veri.[5]

Elucidation through Examples

Why is a game (especially for money) so attractive, and, if it is not too self-serving, why is it the best distraction and recreation after long and exhausting thought? One can recuperate only slowly by remaining idle. A game is a state of incessant movement between fearing and hoping. After a game the evening meal tastes better and agrees with us better. Why are dramas (whether tragedies or comedies) so alluring? Because all entertain certain complications, fears, and dilemmas between hope and joy, and because the play of opposing emotions at the end provides the spectator with an enhancement of life by stirring him inwardly. Why does a love-novel end with a wedding; and why is a sequel (to Fielding's novel) written by a clumsy amateur so repugnant and in bad taste when he continues the story into the married life of the couple? Jealousy before marriage, like the anguish of the lovers between their joys and hopes, is spice for the reader, while in marriage it is poison, because, to use the language of such a novel, "the end of love's grief, is also the end of love" (understood, of course, as love with passion). Why is work the best way of enjoying life? Because it is a troublesome occupation (unpleasant in itself and delightful only in its success), so that relaxation, through the mere disappearance of a long hardship, turns into sensible pleasure, that is, cheerfulness, because otherwise there would not be anything enjoyable. Tobacco (whether smoked or snuffed) is initially linked with an unpleasant sensation. But just because nature instantaneously does away with the pain (by secretion of mucus at the palate or in the nose), tobacco (especially when smoked) becomes a sort of companion who entertains and constantly stimulates sensations and even thoughts, though they are only of the roaming kind. Finally, the one who is not induced to activity by any positive pain will always be affected by a negative one, namely [233] boredom, perceived as a form of emptiness of sensation by the person accustomed to change of sensations. In trying to fill his life with something such a person will often feel compelled to do something harmful to himself rather than do nothing at all.[6]

On Boredom and Amusement

§ 61.[7] To feel one's life, to enjoy oneself, is then nothing else but to feel constantly impelled to pass beyond the present state (which, consequently, has also to be a frequently recurring grief). This also explains the oppressive, distressing difficulty of boredom for all persons who are mindful of their life and their time (cultivated people).* This stimulus or impulse

* Because of his inborn dullness the Carib [see sec. 35, n. 198—Trans.] is free from this difficulty. He can sit for hours with his fishing rod without catching anything; his want of thought is caused by a lack of incentive activity, which always brings grief with it and is therefore dismissed. Our

to forsake every point of time in which we find ourselves, and to pass over into the next moment, has accelerating characteristics and may turn into the determination to put an end to one's life. The luxurious person has experimented with pleasures of every kind, and no pleasure is new to him any longer; just as people in Paris said of Lord Mordaunt: "The English hang themselves in order to while their time away."[8] The dearth of sensations perceived in oneself produces a dread *(horror vacui)*, and, as it were, the presentiment of a slow death is regarded as more agonizing than when fate suddenly cuts the thread of life.

This also explains why pastimes are equaled with entertainment because the quicker we can make time pass, the more we feel ourselves refreshed. Among friends who have talked for three hours while taking a pleasure ride in a carriage, one will at the end look at his watch and ask   [234] "Where did all that time go?" or say, "How short the time has been for us." We would regret the loss of time very little if the attention to time would be a pleasure and not so much directed to the attention to pain which we strive to leave behind us. Conversations which have little exchange of ideas are called tedious, and just because of this tiresome; and an entertaining man may not be considered important but nevertheless pleasant. As soon as he steps into the room, the face of every guest lights up, like the joyfulness resulting from being relieved of a burden.

But how do we explain the phenomenon that a person complains at the end of his days about the brevity of life, when he had been so tormented with boredom most of his life that every day appeared very long to him.

---

world of readers of refined taste is always sustained by the appetite and even the ravenous hunger for reading (a type of idleness) ephemeral literature. Such reading is done not for the sake of self-cultivation, but rather for enjoyment; so that readers' heads always stay empty, and there is no fear of overeating, because they give to their busy idleness the aspect of work, and pretend to themselves a meritorious use of time, which is in no way better than what the *Journal des Luxus und der Moden* offers to the public.

The cause is to be sought in analogy to a similar observation: Why do German miles (not measured or indicated by milestones, like the Russian versts) become ever shorter the nearer we come to the capital (such as Berlin), and become longer, the farther we are away from the capital (as in Pomerania)? The large number of objects seen (villages and farmhouses) leaves the memory with the deceptive conclusion that a vast amount of space has been covered and, consequently, that a longer period of time has passed. The open space[9] in the latter instance produces less recollection of what has been seen, and therefore it is concluded that the journey has been shorter, and that the time also has been shorter than would be shown by the clock. Just as the great number of periods lived through, which characterize the last part of life with numerous and varying tasks already performed, will arouse in an old person the imagination of a longer lived life, than he would think according to the number of years. Filling one's time with harmoniously progressive activities, which have an important and intended purpose in view *(vitam extendere factis),*[10] is the only certain means of becoming happy with one's life and at the same time feeling satisfactorily experienced. "The more you have thought, and the more you have done, the longer you have lived (even in your own fancy)." The conclusion of such a life would occur with contentment.

But what about contentment *(acquiescentia)* during life? It is not attainable for mankind, neither in the moral aspect (to be content with oneself and one's good conduct), nor in the pragmatic   [235] aspect (as to one's well-being which he intends to acquire through skill and cleverness). Nature has given man pain as a goad to activity. Man cannot escape from this goad; he needs it so that he can always progress to what is better. Even in the last moments of life, contentment with the last period lived through can be called only comparative (partly because we compare ourselves with the lot of others, and partly because we compare ourselves with ourselves).

Contentment is, however, never pure and[11] complete. To be (absolutely) contented with life would mean inactive rest, the cessation of all motivation, or the dulling of[12] sensations and associated activities. Such a state of inactivity can not prevail over the intellectual life of man because death would follow inevitably, as at the stopping of the heart in an animal's body, unless a new stimulus (through pain) is forthcoming.

NOTE. In this section we also ought to consider the emotional excitement as a feeling of pleasure and displeasure, which transgresses the limits of man's inner freedom. But since it is frequently confused with the passions, which will be discussed in another section, that is, the one on the faculty of desire,[13] and since it is really closely related to desires, I shall address myself to the emotional excitement at the proper time in the third section.

§ 62.[14]   BEING joyously disposed is usually a temperamental trait, but it may also be a result of principles like Epicurus's principle of feeling happy, so-called by others and accordingly decried, which actually was intended to mean the ever joyful heart of a wise person. Even-tempered is he who neither rejoices nor frets; he is very different from the one who does not care about the events of life because the latter's feeling has become dull. Different from equanimity is the ill-humored disposition (which may at first have been called lunatic disposition). It signifies a person's tendency to have fits of joy or sadness for which no apparent reason can be given by the afflicted. It is a characteristic especially common with hypochondriacs. This disposition is entirely different from the playful talent (of Butler or Sterne),[15] with which the witty person gives, with roguish simplicity, the audience or the reader an opportunity to rearrange on their own those objects which have intentionally been misplaced (by standing them on their heads, so to speak). Sensitivity is not opposed to equanimity, because it is a faculty [236] and a power which either permits the states of pleasure or displeasure, or even keeps them from being felt. Sensitivity is accompanied by a choice. Sentimentality, on the other hand, is a weakness because of its interest in the condition of others who could play the sentimentalist at will, and even affect that person against his will. Sensitivity is masculine because the man who wants to spare his wife or children from hardship or grief must possess such delicate feeling as is necessary to make others judge their sensation not by his own strength but rather by their weakness. The delicacy of his sensation is necessary for generosity. On the other hand, the hypocritical extension of one's feelings in order to appear sympathetically in tune with the feelings of others, thus allowing oneself to remain passive, is silly and childish. There can and should be piety with good humor; difficult but necessary work can and ought to be performed with good humor; indeed one can and should even die with good humor, since all this loses its value when it is done or endured in a bad humor and[16] sullen temper.

Concerning grief which one broods over intentionally as a grief which is never to end except with life itself, it is said that someone has something weighing on his mind (some trouble). However, one does not have to have something weighing on one's mind, since what cannot be changed must be dismissed from the mind. It would be nonsensical wanting to make what has happened into what has not happened. To better oneself[17] is good and it is also a duty, but wishing to better what is already beyond one's power is absurd. On the other hand, taking something to heart, which means accepting good advice and instruction with good intentions, is the deliberate determination to supply one's will with a sufficiently strong feeling for carrying it out. The penitence of the self-tormentor, who should quickly apply his disposition toward finding a better way of life, is simply a lost labor. And it has, in addition, the bad consequence that he regards his guilt as thereby erased (simply through remorse) so that he does not have to subject himself to striving for the better, which under reasonable circumstances should now have been doubled.

§ 63.[18]   ONE kind of self-gratification also brings cultivation with it. It increases the faculty of enjoying more gratification of this sort, and applies to the sciences and the fine arts. Another kind of self-gratification, however, is overindulgence, which makes us less and less susceptible   [237] to further enjoyment. Upon whichever course one may seek gratification, it is a principal maxim, as has already been stated above,[19] for someone to indulge only so far that he could still go further, since being completely satisfied causes that disgusting state which makes life a burden for the spoiled person who has everything, and which consumes women with so-called vapors. Young man! (I repeat)[20] be fond of your work; deny yourself pleasures, not for the sake of denying, but rather in order to keep them always in view as far as possible! Do not dull your capacity for receptivity by indulging yourself prematurely! The maturity of old age, which never makes you regret the loss of a single physical pleasure, will assure, even in this sacrifice, a store of contentment which is independent of chance as well as the laws of Nature.

§ 64.[21]   HOWEVER, we also judge pleasure and sorrow by a higher satisfaction or dissatisfaction within ourselves (namely, the moral). We have to decide whether we ought to refrain or indulge.

1.   The object may be pleasant; but the pleasure we take in it may be dissatisfying. Therefore we have the expression "a bitter joy." A person who is in precarious circumstances and then inherits the estate of his parents or other worthy and generous relatives, cannot avoid rejoicing

over their death, though he also cannot keep from reproaching himself for his joy. This is exactly what takes
place in the mind of a colleague who attends, with sincere
sadness, the funeral of his honored predecessor.

2. The object may be unpleasant, but grieving about it
may be pleasing. Therefore we have the expression,
"sweet sorrow," for example, of a surviving widow who is
otherwise very well off, but who will not allow herself to
be comforted; this is something which is often improperly explained as affectation.

On the other hand, pleasure may also provide satisfaction when a person finds pleasure in such objects
which provide honor to him through his occupation with
them, for example, devoting oneself to the fine arts
rather than to mere sensual enjoyment; thus he has the
added satisfaction that he (as a refined person) is capable
of such pleasures. Likewise, the sorrow of a person can
also be dissatisfying to him. The hate of an insulted
person is pain; and, even after satisfaction, the high-
minded person cannot refrain from reproaching himself
with the fact that he still continues to bear a grudge
against the offender.

[238] § 65.[22]   PLEASURE which someone (lawfully) acquires himself[23] is doubly felt, first as
a prize, and then also as merit (the inner awareness of
being the author himself). Money gained by working is
gratifying; at least for a longer time than money won in
games of chance. Even if one disregards the general
harmfulness of the lottery, there remains, nevertheless,
something which a high-minded man must be ashamed of
if he should win by this means. An evil for which an
external cause is to blame is a source of grief; but an evil
for which oneself is to blame saddens and depresses.
    But how is it to be justified that in the case of an evil
which one person has suffered from another, two kinds

of explanation are given? Thus, for example, one sufferer says: "I would be satisfied if I were in the least to blame for it." But a second sufferer says: "It is consolation to me that I am completely innocent in this case." Innocent suffering is irritating since it is an insult inflicted by another person. Guilty suffering depresses because it is a reproach from inside. One can easily see that of the two the second is the better person.

§ 66.[24]   IT is surely not the loveliest trait of man to increase his pleasure by comparing his own state with the sorrow of others, while their own sorrow is diminished by comparison with similar of even greater sufferings of others. This effect, however, is merely psychological (according to the law of contrasts: *opposita juxta se posita magis elucescunt*)[25] and has no moral implications like wishing suffering on others so that one may feel the comfort of one's own state all the more intensely. By means of the imagination one sympathizes with others (for example, when one sees a person who has lost his balance and is ready to fall, one involuntarily and vainly leans toward the opposite side in order to place him back into balance again); and one is only happy about not being in the same situation.* Similarly, the masses run with greater[26] desire to look at the public exhibition and execution of a criminal, than to the performance of a play. The emotions and feelings, which are expressed on the victim's face   [239] and in his bearing, have a sympathetic effect on the spectator. Such emotions, through

---

*   *Suave mari* [A: *Dulci, mari*—Ed.] *magno, turbantibus aequora ventis,*
    E terra alterius magnum spectare laborem;
    Non quia vexari quenquam est jucunda voluptas
    Sed quibus ipse malis careas, quia cernere suave est.
                                                        LUCRETIUS

[It is sweet, when the winds disturb the waters on the vast deep, to behold from the land the great distress of another; not because it is a joyous pleasure that any one should be-made-to-suffer, but because it is agreeable to see from what evils thou thyself art free. *De Rerum Natura* 2. 1–4, trans. Watson (London, 1851).]

the imagination (heightened by the solemnity of the affair), cause the spectator to be uneasy, but also leave behind a gentle but genuine feeling of exhaustion, which makes the subsequent enjoyment of life even more pleasurable.

Also, if one compares one's own grief with other possible griefs of one's own, it becomes thereby more tolerable. The misfortune of someone who has broken his leg may be made more bearable if he is shown that he might easily have broken his neck.

The most basic and easiest means of alleviating all grief is the thought, which one can well expect a reasonable person to have, that life itself and the enjoyment of it, so far as it depends upon circumstances, has no value of its own; what alone has value is the use to which life is put and the end to which it is directed. The value of life has to be created by man, it cannot be obtained through luck but only through wisdom. He who is anxiously concerned over losing his life will never enjoy life.

B.   On the Feeling for the Beautiful, *i.e.,*
On the Partly Sensuous, Partly Intellectual Pleasure
in the Reflective Perception, or On Taste[27]

§ 67.[28]   TASTE, in the proper sense of the word, is, as has already been stated above,[29] the property of an organ (the tongue, the palate, and the gullet) to be specifically affected by certain dissolved matter in food or drink. According to its use it is to be understood either as a differentiating taste alone or, at the same time, as a pleasant taste (for example, whether something is sweet or bitter, or whether what is tasted [sweet or bitter] is pleasant). Distinguishing taste can provide universal agreement as to how certain things are to be labeled, but pleasant taste can never yield a universally valid judgment: namely, that something (for example, something bitter) which is pleasant to me will also be pleasant to everybody. The reason for this is clear because neither pleasure nor displeasure belong to the cognitive faculty concerning objects; they are rather determinations   [240] of the subject which, therefore, cannot be attributed to external objects. Pleasant taste also contains the concept of a distinction between satisfaction and dissatisfaction, which I relate to the idea of the object in the perception or imagination.

The word taste is, however, also used for a sensory faculty of judgment, which is not merely to choose for myself, according to my own sense perception, but also according to a certain rule believed to be valid for everybody.[30] This rule may be empirical, in which case, however, it can neither lay any claim to true universality, nor, consequently, to necessity (because the judgment of everyone else about pleasant taste would have to agree with my own). This kind of rule is illustrated by the habits of taste which apply to meals. The Germans begin with a soup, whereas the English begin with solid food, because a custom, gradually extended by imitation, has turned into a rule as to the sequence of courses.

There is also a pleasant taste whose rule must be established a priori, because it indicates with necessity, hence it is valid for everybody, how the idea of an object is to be judged in relation to the feeling of pleasure or displeasure (where, consequently, reason is secretly at play, although one cannot derive its judgment from principles of reason, and demonstrate it accordingly). One could classify this taste as a rationalizing taste in distinction to the empirical as the sensuous taste, (the former being the *gustus reflectens,*[31] the other *gustus reflexus*).

Every tasteful reference to oneself or one's own skills presupposes a social intention (to express oneself), which is not always sociable (sharing in the pleasure of others), but initially usually barbaric, unsociable, and merely competitive. No one in complete solitude will dress up[32] and sweep out his house; he will not even do it for his own wife and children, but only for a guest, in

order to present himself in a favorable light. In taste
(discrimination), however, that is, in aesthetic judgment,
it is not directly the sensation (the material of the idea of
an object), but rather how the free (productive) imagination combines it through its creativity, that is, the form,
which produces satisfaction in an object.[33] Only the form
is capable of stating[34]   [241] a general rule for the feeling
of pleasure. One need not expect such a general rule
from sense perception which may vary greatly according
to the different sense-capacity of subjects. One may
therefore explain taste as follows: "Taste is the faculty of
aesthetic judgment which makes universally valid dis-
criminations."[35]

Taste is, therefore, a faculty of the social judgment
of external objects within the imagination. Here the
mind feels its freedom in the play of images (therefore of
sensibility), since sociability with other people presupposes freedom; and this feeling is pleasure. But the universal validity of this pleasure for everyone, whereby
discrimination (of the beautiful) with taste is distinguished from discrimination through mere sense perception (of what is only subjectively pleasing), that is, of
what is agreeable, contains the concept of a law within
itself, because only in accordance with this law can the
validity of satisfaction be universal for the person who
makes the judgment. The faculty of perceiving the universal, however, is the understanding. Thus, the judgment of taste is just as much an aesthetic judgment as it is
a judgment of the understanding; but they are both in
combination, (and therefore the latter is not considered
to be pure). The judging of an object through taste is a
judgment about the harmony or discord concerning the
freedom of play between imagination and the law-
abiding character of the understanding, and, therefore,
applies only to the form of judging aesthetically (the
compatibility of the sense perceptions), and not to the
generation of products in which the form is perceived. It
would otherwise apply to the genius whose passionate

vitality often needs to be moderated and limited by the propriety of taste.

The beautiful alone is that which appertains to taste; the sublime, however, appertains also to the aesthetic judgment, but not to taste. But the idea of the sublime can and should be beautiful in itself; otherwise it would be crude, barbaric, and contrary to taste. Even the portrayal of the evil or ugly (for example, in the figure of the personified Death in Milton) can and must be beautiful whenever an object is to be aesthetically imagined,[36] even if a Thersites[37] were to be portrayed. Otherwise the portrayal would arouse either distaste or disgust which both involve an endeavor to reject an idea that has been offered for enjoyment; whereas the beautiful contains in itself the concept of the invitation to the most intimate union with the object, that is, to immediate enjoyment.   [242] With the expression of a "beautiful soul" one says all that can be said about the purpose of the innermost union with the beautiful. Greatness of soul and strength of soul relate to the matter (the tools for certain purposes); but goodness of soul,[38] the pure form under which all purposes must be united, is therefore, wherever it is encountered, similar to Eros in the world of myth, archetypically creative and also supernatural. Such goodness of soul is still the focal point around which the judgment of taste assembles all its judgments of sensuous pleasure as long as they are compatible with the freedom of the understanding.

NOTE. How might it have happened that the modern languages particularly have chosen to name the aesthetic faculty of judgment with an expression (*gustus, sapor*) which merely refers to a certain sense-organ (the inside of the mouth), and that the discrimination as well as the choice of palatable things is determined by it? There is no situation in which sensibility and understanding, united in enjoyment, can be as long continued and as often repeated with satisfaction as a good meal in good company. The sensibility, however, is regarded in this case only as a vehicle of conversation for the understanding. The aesthetic taste of the host manifests itself in his ability to make a universally acceptable selection, something which he cannot accomplish completely with his own sense of taste, because his guests might perhaps wish to choose other foods or drinks, each according to his own private sense. Consequently, the host makes his decisions with the tastes of his guests in mind, so that everyone finds something to his own liking; such a procedure yields a comparatively universal validity. His skill in choosing guests who can engage themselves in mutual and general conversation (which is indeed also called taste, but in reality it is reason applied to taste, and yet is distinct from taste), cannot enter into the present question. And so the feeling of an organ through a particular sense has been able to yield the name for an ideal feeling, a feeling for a sensory, universally valid choice in general. It is even more strange that the skill to test by sense whether something is an object of enjoyment for one and the same subject (not whether the choice of it is universally valid) (*sapor*) has even been exaggerated to designate wisdom (*sapientia*). Perhaps the reason for this is that an unconditional, necessary purpose requires neither deliberation nor experiment, [243] but comes to mind immediately by, so to speak, the tasting of what is wholesome.

§ 68.[39]   THE sublime (*sublime*) is awe-inspiring magnitude (*magnitudo reverenda*) as to extent or degree which invites approach (in order to test how far one measures up to it); but the fear of diminishing one's own estimation through the comparison with it is at the same time acting as a deterrent (for example, thunder over our heads, or a high, wild mountain). In this connection, if one feels confident enough and tries to collect one's powers to comprehend the phenomenon, and if then, one begins to fear that one cannot measure up to its grandeur, a feeling of astonishment is aroused (a pleasant feeling through the continual overcoming of pain).

The sublime is the counterpoise, but not the reflection of the beautiful; because the effort and attempt to elevate oneself to a grasping *(apprehensio)* of the object awakens in the subject a feeling of his own magnitude and strength; but the idea of the sublime in thought by description or presentation can and must always be beautiful. Otherwise veneration becomes repugnance which differs greatly from admiration as an act of judgment, whereby one cannot satisfy one's own veneration.

Magnitude, which runs contrary to the purpose *(magnitudo monstrosa),* is the monstrous. Writers, therefore, who wanted to extol the vast extent of the Russian Empire, have missed the mark in designating it as monstrous because there is a reproach involved which implies that Russia was too huge for a single ruler. A person is adventurous who has the inclination to involve himself in events whose true account resembles a novel.

The sublime, therefore, is not an object of taste, but a feeling of emotion; however, the artistic presentation of the sublime in description and embellishment (in secondary works, *parerga*) may be and ought to be beautiful, since otherwise it would be wild, crude, and repulsive, and, consequently, contrary to taste.

[244]   Taste Contains a Tendency toward
         External Advancement of Morality

§ 69.⁴⁰   TASTE (as a formal sense) concerns the communication of one's feeling of pleasure or displeasure to somone else. It includes a susceptibility, which through this communication affects others with the pleasure of sharing a satisfaction *(complacentia)* with other persons (that is, sociably). Satisfaction must be considered as generally valid not only for the experiencing subject, but also for anybody else, because it must contain necessity (of satisfaction) and, so that it can be so recognized, an a priori principle of necessity. Satisfaction means contentment with the agreement between the pleasure of the subject and the feeling of any other person according to a general law which has to result from the general mental constitution of the feeling person, consequently from reason. This means that the choice of such satisfaction is subject, according to form, to the principle of duty. Therefore the ideal taste has a tendency toward the external advancement of morality. Training a person to become well-mannered for his own social position will not mean as much as educating him to be morally good; but, nevertheless, the effort prepares him to please (to be liked or admired by) others in his social position. In this way one could call taste morality in external appearance; even though such an expression, understood literally, contains a contradiction because being well-mannered already has the appearance or demeanor of morality, and even though it contains a certain degree of it, namely, the inclination[41] to ascribe value even to the appearance of good manners.

§ 70.[42]   To be well-mannered, proper, polite, and polished (by disposing of rudeness) is, nevertheless, only the negative condition of taste. The representation of these qualities in the imagination can be a tasteful, externally intuitive way of imagining an object, or one's own person, but for two senses only, hearing and sight. Music and plastic art (painting, sculpture, architecture, and gardening) lay claim to taste as a susceptibility of a feeling of pleasure for the mere forms of outer perception, the former in respect to hearing, the latter in respect to sight. On the other hand,   [245] the discursive way of imagining through the spoken or written word embraces two arts wherein taste can manifest itself: rhetoric and poetry.

Anthropological Observations Concerning Taste

a. *On Taste in Fashions*

§ 71.[43] IT is a natural inclination of man[44] to compare his behavior to that of a more important
person (the child compares itself to grown-ups, and the
lowly compares himself to the aristocrat) in order to
imitate the other person's ways. A law of such imitation,
which aims at not appearing less important than others,
especially when no regard is paid to gaining any profit
from it, is called fashion. Therefore it belongs under the
title of vanity, because in its intention there is no inner
value; at the same time, it belongs also under the title of
folly, because in fashion there is still a compulsion to
subject oneself slavishly to the mere example which
many in society project to us. To be in fashion is a matter
of taste; he who clings to custom which is out of fashion is
said to be old-fashioned; and he who even attributes
value to being out of fashion is an odd person. But it is
always better, nevertheless, to be a fool in fashion than a
fool out of fashion, if one chooses to brand this vanity at
all with such a hard name, a title which the mania for
fashion really deserves whenever it sacrifices true uses or
even duties to such vanity. All fashions are, by their very
concept, mutable ways of living. Whenever the play of
imitating becomes fixed, imitation becomes usage, and
that means the end of taste. Novelty makes fashion alluring; and to be inventive in all sorts of external forms,
even if they often degenerate into something fantastic
and even detestable, belongs to the style of courtiers,
especially the ladies, whom others then follow avidly.
Those in low social positions burden themselves with
these fashions long after the courtiers have put them
aside. Therefore, fashion is not properly a matter of taste
(for it may be extremely antagonistic to taste), but a
matter of mere vanity in order to appear distinguished,

and a matter of competition in order to surpass others in it. (The *élégants de la cour,* otherwise called *petits maîtres,* are windbags.)

Something splendid and sublime which is at the same time beautiful, can be combined with true,   [246] ideal taste (like a splendid starry heaven, or, if it does not sound too out of place, a St. Peter's Church in Rome). Even pomp, an ostentatious exhibition for the sake of show, can be combined with taste; but not without objection by taste, because pomp is intended for a great mass of people, including much rabble, whose taste, being dull, calls more for the stimulation of the senses than the capacity of judgment.

b. *On Artistic Taste*

I shall now consider only the speaking arts, rhetoric and poetry, because they are aimed at a mood whereby the mind is directly aroused to activity. They have their place in a pragmatic anthropology in which one seeks to know Man from the point of view of what can be made of him.

The mental principle that animates by means of ideas is called spirit. Taste is a mere regulative faculty which judges form as to the uniting of the manifold in the imagination. Spirit, however, is the productive faculty of Reason, which supplies a pattern (a priori) for that form before the imagination is applied. Consider spirit and taste: spirit is to create ideas; taste is to confine ideas to the proper form which fits the laws of productive imagination, and thus is to create *(fingendi)* in an original way (not imitatively). A product composed with spirit and taste can be called poesy and is a work belonging to the fine arts. Such a product can be presented directly to the senses by means of the eyes or ears. Poesy can also be called the art of poetry *(poetica in sensu lato);*[45] it comprises painting, gardening, architecture, music, and the

art of making verse *(poetica in sensu stricto)*.[46] The art of
poetry, however, to contrast it with rhetoric, is different
from rhetoric only in the mutual submission of understanding and sensibility. The art of poetry is an activity of
the sensibility organized by the understanding; rhetoric
is a transaction of the understanding animated by sensibility. Both however, the orator and the poet (in a broad
sense), are makers[47] who generate out of their own selves
new forms [247] (combinations of what is sensuous) in
their imagination.*

Since the poetic gift implies an aptitude for art and,
combined with taste, a talent for the fine arts which aim
partly at illusion (although it is sweet and often also
indirectly beneficial), it is obvious that not much (often
even harmful) use of the poetic gift has been made in life.
To appreciate the character of the poet and the influence
which his craft has upon himself and others, it is worthwhile to ask some questions and provide some comments.[48]

Why does poetry among the fine (eloquent) arts win
the prize over rhetoric, even when their purposes are
precisely the same? Because poetry is at the same time
music (it can be sung) and tone, it is a sound pleasant for
its own sake, something which does not apply to mere
speech. Even rhetoric borrows from poetry one sound

* Novelty in the presentation of a concept is a principal demand made
by the fine arts upon the poet, even if the concept itself should not be new.
But for the understanding (without regard to taste) one has the following
expressions for the augmentation of our knowledge through new perceptions. To discover something is perceiving something for the first time that
was already there, for example, America, the magnetic force existing at the
poles, or atmospheric electricity. To invent is bringing into being what has
not been there before, for example, the compass and the aerostat. To track
down something is recovering something lost, by searching. To devise and
to contrive have to do with tools for the artist, or machines. To fabricate is
consciously representing the false as true, as in novels where it happens only
for entertainment. Fiction propagated as truth, however, is a lie.

(Turpiter atrum desinit in piscem mulier formosa supern—HORATIUS.)

[The woman, well shaped on top, ends below ugly in a black fish—Ed.]

that approaches tone, namely, the accent, without which speech would lack the necessary interspersed moments of pause and emphasis. Poetry, however, does not only win the prize over rhetoric, but also over any other of the fine arts, like painting (including sculpture), and even music. Music is a fine (not merely pleasant) art only because it serves poetry as a vehicle. Also, there are among poets not so many shallow heads (unfit for business), as there are among musicians, because poets speak also to the understanding, while musicians speak only to the senses. A good poem is the most penetrating means of enlivening the mind. It is true, however, not merely of the poets but   [248] of every artist, that one must be born to it, and that one cannot attain it by industry and imitation. Also, to succeed in his work, the artist needs to be possessed of a good disposition as well as a moment of inspiration (therefore he is also called *vates*), because whatever is made according to instructions and rules turns out to be spiritless (slavish). But a product of the fine arts requires not only taste, which may be based upon imitation, but also originality of thought, which, as self-inspired, is called spirit. The artist who depicts Nature[49] with the paintbrush or the pen (be it in prose or in verse) does not have the beautiful spirit, because he only imitates. The artist who depicts ideas[50] is the only master of fine arts.

Why does one usually understand that a poet is a writer of verse, that is, a discourse which can be scanned (and should be spoken rhythmically like music)? Heralding a work of the fine arts, the poet proceeds with solemnity which must satisfy the most refined taste (in respect to form), otherwise the work of art would not be beautiful. Since such solemnity is mostly required of the beautiful representation of the sublime, a similarly affected solemnity without verse is called (by Hugh Blair) "prose run mad."[51] Versification, on the other hand, is not poetry if it has no spirit.

Why is rhyme in the verses of the poets of modern

times, when the poet is happy to bring his thought to conclusion, such a great prerequisite of taste in our part of the world? On the other hand, why is rhyme[52] a repugnant insult against verse found in the poetry of ancient times, so that now, for example, verse free of rhyme in German is not very pleasing, and Virgil's Latin rendered in rhyme is even less pleasing? Probably because prosody was fixed for the old classic poets; but in the modern languages prosody is, for the most part, lacking, and the ear must make up for this with rhyme which concludes a line with a sound similar to that of the preceding one. In a prosaic, solemn discourse a rhyme occurring accidentally among other sentences becomes ridiculous.

How does it happen that poetic license, which does not belong to the orator, takes the liberty of violating the laws of language every now and then? It is caused probably by the fact that the orator does not feel too much constrained by the law of form when he expresses a great thought.

Why is a mediocre poem intolerable, while a mediocre [249] speech is still bearable? The cause for this appears to lie in the fact that the solemnity of tone in every poetical work arouses great expectation; and, just because this expectation is not satisfied, attention usually sinks lower than the prosaic value of the poem would perhaps merit. Completing a poem with a verse which can be remembered as an aphorism provides a gratifying aftertaste, and thereby makes up for much of this staleness; thus it also belongs to the art of the poet.

In old age, when the sciences still promise good health and activity to a sound mind, the poetic vein dries up. This seems to be so because beauty is a blossom, whereas science is a fruit; that is, poesy must be a free art which, on account of its variety, requires facility; but in old age this facile sense dwindles away (and justly so). Furthermore, the poetic vein dries up because the habit of proceeding only on the same road as the sciences drags facility along with it; therefore poetry, which requires originality and novelty (and a skill for this too) for every one of her productions, does not agree well with old age, except perhaps in matters of caustic wit, in epigrams, and *xenia*,[53] where poetry is more serious than playful.

That poets make no such fortune as lawyers and others in the learned professions lies in the disposition of their temperament which is, on the whole, a characteristic of the born poet. The poet has the ability to drive sorrows away by means of the malleable play with thoughts. A peculiarity, however, which refers to the character, namely, of having no character, but being ill-humored, peevish, and (without malice) unreliable, of intentionally making enemies for oneself, though without hating anyone, and of jeering at one's friend in a sarcastic way, without wanting to harm him, all this goes back to a partly innate disposition of perverted intelligence dominating practical judgment.

On Opulence

§ 72.[54]   OPULENCE *(luxus)* is the excess of tasteful social life of pleasure, within a commonwealth (a life of pleasure which actually runs contrary to the welfare of that commonwealth). Any excess without taste, however, is obvious debauchery *(luxuries)*. If one considers   [250] the effects of both on human welfare, then opulence is a dispensable expenditure which makes us poor, while debauchery is of the kind that makes us ill. Opulence, nevertheless, is still related to the advancing culture of a nation (as to arts and sciences); debauchery, however, overindulges in consumption and finally arouses disgust. Both are more ostentatious (glittering on the outside) than self-pleasing; opulence does this through elegance (as at balls and in the theaters) for the ideal taste; debauchery does this through superabundance and variety for the sense of tasting (the physical sense, as, for example, at the feast of a Lord Mayor). Whether the government has the right to restrict both by sumptuary laws is a question which does not belong here. But to suppress[55] the fine arts as well as the pleasant arts entirely, which partly weaken the nation, so that the people can be more easily governed, would work directly against the intentions of a government if a crude Spartan rule [laconicism] should be introduced.

The art of good living is the proper equivalent to living well as to sociability (that is, to living with taste). One can conclude from this that luxury is injurious to good living. The expression, "He knows how to live," used about an opulent or aristocratic person, means that he is skillful in his choice of lasting social pleasures which include temperance (sobriety) in making pleasures mutually beneficial.

Since opulence can be criticized only in public life, not in domestic life, it must be concluded that the relation of the citizen to the commonwealth as far as the freedom of competition is concerned as to the adornment of one's own person or possession (at feasts, weddings, funerals, and on down to well-mannered behavior) can only with difficulty, for the sake of the anticipation of the useful, be burdened by sumptuary law. This should be so because opulence still offers the advantage of animating the arts, thereby returning to the commonwealth those expenses which such luxuries may have incurred.

Third Book

On the Faculty of Desire

§ 73.[1] DESIRE *(appetitio)* is the self-definition of the power of a subject to imagine something in the future as an effect of such imagination. Habitual sensuous desire is called inclination. Desiring without emphasis on the production of the object is wish. Wish may be directed toward objects for whose production the subject himself feels incapable; in such a case it is an empty (idle) wish. The empty wish to overcome the time between the desire and the acquisition of the desired object is yearning. The undetermined desire, as to the object *(appetitio vaga),* which only incites the subject to get out of his present condition without knowing where he wants to go, can be called a capricious wish (which cannot be satisfied with anything).

The inclination which can hardly, or not at all, be controlled by reason is passion. On the other hand, emotion is the feeling of a pleasure or displeasure at a particular moment, which does not give rise to reflection (namely the process of reason whether one should submit to it or reject it).

To be subject to emotions and passions is probably always an illness of mind because both emotion and passion, exclude the sovereignty of reason. Both are also equally strong according to degree; but in accordance with their quality, emotion and passion are essentially distinct from one another as to the method of prevention as well as in that of cure which the physician of souls would have to employ.

[252] ON EMOTION IN CONTRAST
TO PASSION

§ 74.[2] EMOTION is surprise[3] through sensation, whereby the composure of mind *(animus sui compos)* is suspended. Emotion therefore is precipitate, that is, it quickly grows to a degree of feeling which makes reflection impossible (it is thoughtless). Apathy,[4] which has not diminished the intensity of the stimuli for action, is self-possession which has retained sound understanding. It is a characteristic of the experienced person *(animi strenui)* not to let himself be drawn away from peaceful deliberation by the intensity of these stimuli. What the emotion of anger does not accomplish quickly will not be accomplished at all. The emotion of anger easily forgets. But the passion of hate takes its time to root itself deeply and to associate itself with the energy. A father and a teacher cannot punish as long as they have had the patience to listen to apologies (not to justifications). If a person comes to your room in anger in order to say harsh words in great wrath, politely ask him to be seated, and, if you succeed in this, his scolding will already be milder because the comfort of sitting is a relaxation which does not really conform to the menacing gesticulations and screaming while one is standing. Passion, however violently it may present itself (as a frame of mind belonging to the faculty of desire), takes its time, and is deliberative in order to achieve its purpose. Emotion works like water that breaks through a dam; passion works like a river digging itself deeper and deeper into its bed. Emotion works upon the health like a stroke of apoplexy; passion works like consumption or atrophy.

Emotion is like an intoxicant which one has to sleep off, although it is still followed by a headache; but passion is looked upon as an illness having resulted from swallowing poison, or a handicap which requires an inner or an outer physician for the soul, one who knows how to prescribe cures that are generally not radical, but almost always only of a palliative nature.

Wherever there is much emotion, there is generally little passion; as in the French, who are fickle, in comparison to the vivacity of Italians and Spaniards (as well as Indians and Chinese) who are consistent in their brooding rage concerning revenge, and consistent in their affairs of love right to the point of insanity. Emotions are honorable and unconcealed, while passions are deceitful and hidden. The Chinese reproach the English   [253] with being impetuous and hotheaded "like the Tartars," but vice versa the English reproach the Chinese with being perfect (though tempered) deceivers whose passion is not shaken by this reproach. Emotion is like an intoxicant which can be slept off; passion is to be regarded as an insanity which broods over an idea that is imbedding itself deeper and deeper. Whoever loves can keep his vision intact; but the person who is in love is inevitably blind to the mistakes of the beloved object, although the latter will usually regain his vision a week after the wedding. Whoever is customarily seized by emotion with rapture, no matter how good-natured he may be, still resembles a deranged person; just because he regrets his rapture so soon afterward, it is only a paroxysm, which they call thoughtlessness. Many a person even wishes that he could be angry; and Socrates was in doubt whether it would not be good to be angry sometimes; but to have emotion so much under control that one can cold-bloodedly deliberate whether or not one ought to be angry appears to be something paradoxical. Passion, on the other hand, no man[5] wishes for himself. Who wants to have himself put in chains when he can be free?

ON THE EMOTIONS IN PARTICULAR

a. On the Regulation of the Mind
with Regard to Emotions

§ 75.[6] THE principle of apathy, that is, that the prudent man must at no time be in a state of emotion, not even in that of sympathy with the woes of his best friend, is an entirely correct and sublime moral precept of the Stoic school because emotion makes one (more or less) blind. Nevertheless, the wisdom of Nature has planted in us a disposition for apathy in order to hold the reins provisionally, before reason attains the necessary control. For the purpose of enlivening us Nature has done so by adding to the moral motives for the Good those motives of pathological (sensuous) inducement as a temporary surrogate of reason. Moreover, emotion taken by itself alone is always imprudent; it makes itself incapable of pursuing its own purpose, and it is therefore unwise to allow it to arise intentionally. However, in projecting the morally good, reason can produce the enlivening of our will (in sermons, political speeches to the people,   [254] and speeches just to oneself) by combining its ideas with illustrations (examples) which have been attributed to the ideas; consequently it is enlivening, not as effect, but as the cause of an emotion with respect to the good, wherein reason still holds the reins, creating an enthusiasm of good intentions which, however, must be attributed to the faculty of desire and not to the emotion as a stronger sensuous feeling.

Nature's gift of apathy, in the case of sufficient spiritual strength, is, as has been said already, happy self-possession (in the moral sense). He who is gifted with it, is not yet a wise man, but he enjoys the favor of Nature to become wise more easily than others.

On the whole, it is not the intensity of a certain feeling which creates the emotional state, but the want of reflection in the comparison of this feeling with the sum of all feelings (of pleasure or displeasure) in one's own condition. The rich person, whose servant clumsily smashes a beautiful and rare crystal goblet while waiting on table, would consider this incident of no importance if he compared at that moment this loss of a single gratification with the multitude of all gratifications which his fortunate position as a rich person affords him. But if he completely gives himself to this one feeling of grief (without making such a quick survey in his thoughts), then it is no wonder that he feels as if his whole state of bliss were lost.[7]

b.   On the Various Emotions Themselves

§ 76.[8]   THE feeling which motivates the subject to remain in the state in which he currently finds himself is pleasant; but the feeling which motivates him to abandon it is unpleasant. Combined with consciousness, the first feeling is called gratification *(voluptas)*, and the second is called dissatisfaction *(taedium)*. As emotion, the first feeling is called joy, the other sadness. Exuberant joy (untempered by any concern for grief) and absorbing sadness (unmitigated by any hope), or sorrow, are emotions which threaten life. Nevertheless, one [255] can see from the death lists that more persons have lost their lives suddenly on account of exuberant joy than on account of sorrow. The mind embraces hope as an emotion without reservation because of the unexpected emergence of a prospect of immeasurable good fortune; consequently, the emotion keeps rising until it reaches the point of suffocation. However, the continually fearful sorrow is naturally and always opposed by the mind, so that sorrow can only kill slowly.

Fright is suddenly aroused fear which disturbs the mind's composure. Similar to fright is the shocking, something which disconcerts (though not yet dismays) and which awakens the mind to collect itself for reflection; it is the stimulus to astonishment (which already contains reflection). To the experienced person this does not happen so easily, but it is characteristic of art, to represent the usual in a striking way, so that it will be startling. Wrath is a fright which immediately stirs up the forces for opposing evil. Fear of an object which threatens an undetermined evil is anxiety. One may experience anxiety without having a particular object in mind, in which case it is an uneasiness arising from merely subjective causes (an unhealthy condition). Shame is anguish arising from a committed contempt of a person who is present, and as such it is an emotion. Moreover, a person may feel considerably ashamed without the presence of the person concerned; in such a case, however, we have not emotion, but rather, as with sorrow, we have a passion to torture oneself with contempt continuously, but in vain; shame, on the other hand, as an emotion, must occur suddenly.

Emotions are generally morbid occurrences (symptoms) and may be divided (according to analogy with[9] Brown's system) into sthenic emotions as to strength and asthenic emotions as to weakness. Sthenic emotions are of the exciting and frequently exhausting nature; asthenic emotions are of a sedative nature which often prepare for relaxation. Laughing with emotion is a convulsive gaiety. Weeping accompanies[10] the diminishing sensation of a helpless quarrel with fate or other people, like a sensation of insult that has been suffered; but this latter[11] sensation is called melancholy. Both, laughing as well as weeping,[12] have a way of cheering one up because they liberate from whatever curbs vitality through their overflowing (one may also laugh oneself to tears if one laughs until exhaustion). Laughing is masculine, while weeping is feminine (effeminate   [256] in the case of men). Only the becoming overwhelmed by tears, which arises from magnanimous but helpless sympathy with the sorrows of others, can be excused in a man whose eyes are shining with tears, as long as he does not allow them to fall in drops, and as long as he can avoid accompanying the tears with sobbing, thus making disagreeable music.

On Cowardice and Bravery

§ 77.[13]   ANGUISH, anxiety, horror, and dread are degrees of fear, that is, of the aversion to danger. The composure of mind which is determined to overcome fear with reflection is courage; the strength of the inner sense *(ataraxia)* which does not allow itself to be put easily into a state of fear is intrepidity. The want of such courage is cowardice;* the want of intrepidity is shyness.

Stouthearted is he who does not become startled; courage has he who uses his mind and does not retreat upon danger; brave is he whose courage persists during dangers. Foolhardy is the frivolous person who risks facing dangers because he does not know them. Bold is he who risks his life although he is aware of the dangers; rash is he who, in the face of a manifest impossibility, tries to reach his goal by subjecting himself to the greatest danger (like Charles XII at Bender).[14] The Turks call their brave men madmen (perhaps because of opium). Cowardice is, consequently, shameful despair.

Fright is not the habitual tendency to be scared easily, because this tendency is called timidity; but fright is only a condition and accidental disposition, mostly dependent upon bodily causes alone, of feeling not prepared enough for suddenly arising danger. When the unexpected approach of the enemy is announced to a field marshal, who is still in his dressing-gown, his blood may well freeze for an instant in the chambers of his heart; a physician once observed that a certain general was fainthearted and shy whenever he had acid indiges-

---

* The word poltroon (derived from *pollex truncatus*) was rendered with *murcus* in later Latin, and signified a person who chops off his thumb so that he will not be drafted into the war.

tion. But stoutheartedness is only[15] a characteristic of temperament. Courage, on the other hand, rests upon principles and is a virtue. Reason gives the resolute man strength when nature sometimes denies it to him. Fright in [257] battle even produces salutary evacuations which have proverbially given rise to jesting (not having one's heart in the right place);[16] however, one will have noticed that those very sailors, who at the summons to fight hasten to the place of riddance, are afterward the most courageous in the hour of battle. The same holds true also of the heron preparing himself for battle when the swooping falcon hovers over him.

Patience is, accordingly, not courage. Patience is a feminine virtue because it does not muster the strength for opposition, it only hopes to make sorrows (suffering) bearable through habit. He who shrieks under the surgeon's knife or under the pains of gout or stone is therefore not cowardly or weak in such a situation. Shrieking is like the cursing when one is out walking and hurts one's toe on a cobblestone in the street (the big toe, from which the word *hallucinari* is derived).[17] This cursing is rather an outburst of anger, in which nature tries to break up the constriction of blood in the heart with words. Patience of a particular kind is shown by the Indians in America, who throw away their weapons when they are encircled and, without begging for pardon, let themselves be slain quietly. Does this indicate more courage than the Europeans display, who in such a situation tend to defend themselves to the last man? To me it seems to be just a barbaric vanity intended to preserve the honor of the trible so that the enemy could not force them to lament and beg as indications of submission.

Courage as emotion (belonging partially to sensuality) can also be aroused by reason and thus be genuine bravery (virtuous strength). Not allowing oneself to be intimidated by something that is sacred, by sarcastic derision even when it is more temptingly seasoned with taunts and trickery, but instead pursuing one's own course steadfastly, is a moral courage which many a person does not possess who otherwise excels as brave on the battlefield or in a duel. It takes a high degree of determination to do what duty demands, even at the danger of being ridiculed by others. It takes a high degree because love of honor is the constant companion of virtue; and he who can otherwise well withstand force seldom feels strong enough to endure ridicule if his claim to honor is sneeringly refused.[18]

[258] Proper behavior which presents an external appearance of courage, so that one does not lose one's honor in comparison to others, is audacity.[19] Audacity is opposed to timidity, a kind of bashfulness and concern not to appear favorably in the eyes of others. Audacity cannot be criticized as cheap confidence in one's self. But the kind of audacity* in behavior, which gives the appearance of not caring about the judgment of others, is foolhardiness, effrontery, or, in a milder term, pretentiousness; it does not belong to courage, in the moral sense of the word.[20]

Whether suicide also presupposes courage, or always despair only, is not a moral but merely a psychological question. If it is committed just for the sake of not outliving one's honor, hence committed out of anger, then it appears to be courage; however, if it is due to consuming grief after the exhaustion of patience with suffering, then it is a case of despair. Looking death straight in the eye and not being afraid of it seems to fill man with a kind of heroism when he cannot love life any longer. If, however, although someone may fear death,

---

* The German word for audacity should really be spelled *Dräustigkeit* (from *dräuen* or *drohen*) instead of *Dreistigkeit,* because the tone or countenance of such a person may cause others to be afraid that he could also be impolite. The same holds true for the spelling of the German word *liederlich* (untidy) as *lüderlich* (disgusting), because the former signifies an easygoing, playful, but still useful and well-meaning person, whereas the latter refers to an outcast who arouses disgust in other people (relating to the word *Luder,* carrion).

he still cannot stop loving life in every respect, a state of mental bewilderment stemming from anxiety must inevitably have occurred first, so that the step toward suicide can be taken. Such a person dies from cowardice because he can no longer bear the agonies of life. To some extent the manner of execution of the suicide reveals the following differentiations of mental attitude. If the chosen means is sudden and fatal beyond possible rescue, as, for example, the firing of a pistol, or a dose of acid sublimate (as once carried by a great monarch[21] during time of war, in case he should be captured by the enemy), or deep water together with pockets weighted with stones, then one cannot dispute the courage of the person who has committed suicide. However, there are attempts in which the life of the victim can be saved, and if it is saved, he is usually   [259] happy once more and will not attempt to take his life again. Such means of suicide are, for example, the rope which still can be cut by someone else, an ordinary poison which a physician can remove from the body, or a slitting of the throat which can be sewn up again and healed. These means indicate cowardly despair born of weakness, and not vigorous despair which still requires strength of mind for such an act.

They are not always merely dejected and worthless souls who decide to rid themselves of the burden of life in this manner. Indeed, those who have no feeling for real honor rarely commit the deed. Since such a deed will always remain hideous, and since by committing it man makes a monster of himself, it is noteworthy that in periods of public and legally declared injustice during a revolutionary situation (for example, the Public Welfare Committee of the French Republic) honor-loving men (for example, Roland)[22] have tried to forestall such legal execution by resorting to suicide, an act which under normal constitutional conditions they themselves would have referred to as objectionable. The reason for this is that in every legal execution there is something disgraceful, because it is punishment; and, if the punishment is unjust, the victim who is sacrificed to the law cannot acknowledge the punishment as being deserved. He proves through his act, however, that, when sentenced to die, he would rather choose to die as a free man and carry the sentence out himself. Consequently, tyrants (like Nero) considered it a gesture of favor to permit the condemned person to kill himself, because it then was done with more honor. The morality of this, however, I do not claim to justify.

The courage of the warrior is quite different from that of the duelist. Dueling is not explicity permitted by law, but the government is lenient about duels. The military has made dueling an affair of honor, a self-defense against insult in which the supervisors do not interfere. Not keeping a strict eye on the terrible aspects of dueling is an oversight by the head of state, because there are infamous people who like to risk their lives only in order to draw attention. Those who put their life on the line for the state are not being spoken of here.

Bravery is courage within the framework of the law, where duty commands that not even the potential loss of life should discourage action. Fearlessness alone is of no account, but moral integrity *(mens conscia recti)*[23] must be combined with it, as in the case of Seigneur de Bayard *(chevalier sans peur et sans reproche)*.[24]

[260]   On Emotions which Weaken Themselves
      as to Their Purpose *(impotentes animi motus)*[25]

§ 78.[26]   EMOTIONS of anger and shame share the characteristic that they weaken themselves with regard to their purpose. They are suddenly[27] aroused feelings against an evil which has been interpreted as an insult. However, these feelings are also incapacitating because of their intensity, so that the evil cannot be effectively averted.

Who is more to be feared, he who grows pale in violent anger, or he who flushes in the same situation?

The first one is to be feared instantly; the second is more to be feared later (because of his vindictiveness). In the first case the upset person is terrified of himself because he fears being driven to violence which he might later repent. In the second case terror suddenly changes into the concern that his own awareness of his inability to defend himself should not become apparent. If people are able to unburden themselves by quickly expressing their feelings, neither emotion is detrimental to health; however, when people cannot do so, these emotions can either in some degree be dangerous to life itself, or, if the outburst is suppressed, the feelings leave resentment behind, that is, a grieving over not having responded to insult with proper means. Such resentment, however, is avoided if people can verbalize their concerns. However, left alone both emotions are of the sort that make people speechless. For this reason these emotions present themselves in a disadvantageous light.

Hot temper can be controlled gradually by inner discipline of the mind; but the weakness of an oversensitive feeling of honor at moments of shyness does not lend itself so easily to control. Hume says[28] (who himself was afflicted with such an infirmity, namely shyness of making public statements), that if the first attempt at boldness fails, the result is more bashfulness. As remedy, nothing else remains but to begin to be with persons whose judgment concerning behavior one does not care much about, so that one can gradually overcome the supposed important judgment of others concerning ourselves and thereby rank the importance of our own judgment equally with theirs. Such a habit produces freedom of mind, which is far from shyness and insulting audacity.

We sympathize with someone else's shyness as if it were a pain, but we do not sympathize with the anger of a person when he actually demonstrates to us with emotion the motive of his anger.   [261] If a person is in such a state, the other person, who has to listen to his story (of the insult which has been inflicted), cannot feel safe himself.

Surprise (embarrassment at finding oneself in an unexpected situation) at first impedes the natural flow of thought; it is unpleasant; but later it promotes the influx of thoughts beyond expectation and becomes an agreeable excitement of feeling. This emotion is legitimately called astonishment only if one is uncertain whether the perception occurs when one is awake or dreaming. A neophyte in the world gets excited about everything; but he who has become acquainted with the course of things through varied experience makes it a rule of conduct to be surprised at nothing *(nihil admirari)*. On the other hand, he who thoughtfully and with a searching eye investigates the laws of Nature in all their immense variety is stricken with astonishment when he stumbles upon a wisdom he was not aware of. It is a wonderment from which he cannot tear himself away (and about which he cannot be surprised enough). Such an emotion can only be aroused by reason, and it is a kind of sacred shudder to feel the abyss of the transcendental opening up before one's feet.

On the Emotions by which Nature Mechanically Strengthens Health

§ 79.[29]   BY means of several emotions good health is mechanically promoted by nature. Laughing and weeping especially serve this end.[30] Anger[31] too, if one can scold freely (without fear of opposition), is a rather sure way to aid digestion; and many a housewife has no other emotional exercise than the scolding of her children and[32] servants. If the children and servants submit patiently[33] to this, a pleasant feeling of fatigue will spread vitality[34] uniformly through the organism. However, this remedy is not without danger because of potential resistance by the members of the household.

Good-humored (not malicious and bitter) laughing is, however, more highly esteemed and more beneficial. It is exactly what should have been recommended to the Persian king who offered a prize to the person   [262] "Who would discover a new means of delectation." Jerky (nearly convulsive) exhalation of breath (of which sneezing is only a small but enlivening effect, if its sound is allowed to go unrestrained) strengthens the feeling of vitality through the wholesome exercise of the diaphragm. It may be a hired jester (harlequin) who makes us laugh,[35] or a cunning knave among our friends who seems to have nothing mischievous on his mind. Waiting for his moment, he does not laugh with the others, but then with apparent innocence he suddenly makes his crack (like a taut string). The resulting laughter is always an exercise of muscles which are used for digestion. Laughing helps digestion better than the wisdom of the physician. Even[36] a great absurdity of faulty judgment[37] may have the same effect, though at the expense of the one who claimed to be the smartest.*

Weeping, inhaling, accompanied by (convulsive) sobbing and tear-shedding, is a soothing remedy as well as a provision of nature for one's state of health. A widow who, as the saying explains, will not allow herself to be comforted, that is, who does not want to know how to dry

---

* Many examples of this can be provided. But I shall give only one, which I have heard from the lips of the late Countess of K——g, a lady who was the shining ornament of her sex. [Countess von Keyserling—Trans.] Count Sagramoso, who once had the commission to establish the Order of the Knights of Malta in Poland (of Ostrogothic appointment), had paid her a visit, and it happened that a man joined them, who was born in Königsberg, but who was now employed by several rich merchants in Hamburg as a collector and curator of collections which they had gathered as a hobby in their private galleries. This man was visiting his relatives in Prussia. In order to strike up a conversation the count said to him in broken German: "I 'ave 'ad an aunt in 'Amburg (I used to have an aunt in Hamburg), but now she is dead." Quickly the curator replied: "Why don't you have her skinned and stuffed?" He had taken the English word aunt, which means *Tante* in German, for *Ente* (duck); and, because it occurred to him that it must have been a very rare specimen, he was bewailing the great loss. You can imagine what laughter this misunderstanding must have stirred up.

up the flow of tears, unknowingly or unintentionally takes care of her health. Anger, which might arise in this situation, would quickly stem the flow of tears, but it would also damage her health; although women and children are brought to tears not only by suffering but also by anger. The sensation of one's   [263] helplessness against an evil, together with a strong emotion (be it anger or sadness), calls for the assistance of the external natural signs which then (according to the right of the weaker one) disarm the person, at least if it is a male. This expression of tenderness, as a weakness of the sex, however, must not permit the male involved to be moved to shedding tears, but only to have tears in his eyes; because in the first instance he would be transgressing against his own sex, and so, with his femininity, he would not be able to serve as protector of the weaker sex; and in the second instance he would not be showing the other sex any of the sympathy which his masculinity demands of him, namely, to provide protection for the other sex as befits the character which books about knights attribute to a man of valor.

But why do young people prefer tragic drama and prefer to perform it whenever they want to offer entertainment to their parents? And why do older people prefer comedy, even burlesque? The reason for the former is partly the same as the one which moves children to probe the dangerous; they are probably motivated by the instinct of nature to test their strength; given the lightheartedness of youth, another reason for it is also partly due to the fact that no melancholy remains of oppressive and terrifying impressions when the play has ended, but rather there is only a pleasant feeling of fatigue after a strong internal emotion, which disposes people to new joy. On the other hand, such impressions are not so easily forgotten by older people, who are not able to bring back the disposition of joyfulness so easily. By his antics a harlequin with his nimble wit causes a beneficial exercise of the diaphragm and the intestine so that the appetite for the ensuing social supper is whetted and the conversation at the table is inspired.

General Observation

Certain interior physical feelings are related to the emotions, but they are not identical with them since they[38] are only momentary and transitory, leaving no trace behind. Of the same nature is the shuddering which seizes children when they listen at night to their nurses' ghost stories. Shivering, as when being doused with cold water (as in a rainstorm), is related to the same thing. Not the perception of danger, but the mere thought of danger,   [264] although one knows that none is present, produces this sensation which, as a mere sensation and not as an explosion of fright, seems not to be unpleasant.

Giddiness and even seasickness,[39] according to their origin, seem to belong to the class of such hypothetical dangers. Without hesitation one can proceed to walk across a board that is lying on the ground, but if it bridges an abyss or even, for one with weak nerves, a ditch, then the mere concern about danger will often be perceived as real danger. Even the tossing of a ship in a gentle wind is a change between sinking and rising. With the sinking goes the effort of nature to rise again (because all sinking is associated with danger). Therefore the up-and-down movement of the stomach and the bowels is mechanically accompanied by an inducement to vomiting which increases when the patient looks out of the window of his cabin, catching alternate glimpses of the sky and the sea, whereby the illusion increases that the seat is sinking from underneath him.

An actor who is unmoved himself, but otherwise possesses understanding and strong imagination, may often arouse us more by his affected (artificial) emotions than by genuine emotions. A serious lover is often restrained, awkward, and uncaptivating in the presence of his beloved. But he who only pretends to be madly in love, and who has no other talent, can play his role so naturally that he lures the poor, deceived maiden wholly into his snare, just because his heart is uninhibited and his head clear; consequently, he has full command of the free use of his skill and craft to imitate the appearance of a lover very naturally.

Good-natured (openhearted) laughter (which belongs to the emotion of joyfulness) is sociable; malicious (sneering) laughter is hostile. The distracted person (like Terrasson[40] entering solemnly with his nightcap instead of his peruke on his head, and holding his hat in his hand, still in deep thought about the contention of superiority of the ancients over the moderns with respect to knowledge), often causes the first type of laughter; he is laughed about but still not ridiculed. The not so imprudent odd person is smiled about, without it costing him anything, for he joins in the laughter. A person who has a mechanical (spiritless) laughter is insipid and makes his presence unsavory. The person[41] who does not laugh in company at all is either peevish or pedantic. Children, [265] especially girls, must be accustomed early to frank and unrestrained smiling, because the cheerfulness of their facial features will gradually make an imprint on the inner self and establish a disposition of joyfulness, friendliness, and sociability, which can be achieved through this early preparation for the virtue of kindliness.

It is a good-natured and at the same time a refined means of animating a conversation to use a person in one's company as a butt for witty remarks (pull his leg) without being cutting (joking without invective), especially when the other person's remarks can reply in kind, thus seasoning the conversation with merry laughter. But if this occurs at the expense of a simpleton whom one tosses back and forth like a ball, then the laughter, being malicious joy, is unmannerly, to say the least. Again, if it happens to a sponger who for indulgence gives himself to reveling or allows himself to be made a fool of, then it is evidence of bad taste and also evidence of the callous moral feeling of those who can laugh about this till their sides split. The task of the court jester, however, who is to season the meal and to shake the diaphragm of the chief person with laughter by teasing his most distinguished servants, is, whichever way one takes it, either above or beneath all criticism.

ON PASSIONS

§ 80.[42]   THE subjective possibility of having a certain desire arise, which precedes the representation of its object, is propensity (propensio). The inner compulsion of the faculty of desire to take this object into possession, before one is acquainted with it, is instinct (like the mating instinct, or the parental instinct of an animal to protect its offspring, and so forth). A subject's sensuous desire which has become customary (habit) is called inclination (inclinatio).[43] Inclination, which hinders the use of reason to compare, at a particular moment of choice, a specific inclination against the sum of all inclinations, is passion (passio animi).

Since the passions can be coupled with the calmest reflection, one can easily see that they must neither be rash like the emotions, nor stormy and transitory; instead, they must take roots gradually and even be able to coexist with reason. One can also easily see that passions do the greatest harm to freedom; and if emotion   [266] is a delirium, then passion is an illness which abhors all medication. Therefore, passion is by far worse than all those transitory emotions which stir themselves at least to the good intention of improvement; instead, passion is an enchantment which also rejects improvement.

One labels passion with the word mania (ambition, thirst for revenge, lust of power, and so forth), the only exception is love when it refers to having fallen-in-love. This is so because when love has been satisfied (by indulgence), the desire, at least with regard to the very person involved, ceases altogether. For this reason only an impassioned state of love can be displayed (as long as the partner remains steadfast in refusal), but no physical love can be displayed that may be specified as passion, because, as to its object, it does not contain any persevering principle. Passion always presupposes a maxim of the subject, namely, to act according to a purpose prescribed for him by his inclination. Passion is, therefore, always associated with the purposes of reason, and one cannot attribute passions to mere animals any more than to purely rational beings. Ambition, thirst for revenge, and so forth, just because they[44] are never completely satisfied, are counted, therefore, among the passions as illnesses for which there is only a palliative remedy.

§ 81.[45]   PASSIONS are cancerous stores for pure practical reason, and most of them are incurable because the sick person does not want to be cured and avoids the dominion of the principle by which alone a cure could be effected. In the area of what is sensuously practical, reason proceeds from the general to the particular, according to the axiom not to please only a single inclination by placing all the rest in the shade or in a dark corner, but rather to see to it that it shares properly with the totality of *all* inclinations. The ambition of a person may always be an inclination whose direction is sanctioned by reason; but the ambitious person desires, nevertheless, to be loved by others also; he needs pleasant relations with others, maintenance of his assets, and so forth. But if he is, however, passionately ambitious, then he is blind to those other purposes which his inclinations also offer to him. Consequently he ignores completely that he is hated by others or that he runs the risk of impoverishing himself through his extravagant expenses. This is foolishness (making one's partial purpose the whole of one's purpose) which even in its formal principle smacks reason right in the face.

[267]   Therefore passions are not, like emotions, merely unfortunate moods teeming with many evils, but they are without exception bad. Even the most well-intended desire if it aims (according to matter) at what belongs to virtue, that is, to charity, is nevertheless (according to form), as soon as it changes to passion, not merely pragmatically pernicious, but also morally reprehensible.

Emotion produces a momentary loss of freedom and self-control. Passion surrenders both, and finds pleasure and satisfaction in a servile disposition. But because reason does not desist from its summons to inner freedom, the unfortunate victim is suffering under the chains from which he cannot free himself, because they have already grown into his limbs, so to speak.

Nevertheless, the passions have also found their panegyrists (where are they not found, once malice has found its way into the rules of conduct?) who say that nothing great in this world has ever been accomplished without strong passions; and that Providence itself has wisely planted passions like elastic springs into human nature. Concerning all those many inclinations it may be readily admitted that those of a natural and animal necessity are the ones which the living nature (even man) cannot be without. But Providence has not intended that inclinations become passions, nor that they should. The poet who represents passions from this point of view can be forgiven (Pope says: "If Reason is a magnet, then the passions are wind");[46] but the philosopher must not apply this principle, not even in order to praise the passions as a provisional arrangement of Providence which had intentionally placed passions into human nature before the human race had reached the proper degree of culture.

Classification of the Passions

Passions are divided into those of natural inclination (innate) and those arising from the culture of mankind (acquired).

Passions of the first kind are the inclinations of freedom and sex; [268] both are linked with emotion. Those of the second kind are ambition, lust of power, and avarice, qualities which are not linked with vehement emotion but with the persistence of a maxim meant for a certain purpose. The first kind can be called burning passions (*passiones ardentes*); while the second kind, like avarice, can be called cold passions (*frigidae*). All passions, however, are always desires directed only by men to men, not to things. For the use of a fertile field, or a productive cow, one can have much inclination, but no emotion (which consists in the inclination for fellowship with others), or, even less, a passion.

a. *On the Inclination to Freedom as a Passion*

§ 82.⁴⁷   FOR natural man this is the strongest of all inclinations, which creates a condition in which he cannot avoid getting involved in mutual interrelations with other persons.

Whoever is able to be happy only at the option of another person (be this person as benevolent as you please) justly feels that he is unhappy. What guarantee does he have that his powerful fellow human will concur with the person's own judgment concerning well-being? The uncivilized person (not yet accustomed to submission) knows no greater misfortune than to have this befall him; and justly so, as long as no public law protects him until the time when discipline has gradually made him ready for it. Therefore his lot is one of continuous rebellion, with the intention of keeping others as far away from him as possible, and living as a wanderer in the wilderness. In fact, the child who has just come from its mother's womb, unlike all other animals, seems to enter the world with a loud shriek just because it considers the inability to make use of its limbs a restraint; consequently it announces this claim to freedom (which no other animal knows).* Nomadic peoples [269] (like pastoral tribes) who are not attached to land property, for example the Arabs, although their mode of life is not entirely free from restraint, are so proud of their way of life that they look with contempt on settled peoples, because the toil connected with this way of life has not been able to alienate these peoples from their occupation over thousands of years. Mere hunting peoples (like the Olenni-Tungusi), by separating themselves from the other families which are related to them, have really dignified themselves by this feeling of freedom. Thus, under moral laws, the concept of freedom awakens not

---

* Lucretius, the poet, interprets this indeed remarkable phenomenon of the animal kingdom in another way:

Vagituque locum lugubri complet, ut aequumst
Cui tantum in vita restet transire malorum!
[And fills the air with lamenting cries
As it befits someone who still has to go through so much evil in his life—Ed.]

But the newborn child cannot very well have this prospect! However, the fact that the baby's feeling of discomfort does not originate from bodily pain, but from a vague idea (or an analogous representation) of freedom and its suppression, perceived as an injustice, is disclosed a few months after the birth by tears which accompany the shrieking. This indicates a sort of exasperation when he strives to get near certain objects or only tries to change his position and finds himself hindered. This impulse to have one's own way and to perceive any hindrance in this respect as an insult, expresses itself particularly in the tone of the shriek and in the display of bad temper, which the mother finds necessary to punish, although it is usually countered with still louder shrieking. The same thing occurs when the child happens to fall through his own fault. The young of other animals play, while the young of human beings already begin to quarrel with each other. It appears as if a certain concept of justice (which applies to external freedom) evolves together with the animal nature; consequently, it is not something that is gradually learned.

only the emotion which is called enthusiasm, but the mere sensory-projection of external freedom arouses the inclination to persist in it or to extend it into a strong passion by analogy with the concept of justice.[48]

Even the strongest inclination (such as the mixture of breeds) is not called passion among mere animals, because they have no reason. Reason alone establishes the concept of freedom, and passion collides with it. The outbreak of passion must be attributed to human beings. It is said of humans that they love certain things passionately (such as drinking, gambling, and hunting) or that they hate certain things (such as the musk and brandy). But these various inclinations or disinclinations are not called passions, because only a certain number of various instincts deserve to be classified. There are so many states of passivity in the faculty of desire which should, according to the (innumerable) objects of the faculty of desire, not be classified as *things,* but rather according   [270] to the principle of use or misuse which men make of their person and of their freedom, since one man makes another man a mere means to his own ends. Passions actually belong to human beings alone; they can be satisfied only by them.

These passions are *ambition, lust of power,* and *avarice.*

Since passions are inclinations concerned merely with the possession of means, and since all inclinations have to be satisfied that concern this purpose directly, passions seem to manifest characteristics of reason. Particularly, passion appears to imitate the idea of a faculty which is closely linked with freedom, by which alone those purposes can be attained. Possessing the means to any desired ends, however, reaches much farther than the inclination directed at a single inclination and its satisfactions. Therefore they may also be called inclinations[49] of delusion. The delusion consists in equalizing the mere opinion of someone regarding the value of a thing with the actual value of the thing.[50]

b.   *On the Thirst for Vengeance as a Passion*

§ 83.[51]   WHILE passions can only be inclinations di-
            rected by men toward men, as long as they
are based on either agreeing or disagreeing purposes like
love or hate, the concept of justice, just because it origi-
nates directly from the concept of external freedom, is a
much more important and a much more strongly motivating impulse than the impulse of goodwill. Therefore,
hatred, grown out of injustice suffered, and causing a
thirst for vengeance, is a passion which arises irresistibly
from human nature; but, evil as it may be, it still remains a
maxim of reason, based on a legitimate thirst for justice
whose analogue it is. Thirst for vengeance is related to
inclinations, and thus one of the most violent and most
deeply rooted passions; even if it appears extinguished, it
still harbors secretly the smoldering remains of a hatred
called grudge.

The desire to be in[52] the same state as one's fellow
humans and have a relation with them that grants everyone his share as justice requires is surely no passion, but
only a defining ground   [271] for the free will provided
by pure practical reason. However, excitability of this
desire by sheer self-love, that is, just for one's own advantage, and not for legislation beneficial to all, is a sensuous
impulse of hate, not caused by injustice, but directed
against those who are unjust to us. Such an inclination (to
pursue and to destroy), especially since an idea, though
selfishly applied, lies at the bottom of it, transforms the
desire for justice into the passion of revenge against the
injuring person. The passion for vengeance often mounts
to frenzy, to the point of exposing oneself to ruin, as long
as the enemy cannot escape the same fate. This hatred (in
the case of a blood feud) is intended to become a hereditary affair even between nations, because, as it is said, the
blood of an offended, though not yet avenged, person
clamors until the innocently spilled blood has once again

been washed away with blood, even if this blood should be from one of the offending man's innocent descendants.

c.   *On the Inclination Concerning the Ability of Having Influence over Others*

§ 84.[53]   THIS inclination comes closest to techno-practical reason, that is, the maxim of cleverness. Controlling the inclinations of other people in order to direct and manage them according to one's own intentions, almost amounts to being in possession of them as mere instruments of one's own will. It is not surprising, then, that striving after the faculty to have influence over others is a passion.

This faculty controls three powers, which are honor, authority, and money. By possessing these three powers, one can influence everybody, if not by means of one, then by means of another, and thus make a person subject to one's intentions. The inclinations for this, if they become passions, are ambition, lust of authority, and avarice. In such a situation a person becomes the fool (the deluded) of his own inclinations and fails in his purpose when he uses such means. However, we are not now speaking of wisdom, which admits of no passions, but rather only of cleverness by which one can manage fools.

However, the passions, in their entirety, as strong as they may be as sensuous   [272] motives, are nothing but weaknesses in view of what reason demands of people. Consequently, the judicious man's ability to make use of those weaknesses can be proportionately smaller, the greater the passion is which rules the other person.[54]

Ambition is a weakness of people, which allows them to be influenced through their opinions; lust of authority allows them to be influenced through their fear; and avarice allows them to be influenced through their own interest. Servile submission will always result when a person has been seized by someone who has the faculty to use that person's inclinations for his own purposes. But being conscious of this faculty and being aware of possessing the means to satisfy one's inclinations arouses the passion even more than the actual use of it.

a. *Ambition*

§ 85.[55]   MAN cannot expect that others respect him for his love of honor just because of his inner (moral) values; but what gives him respect is his striving for a reputation which provides ample proof of his good intentions. (Arrogance is directed toward others who are to think little of themselves when they compare themselves to us. It is a foolishness which acts contrary to its own purposes). Arrogance, I say, needs only to be flattered, and one already has control over the fool by means of his passion. Flatterers* and yes-men, who gladly hang on every word of an important personage, nurse this passion which weakens their master; and they become the destroyers of the great and mighty who fall for such charms.

Arrogance is a mistaken desire for honor which defeats its own purpose; it cannot be regarded as an intentional means of using other people   [273] (whom it repels) for one's own purposes. The arrogant person is rather the instrument of the knave, who is called a fool. Once a very intelligent and honest merchant asked me why the arrogant person was always mean. (He had observed that a rich merchant was bragging about his wealth; but later, when he lost his assets that same man

* Flatterer *(Schmeichler)* may originally have been spelled *Schmiegler* (one who stoops and bends) in order to manage a conceited potentate [MS: dandy—Ed.], *ad libitum,* just by his arrogance; as the word hypocrite *(Heuchler),* which really should be written *Häuchler* (puffer), ought to have designated a deceiver who expresses his false show of sanctimonious humility before a very powerful ecclesiastic by means of deep sighs mixed with his speech.

had no compunction about cringing and fawning.) I replied that since arrogance is directed toward another person so that he despises himself in comparison to others, such a thought could only enter the head of someone who feels himself ready for such base action. Arrogance itself seems to provide a never-deceiving and forboding indication of the baseness of such persons.

b. *Lust of Authority*

This passion is unjust per se, and its manifestation aligns everything against it. It arises from the fear of being ruled by others, and it then concerns itself with gaining a vantage point over this danger before it is too late. But such a step is, nevertheless, a false and unjust means of using other people for one's own designs; partly, it is unwise because it arouses opposition; and partly, it is unfair because it runs contrary to freedom under the law, which is everyone's right. The indirect art of domination, for example, the power of the feminine sex to influence the male through sex and to use the man for her purposes, does not belong under this title, because it holds no authority of its own, but rather it knows how to rule and to fascinate the person into submission through his own inclination. This is not to say that the feminine part of our species is free from wanting to rule over the masculine element (just the opposite is true), but it does not use the same means to this end as the masculine. The feminine sex does not use the quality of strength (which refers in this context to domination), but rather the quality of charm which directs itself toward the inclination of the other sex to submit.

[274] c. *Avarice*

Money is the password, and all doors, which are closed to the man of lesser means, fly open to those whom Plutus favors. The invention of money, which has no other usefulness (or at least it should not have any) except for the commercial exchange of the products of man's industry, now serves all that is physically good among men. Especially after money was represented by metal, it has produced avarice which, finally, without indulgence, but by its mere possession, and even with the resolution (of the stingy) not to spend it, still contains a power which people believe can sufficiently compensate for the lack of any other power. This passion is quite shallow, even though it is not always morally reprehensible. It is merely cultivated mechanically and belongs chiefly to older persons (as a substitute for their natural impotence). Because of its great influence, this passion has gained the reputation of a faculty.[56] Once a person has been seized by avarice, no modification is possible; and, while the first of the three passions [ambition] makes one hated, and the second [lust of authority] makes one feared, this third one [avarice] makes one despised.[57]*

On the Inclination to Delusion, as a Passion

§ 86.[58]   BY delusion, as a motive of desires, I understand the internal practical deception of taking subjective reasons for objective ones. So that a man does not lose the feeling of life in mere enjoyment, Nature likes, from time to time, stronger excitement of vitality in order to rejuvenate the human activity. To this end, a very wise and benevolent Nature has offered objects to the characteristically lazy man, which he takes in his imagination for real goals (modes of acquiring a

* Despise is here to be understood in the moral sense; because in a bourgeois sense, when it turns out to be true, as Pope says, that "the devil in a golden rain of fifty to a hundred falls into the lap of the usurer and takes possession of his soul," the great majority marvels at the man who demonstrates such great business acumen. [This quotation could derive from Alexander Pope, "Moral Essays" (3): "Of the Use of Riches, lines 369–74 in *The Poetical Works* (New York: Worthington, 1884), p. 252—Trans.]

reputation, power and money. These give the idle person enough trouble   [275] and provide him with much to do about nothing, so that the interest which he takes in it is an interest of mere delusion. Nature really plays with the person and spurs him (the subject) on to its[59] purpose, although the person is convinced (objectively) that he pursues his own purpose. Such inclinations of delusion, just because fantasy acts as a self-creator in them, are well suited to become highly passionate, especially when they are intended for competition between human beings.[60]

Boys' games, like playing ball, wrestling, running races, and playing soldier, or men's games, like playing chess or cards (one of these activities gives full preference to the understanding, whereas the other also stresses profit), and, finally, the games of the townsman who tries to make his fortune with faro or dice are altogether daring enterprises deliberately spurred on by the wisdom of Nature so that they all test their strength in a competition with others. Actually this is done so that the force of life is prevented from weakening and is kept strong instead. Two such contenders believe they are playing between themselves; but in reality nature plays with both of them. Reason can clearly convince them of this fact if they consider how badly the means they have selected are suited to their purpose. But satisfaction arising from this excitement, just because it is closely related to ideas of delusion (though ill-judged), is for this very reason the cause of a propensity to the strongest and longest-lasting passion.*

Inclinations to delusion make the weak man superstitious and the superstitious man weak, that is, they make him inclined to expect interesting results from circumstances which cannot be natural causes at all

---

* A man in Hamburg, who had gambled away considerable wealth in that city, now spent his time watching the players. Someone asked him how he feels when he thinks of having once had such wealth. The man replied: "If I had possession of it again, I should not know how to use it in a more delightful way."

(something to fear or something to hope for). Hunters, fishermen, and gamblers (particularly in the lottery) are superstitious; and the delusion which seduces us into imagining the subjective to be the objective, and thereby taking the mood of the inner sense for knowledge of the thing itself, makes the propensity to superstition also conceivable.

[276] On the Highest Physical Good

§ 87.[61]   THE greatest sensuous pleasure, which is not accompanied by any loathing at all, is found under healthy conditions in resting after work. The propensity to rest without previous labor is laziness. Nevertheless, a somewhat long refusal to return to one's business, and the indulgence in a sweet *far niente*[62] for the purpose of regaining strength, is not yet laziness, because (even in play) one can be occupied pleasurably and usefully at the same time. Even changing the type of work as to its specific nature is a varied recreation, whereas it takes a rather strong determination to return to hard work which has been left unfinished.

Among the three vices of laziness, cowardice, and deceit, the first appears to be most contemptible. In judging laziness, however, one may often do injustice to a person. For his own well-being and that of others, Nature has wisely provided many a subject with a healthy instinct of distaste for continuous work. Man cannot tolerate any prolonged and frequently repeated expenditure of energy without exhaustion; but rather he requires certain pauses for recreation. Not without good reason, Demetrius could have allotted an altar to this fiend (laziness);[63] because, if laziness did not intervene, then restless wickedness would cause far more trouble in this world than it already does. If cowardice did not have pity on man, then belligerent bloodthirst would soon annihilate him; and if there were no deceit (for among the many scoundrels united through conspiracy, for example, in a regiment, there will always be one to betray it), then, because of the inborn wickedness of man, whole states would soon be overthrown.

The strongest motives of Nature, which take the place of reason (the ruler of the world), are love of life and love of the other sex.[64] By means of a higher reason they invisibly provide the human race in general with the best physical state in the world, without making it necessary that human reason involve itself to that end. Love of life is to maintain the individual, love of the other sex is to maintain the species. Through the general mixing of the sexes, the life of our species, which is endowed with reason, will be progressively maintained, despite the fact that this species works intentionally on its own destruction (by war). This [277], however, does not keep the rational creatures of such a constantly advancing culture, even in the midst of war, from promising to mankind in coming centuries an unequivocal prospect of bliss which will never end.[65]

ON THE HIGHEST ETHICOPHYSICAL GOOD

§ 88.[66]   THE two kinds of good, the physical and the moral, cannot be mixed together, because they would then neutralize each other and have no effect on the purpose of true bliss. Rather, inclination to pleasurable living and inclination to virtue are in conflict with each other, and the restriction of the principle of physical good by the principle of moral good constitute through their very conflict the whole purpose of a well-bred, partly sensuous and partly ethicointellectual[67] human being. But, since mixture can hardly be avoided in practice, a dissolution by counteracting means *(reagentia)* are needed in order to know which elements exist in what proportion in this mixture which, if properly combined, can provide the enjoyment of civilized bliss.

The kind of thought characteristic of the union of good living and virtue in society is humaneness. The degree of good living does not matter here because one person demands much and the other less of it according to what he deems necessary. What really counts, however, is the kind of relationship whereby the inclination to good living is curbed by the law of virtue.

Sociability is also a virtue; but the inclination to be sociable often becomes a passion. But, if sociable enjoyment is boastfully heightened by squander, then this false sociability ceases to be virtue, and becomes merely high living, injurious to humanity.

Music, dance, and play are conducive to company without conversation (because those few words which are needed for play establish no conversation which encourages a mutual exchange of thought). Some people claim that play should serve only to fill out the emptiness of conversation   [278] after dinner, but it is commonly made the principal affair. It is used as a means of acquisition by which the emotions are strongly stirred, and where a certain habit of self-interest is established in order to plunder each other with the greatest politeness. As long as the play lasts, nobody denies that complete egoism is determined to be the rule of conduct. Despite all that culture springing from those mannerisms,[68] such conversation does not further the union of social good living with virtue, and, consequently, it would thereby hardly further the cause of true humaneness.

The good living which still seems to harmonize best with virtue is a good meal in good company (and if possible with alternating companions). Chesterfield says that the number of companions must not be fewer than that of the Graces, nor more than that of the Muses.[69]*

* Ten per table, because the host, who serves the guests, does not count himself.

When I think of companions for a dinner party to be composed solely of men of taste (aesthetically united),* who are not only interested in having a meal together but also in enjoying one another, then this little dinner party (since their number cannot amount to many more than the number of the Graces) must not only try to supply physical satisfaction—which everyone can find for himself—but also social enjoyment for which the dinner must appear only as a vehicle. If the number of participants is right, it need not be feared[70] that the conversation will come to a standstill or that the guests will break up into small groups with those seated nearest them. The latter situation does not follow the rules of taste which are always observed when one person speaks   [279] to everybody (not only to one's neighbor). Those so-called festive entertainments (feasting and gorging), on the other hand, are pretty much in bad taste. There can be no question that whatever is publicly said by an indiscreet table-companion at all dinner parties or even at an inn, to the detriment of someone absent, should not be used outside this company and should not be gossiped about. Even without any special agreement any such gathering has a certain sanctity and duty of secrecy about it in consideration of what embarrassment fellow members of the dinner party might be caused afterward. Without such confidence the wholesome gratification of enjoying moral culture within society and of enjoying culture itself would be denied. Therefore, if something derogatory

---

* There are occasions at a festive table, where the presence of ladies automatically limits the freedom of the conversation to what is polite. Sometimes a sudden silence threatens the conversation when no one dares to bring up a new subject suitable for keeping the conversation alive. People do not want to raise a new subject but rather they prefer to make it interesting by relating it to the news of the day. A single person, particularly the lady of the house, can often all by herself avoid such a stagnation and keep the conversation flowing, so that, as at a concert, the conversation can conclude with general and complete joyfulness, which makes it all so much more wholesome. It is like Plato's *Symposium* in which the guest said: "Your dinners are pleasing not only when one enjoys them, but also as often as one thinks of them."

were said about my best friend in a so-called public company (even the largest dinner party is really always only a private party, whereas only a state dinner is public by definition) I shall defend him; and, in any event, I shall, at my own risk, come to his aid with severity and bitterness of expression. But I shall not allow myself to become a tool in spreading this evil report or in carrying it to the man concerned. Not merely social taste must guide the conversation, but also principles which are meant to serve the open exchange of ideas among men within the limiting conditions of freedom.

There is something analogous to the confidence between men, who eat together at the same table, and[71] their familiarity with ancient customs like those of the Arab, with whom a stranger may feel safe as soon as he has been able to obtain a refreshment (a drink of water) in the Arab's tent; or by accepting salt and bread offered by deputies coming to her from Moscow, the Russian Czarina could regard herself as secure from all snares by the bond of hospitality. Eating together at the same table is regarded as formal evidence of such a covenant of security.

Eating alone (*solipsimus convictorii*)[72] is unhealthy for a philosophizing [280] man of learning;* it does not restore his powers but exhausts[73] him (especially when it

---

* The philosophizing man must carry his thoughts continuously with him in order to find out by numerous experiments to what principles he should tie them systematically; and ideas, because they are not intuitions, also float in the air and offer themselves to him. The historian or mathematician, on the other hand, can write down his thoughts and ideas; and so, with his pen in hand, according to general rules of reason, he can arrange them empirically right away as facts. Because his thoughts and ideas have already been arranged as to certain points, he can continue his work on the following day just where he left off. The philosopher must not be considered as a laborer working at the building of a system of the sciences, that is, not in the way in which scholars are engaged, but rather he must be considered as an investigator of wisdom. It [A: He—Ed.] is the bare idea of a person which determines the final purpose of all practical and also theoretical knowledge. One cannot use the title philosopher in the plural, but only in the singular (the philosopher judges such or such), because he determines the bare idea, wheras speaking of philosophers would imply a plurality of something that is an absolute unity.

becomes a solitary feasting); it turns into exhausting work, and not into the refreshing play of thoughts. The indulging person who wastes himself in self-consuming thought during the solitary meal gradually loses his vivacity which, on the other hand, he would have gained if a table companion with alternative ideas had offered stimulation through new material which he had not been able to dig up himself.

At a full dinner, where the multitude of courses is only intended to keep the guests together for a long time (*coenam ducere*),[74] the conversation usually goes through the three stages of   *1*) narration,   *2*) reasoning, and   *3*) jesting.   *A.*   The first stage concerns the news of the day, first domestic, then foreign, received from personal letters and newspapers.   *B.*   During the second stage, when this first appetite[75] has been satisfied, the company gets livelier, because, in arguing back and forth, it is hard to avoid a variety of judgment about one and the same object under discussion. Since no one has a low regard for his own judgment, a dispute arises which continues to whet the appetite for food and drink; and in proportion to the liveliness of the dispute and the participation in it, the food is felt to be beneficial.   *C.*   In the third stage, because reasoning is always a kind of work and exertion of energy, this finally becomes difficult after eating rather copiously during the dinner. Consequently, the conversation turns naturally to the mere play of wit, partly also to please the lady   [281] in the company who is encouraged by the minor, intentional, but not insulting attacks on her sex to shine in her own display of wit. Thus the meal ends with laughter. Such laughter, if it is loud and good-natured, has ultimately been determined by nature to help the stomach in the digestive process by moving the diaphragm and intestines, consequently[76] contributing to the physical well-being. Meanwhile the participants in the dinner (how many, I do not know!) fancy that they have found culture of the intellect—one wonders how much!—in the purpose of Nature. Dinner music at festive banquets of great gentlemen is the most tasteless absurdity that revelry has ever concocted.

A tastefully arranged dinner[77] that animates the company obeys the following rules: *a*) choose topics for conversation which interest everybody, and always give everyone a chance to add something appropriate; *b*) do not allow deadly silence to fall, but permit only momentary pauses in the conversation; *c*) do not change the subject unnecessarily, nor jump from one subject to another. The mind at the end of the meal, as at the end of a drama (the same applies to the entire life lived by a rational human being), inevitably looks back on several phases of the conversation. If the mind cannot find a connecting thread, it feels confused and realizes with displeasure that it has not progressed in matters of culture, but rather regressed. An entertaining subject must nearly be exhausted before one can pass on to another; and, when conversation stagnates, one must know how to suggest skillfully, as an experiment, another related topic for conversation. In such a way one individual in the company can direct the conversation, unnoticed and unenvied. *d*) Do not tolerate the beginning or continuation of anything dogmatic, neither for yourself nor the companions in the group. Rather, since this conversation ought not to be business but merely a pastime, avoid such seriousness by means of a jest deftly introduced. *e*) In a serious conflict, that cannot be avoided, control yourself and your emotions carefully so that mutual respect and good faith always prevail. What counts more is the *tone* (which must neither be ranting, nor arrogant), not the content of the conversation, so that none of the guests should go home from the company at variance with another.

[282]   No matter how insignificant these laws of refined humanity may seem, especially if you compare them with purely moral laws, then everything that furthers compan-

ionship, even if it consists only of pleasant maxims or manners, is a dress that properly clothes virtue. Such a dress must also be recommended to virtue even in a serious context.[78] The cynic's purism and the hermit's mortification of the flesh, without social good-living, are distorted interpretations of virtue and do not make virtue attractive; rather, being forsaken by the Graces, they can make no claim of humanity.

ANTHROPOLOGY

Part Two

Anthropological Characterization

On How to Know a Man's Interior

from His Exterior

[285] *Classification*

1) The character of the person,   2) the character of the sex,   3) the character of the nation,   4) the character of the race,   5) the character of the species.[1]

A. THE CHARACTER OF THE PERSON

§ 89.[2] IN pragmatic consideration, the universal, natural (not civil) signification *(semiotica universalis)* of the word character is twofold; sometimes people say that a certain person has this or that (physical) character; and sometimes people say that a person has simply character (a moral character) which defines him as an individual and no one else. The first is man's mark of difference as a creature with senses or a being of Nature; the second is the distinguishing mark of a reasonable being endowed with freedom. The man of principles has character. Of him we know definitely what to expect. He does not act on the basis of his instinct, but on the basis of his will. Therefore, without being redundant one can classify characteristics according to a person's faculty of desire (what is practical), as   a) his nature, or natural talent,   b) his temperament, or disposition, and   c) his general character, or mode of thinking. The first two dispositions indicate what can be made of a person; the third (which is moral) shows what man is prepared to make of himself.

I. On Nature[3]

To say that the human being has a good disposition means that he is not stubborn, but compliant; he may get angry, but can easily be appeased, [286] and will bear no grudge (he is good in a negative way). But to be able to say of him that "he has a good heart" does tell us more about him, although such a statement is also based on sense impressions. It is, however, an incentive to the practical-good, even though such a characterization is not bestowed according to principles. Consequently, the good-humored and the good-hearted are both people whom a crafty guest can use as he chooses. Accordingly, man's nature is conditioned (subjectively) more by the feeling of pleasure or displeasure, as to how one person is affected by another (and in this reaction may be found something characteristic), than (objectively) by the faculty of desire, wherein life manifests itself not merely in feeling, that is, internally, but also in activity, that is, externally, though manifested merely in accordance with incentives pertinent to sensibility. Temperament exists in this relation, and it must be distinguished from habitual disposition (which has been acquired by custom) because a habitual disposition is not a natural disposition, but only a result of chance.

II. On Temperament[4]

When we speak of temperament from a physiological point of view, we mean physical constitution (the strong or weak build) and the complexion (the fluid moving regularly through the body by virtue of the vital power, which also includes the heat or cold necessary for the treatment of these humors).

However, speaking of temperament from a psychological point of view, when we mean the temperament of the soul (the faculty of feeling and desire), those terms borrowed from the constitution of the blood are understood as having physically motivated causes (the principal of which is the blood) analogous to the play of feelings and desires.

Thus it follows that the temperaments, which we attribute only to the soul, may perhaps also be influenced mysteriously by the physical condition of a person. Furthermore, since, first, they permit principal classification into temperaments of feeling and activity, and since, second, each of them can be linked with the excitability (*intensio*) or the slackening (*remissio*) of the vital power, it follows that only four simple temperaments (similar to the four syllogistic figures through the *medius-terminus*)[5] can be established: the sanguine, the melancholy, the choleric, and the phlegmatic. Hereby   [287] the old forms can be retained;[6] and only a more comfortable interpretation suited to the spirit of this doctrine of temperaments needs to be offered.

Describing the constitution of the blood does not suffice to state the cause of phenomena observed in a sensuously affected person, even[7] according to the pathology of humors or nerves.[8] Description can only classify phenomena according to observed effects. One does not need to know in advance what chemical blood-mixture it is that justifies the designation of a certain property of temperament, but rather one has to know which feelings and inclinations one collects during the observation of the person, in order to place him properly into a particular class.

The principal classification of the doctrine of temperaments can be the division into temperaments of feeling[9] and temperaments of activity, and, by subdivision, the classification can again be divided into two kinds which together provide us with the four temperaments.[10] I count *A.* the sanguine, and its opposite, *B.* the melancholy among the temperaments of feeling. The sanguine has the peculiarity that sense impressions are quick and strong, but not deeply penetrating (not of a lasting nature). On the other hand, in the melancholy, sense impressions are less obvious but more deeply rooted. The distinction between the temperaments of feeling[11] must be assigned to this, and not to the propensity to joyfulness or sadness. The lightheartedness of the sanguine disposes to gaiety; while heaviness of heart, which broods over a sense impression, deprives gaiety of its easy fluctuations, but still without producing sadness. However, since every change, which one has under one's control stimulates and strengthens the mind, then the person who lightly bears everything that he encounters is, if not wiser, at least certainly happier than the person who clings to impressions which benumb his vital power.

I.   Temperaments of Feeling[12]

a.   *The Sanguine Temperament of the Light-Blooded*

The sanguine person reveals his temperament as follows: He is carefree and full[13] of expectation; he attributes great importance to   [288] everything for the moment, and at the next moment he may not give it another thought. He makes honest promises but fails to keep his word because he has not considered deeply enough beforehand whether he will be able to keep them. He is good-natured enough to give help to others, but he is a poor debtor and always asks for new terms. He is a good companion, jocular, and high-spirited; he does not like to attribute great importance to anything *(Vive la bagatelle!)*,[14] and he has everybody for a friend. Usually he is not a bad fellow, but as a delinquent he is hard to convert; indeed, he repents of something very much, but quickly forgets this repentance (which is never an affliction to him). Business tires him, and yet he is restlessly busy with things that are mere play, because this provides change, especially since perseverance is not his strength.

b.   *The Melancholy Temperament of the Heavy-Blooded*

He who is disposed to melancholy (not the person afflicted with melancholy, since this signifies a condition, rather than the mere propensity to a condition), attributes great importance to all things that concern him. Everywhere he finds cause for concern and he directs his attention first of all to difficulties, while the sanguine person relies on the hope of success. Therefore the melancholy person thinks deeply, just as the sanguine thinks only superficially. He makes promises with reluctance because to him keeping his word is precious, but the ability to keep his promise is problematic. All this does not arise from moral causes (because we are talking here about sensuous motives), but rather from potential opposition which makes him uneasy, mistrusting, and critical, thereby also incapacitating him for joyfulness. Moreover, this mental disposition, when habitual, contrasts with a philanthropist's disposition which is more akin to the sanguine person, at least in motive, because he who is himself deprived of joy will hardly be able to tolerate it in others.

[289]   II.   Temperaments of Activity[15]

c.   *The Choleric Temperament of the Hot-Blooded*

We say of the choleric person that he is hot-tempered, and that he is quickly ablaze like a straw fire. He readily allows himself to be appeased if the other person is willing to give in. He is still angry then, but he does not hate; on the contrary, he loves the other person all the more for giving in to him. His activity is impetuous, but not lasting. He is busy, but reluctant to undertake business himself, just because he is not persistent. He likes to be the chief who makes the decisions, but does not like to carry them out. Consequently, his dominant passion is ambition; he likes to be involved with public affairs and wants to be loudly praised. Accordingly he is fond of appearance and the pomp of formalities; he gladly plays the role of protector, and is magnanimous as appearances go, though not magnanimous out of love but from pride, because he loves himself most.[16] He values order highly and consequently appears smarter than he is. He is avaricious in order not to be stingy; he is polite, but because of his emphasis on ceremony, he is stiff and affected in society. He likes any flatterer who is the butt of his wit; he suffers more offenses from the opposition of others to his haughty arrogance than the miser ever suffers from the opposition against his avaricious arrogance, especially since a bit of caustic wit directed at him will completely dispel the aura of his importance, whereas the miser is compensated for this by his profit. In short, the choleric temperament is the least happy of all, because it calls most strongly for opposition against itself.

d. *The Phlegmatic Temperament of the Cold-Blooded*

Phlegm[17] signifies apathy, not indolence (inertia), and on that account one should not call a person who has much phlegm a phlegmatic, or lethargic, and thereby classify him in the group of idlers.[18]

Phlegm, as a weakness, is the tendency to inactivity, it is not letting oneself be moved to business even by strong motives. Such insensitivity to stimuli [290] is voluntary uselessness, all inclinations are directed only to the satisfaction of hunger and to sleep.

Phlegm as a strength, on the other hand, is characteristic of not being stirred easily or quickly, but, if slowly, then persistently. He who has a good dose of phlegm in him warms up slowly; but he holds the warmth longer. He does not get angry easily; he first considers whether he should become angry. The choleric person on the other hand, may fall into a rage just because he has found himself unable to stir the resolute man out of his cold-bloodedness.

The cold-blooded person has nothing to regret particularly if he has been equipped by nature with a rather average share of reason, in addition to his phlegm; without being brilliant, he will still proceed from principles and not from instinct. His fortunate temperament takes the place of wisdom, and even in ordinary life people often call him the philosopher. By virtue of this temperament he is superior to others without offending their vanity. Frequently he is also called cunning, because all the bullets and missiles fired at him bounce off him as from a sack of wool.

He is a peaceable husband and knows how to establish authority over his wife and relatives by seemingly humoring everyone. By his firm but well-considered will he knows how to make others follow him, just as bodies with small mass and great velocity penetrate other bodies on impact, and just as bodies with less velocity and greater mass carry along with themselves the obstacle that stands in their path without destroying it.

If one temperament is said to be an associate of another, as it is commonly believed, for example, then

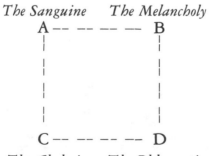

they either oppose or else neutralize each other. They oppose each other if the sanguine is considered united with the melancholy,   [291] and likewise if the choleric is thought to be united with the phlegmatic in one and the same subject, because they (A and B, likewise C and D) stand in opposition to each other. If the sanguine were mixed (chemically, so to speak) with the choleric, and the melancholic with the phlegmatic (A and C, likewise B and D), then they would neutralize each other. Good-natured joyfulness cannot be conceived as being fused with forbidding anger in one and the same act, nor can the agony of the self-tormentor go together with the peaceful serenity of the self-sufficient mind. But if one of these two states should alternate with the other in the same person, the result would be a mere freak, but no specific temperament.

Therefore there is no composite temperament like a sanguine-choleric temperament (which all windbags want to have because then they can claim not only to play the role of the gracious but also the stern gentleman). In all there are but four temperaments, and each of them is simple. We do not know what to make of the person who claims to have a mixture of temperaments.

Happiness and recklessness, melancholy and insanity, high-mindedness and stubbornness, finally cold-bloodedness and feeblemindedness are only distinguished as effects of temperament in relation to their causes.[19]*

---

* What influence the variety of temperament has upon public affairs, or vice versa (the effect which the customary exercise of affairs has on the temperament), is claimed to have been discovered partly by experience and partly also by conjecture of assumed occasional causes. Thus, for example, it is said that

> In religion the choleric is Orthodox,
>   the sanguine is Free-spirit,
>   the melancholy is Enthusiast,
>   the phlegmatic is Indifferentist.

But these are hastily written judgments which have as much value for the topic of Characteristic as a scurrilous wit will allow (vale[a]nt, quantum possunt [they are worth as much as is attributed to them—Ed.]).

III.   On Character as a Way of Thinking[20]

If we are simply able to say of a person "He has character," then we not only tell much about him, but we also praise him, for he is a rarity that calls for respect and admiration   [292] as well.

If one usually understands by character those qualities which accurately describe a person, be they good or bad, it is customarily added that he has this or that character; in that case the term refers to his way of sensing. But simply to have a character relates to that property of the will by which the subject has tied himself to certain practical principles which he has unalterably prescribed for himself by his own reason. Although these principles may sometimes indeed be false or defective, nevertheless the formal element of the will as such, which is determined to act according to firm principles (not shifting hither and yon like a swarm of gnats), has something precious and admirable[21] to it, which is also something rare.

Here it does not depend on what Nature makes of man, but what man makes of himself. What Nature makes of man belongs to temperament (wherein the subject is for the most part passive), and only what man makes of himself reveals whether he has character.

All other good and useful properties of character have a price in exchange for others which have just as much use. Talent has a market price, since the sovereign or estate-owner can use a talented person in all sorts of ways. Temperament has a fancy price,[22] since one can converse well with such a person; he is a pleasant companion. But, character has an inner value* and it is above all price.

---

* Once a seafarer had occasion to listen to a dispute led by learned men concerning the rank of their respective faculties. He decided the question in his own way, namely: How much would a captured man bring at the sale in the market in Algiers? No one would need a theologian or a jurist in that

[293]   On the Qualities which Result
from Having or not Having Character[23]

1. The imitator (as far as morals are concerned) is without character, because character has its being in the originality of the mode of thinking. The conduct of character is based on a source which the person himself has discovered. However, the rational person must not be an eccentric; indeed he never will be, because he depends upon principles that are valid for everybody. The eccentric only mimics a person who has character. Kindness arising from temperament is a painting of watercolors and not a trait of character. But, depicted in caricature, a trait of character is an outrageous ridicule of the man of true character, because he does not indulge in the evil conduct which has become public custom (the fashion), and, consequently, he is represented as an eccentric.

2. However, being temperamentally bad-natured is less bad than being temperamentally good-natured without character, because by character we can get the upper hand over bad nature. A person of bad character (like Sulla),[24] even though the violence of his strict maxims provokes disgust, is, nevertheless, also an object of admi-

---

place; but the physician has learned a trade and might have a cash value. King James I of England was besought by the wet-nurse who had suckled him, that he should make her son a gentleman (a man of distinction). James replied: "That I cannot do; I can make him a count, but he must make himself a gentleman." Diogenes (the Cynic), as the story goes, was captured on a sea voyage near the island of Crete and offered for sale at a public slave market. "What can you do? What do you know?" asked the broker who had put him upon the stand. "I know how to rule," answered the philosopher, "and you better find a buyer who needs a master." The merchant, moved by this unusual request, decided to participate in this strange transaction. He turned his son over to Diogenes for the purpose of education; he told Diogenes to make of him whatever he wished. The merchant himself had to conduct business in Asia for several years and upon his return he received his heretofore uncivilized son now transformed into a skillful, well-mannered, and virtuous person. Thus approximately can the gradation of human worth be appraised.

ration, because we generally admire strength of soul in comparison with kindness of soul. Both must be found united in the same subject in order to bring out what is more ideal than real, namely, the right to the title of magnanimity.

3.   The rigid, inflexible[25] temper which accompanies a resolution (as was the case with Charles XII)[26] is indeed a natural disposition very favorable to the character, but it is not yet a particular character as such. Character requires maxims, which proceed from reason and from ethicopractical principles. Therefore one cannot properly say that the wickedness of this person is a quality of his character, because then it would be diabolic. Man never sanctions the evil in himself, and so there is actually no evil coming from principles, but only from the forsaking of them.   [294] Accordingly, it is best to explain negatively those principles which have to do with character. They are:

a)   Not to speak an untruth intentionally; consequently, we should also speak with caution in order that we do not bring upon ourselves the disgrace of retracting.

b)   Not to dissemble; that is, to appear well-intentioned to one's face, but hostile behind one's back.

c)   Not to break one's (legitimate) promise; this includes honoring the memory of a friendship that has now deteriorated, and not misusing afterward the former confidence and candor of the other person.

d)   Not to join the company of evil-minded people, and, bearing in mind the *noscitur ex socio* etc.,[27] to confine the association only to business.

e)   Not to pay attention to slander derived from people's shallow and malicious[28] judgment, because listening to it already indicates weakness. Also, to restrain[29] our fear of a breach of etiquette which, again, is a fleeting, changeable thing; and, if its influence has already acquired some weight, not to extend its command over morality.[30]

The person who is conscious of the character in his mode of thinking does not have that character by nature, but must always have acquired it. One may also take it for granted that the establishment of character is, similar to a kind of rebirth, a certain solemn resolution which the person himself makes. This resolution and the moment at which the transformation took place remain unforgettable for him, like the beginning of a new epoch. This stability and persistence in principles can generally not be effected by education, examples, and instruction by degrees, but it can only be done by an explosion which suddenly occurs as a consequence of our disgust at the unsteady condition of instinct. Perhaps there will be only a few who have attempted this revolution before their thirtieth year, and fewer still who have firmly established it before their fortieth year. Wishing to become a better person in a fragmentary manner is a vain endeavor because one impression fades away while we labor on another.   [295] The establishment of a character, however, is absolute unity of the inner principle of conduct as such. Also, it is said that poets have no character, for example, they would rather insult their best friends than give up a bright idea; or that character cannot be found at all among courtiers who have to accommodate themselves to all fashions; and to clergymen who pay homage both to the Lord of Heaven and to the lords of the earth in the identical mood, stability of character can only be doubtfully attributed; and, accordingly, it probably is and will remain a pious wish to assume that they have an inner (moral) character. But perhaps the philosophers[31] must be blamed, because they have never yet singled out this concept and shed a sufficiently clear light on it. They have tried to represent virtue only in fragments, but never have they tried to make virtue interesting as a whole to all people in its beautiful form.

Briefly, as the highest maxim, uninhibited internal truthfulness toward oneself, as well as in the behavior toward everyone else, is the only proof of a person's consciousness of having character. And since having character is the minimum requirement that can be expected of a rational person, and at the same time also the maximum of his inner value (of human dignity), then being a man of principle (having a certain character) must be possible for the most ordinary human mind that can[32] thereby be superior to the greatest talent, thanks to dignity.

On Physiognomy[33]

Physiognomy is the art[34] of judging a person's disposition or way of thinking by his visible form; consequently, it judges the interior by the exterior. Here one does not judge him in his unhealthy, but in his healthy condition; not when his mind is stirred up, but when it is quiet. When someone, who is being judged for this purpose, realizes that someone is watching him and seeking to detect his inner nature, it goes without saying that his mind is not at rest but in a state of constraint, internal agitation, and indeed even in a state of annoyance at seeing himself under scrutiny by someone else.

If a clock is in a fine case (says a famous clockmaker), one cannot judge with certainty from this that the inside is also of good quality; but, if the case is badly constructed, one can   [296] conclude with reasonable certainty that the inside is not worth much either, because the craftsmen will not discredit a product on which he has worked diligently and well by neglecting its exterior, which costs him the least labor. However, it would be absurd to conclude that, by analogy to the human craftsman, the same holds true for the inscrutable creator of Nature; that He would have combined a beautiful body with a good soul in order to recommend the person, whom He created, to other persons and so bring him into favor, or, vice versa, scare them away (by means of the *hic niger est, hunc tu, Romane, caveto*).[35] Taste, which merely expresses the subjective basis of satisfaction or dissatisfaction of one person with another (depending upon their beauty or ugliness), cannot serve as a model for wisdom. Wisdom shares (with a purpose which we cannot absolutely comprehend) its existence objectively with certain natural qualities, but it is wrong to assume that these two heterogeneous things[36] are united in a person for one and the same purpose.

On How Nature Guides Us to Physiognomy

If we are to put ourselves into somebody's hands, it is only natural that we first look him in the face and particularly in the eyes, no matter how well-recommended he comes to us. We want to find out what we have to be on guard against. His repelling or attractive gestures determine our choice, or also[37] make us suspicious even before we have come to conclusions about his morals. Hence it cannot be disputed that there is characterization by physiognomy. Yet it can never become a science, because the peculiarity of a human form, which indicates certain inclinations or faculties of the subject under consideration, cannot be understood by terminological description. It can only be done through images and representation (by intuition)[38] or through imitation, whereby the human form in general is judged according to its varieties, every one of which is supposed to point to a special inner quality of the person.

The caricatures of human heads by Baptista Porta have long been forgotten. They represent animal heads painted in analogy to certain characteristic human facial traits, and from these pictures conclusions were to be drawn about a similarity of   [297] natural predispositions in both. Lavater popularized this taste by silhouettes which were well-liked and cheap merchandise for some time, but recently they have been entirely abandoned. Almost nothing remains of this except, perhaps, the ambiguous observation (of Herr von Archenholz) that the face of a person, which we may only imitate for ourselves by making a grimace, also calls forth certain thoughts or sensations, which agree with the imitated person's character. Thus there is now no longer any demand for physiognomy as an art of investigating the human interior through external, involuntary signs, and nothing is left of it but the art of cultivating taste, not taste in things, but rather in morals, manners, and customs, in order to add to the knowledge of man through a critique which would enhance human relations and the knowledge of man in general.

Classification of Physiognomy[39]

On characteristics: *1*) in the structure of the face; *2*) in its features;   *3*) in habitual expression (mien).

a.   *On the Structure of the Face*

It is remarkable that in statues, cameos, and intaglios the Greek artists also had in their minds an ideal of the structure of the face (for gods and heroes), which was to express perpetual youth and at the same time a repose free from all emotions. This quality speaks from their statues,[40] cameos, and intaglios without the superaddition of any alluring charms. The Greek perpendicular profile has the eyes set deeper than they ought to be according to our taste (which looks for charm); even the Venus dei Medici lacks charm. The cause of this may be that, since the ideal should be a definite, unchangeable norm, a nose springing out of the face from the forehead at an angle (the angle may be larger or smaller) would yield no definite rule of form as required of that which belongs to the norm. The later Greeks, despite their beautiful physical build, do not have in relation to the shape of the rest of the body [298] that severe perpendicular profile in their faces, which seems to prove that these ideal facial structures found in works of art[41] were prototypes. In imitation of these mythological models, the eyes have become more deeply set, and they have been placed slightly in the shade at the base of the nose. Nowadays, however, one deems human faces more beautiful that have a nose with a slight deviation from the direction of the forehead (an indentation at the base of the nose).

If we pursue our observations of how people actually are, it is apparent that a strictly measured adherence to the rule generally signifies a very ordinary person who has no spirit. The happy mean appears to be the basic measure and the foundation of beauty, but it is still far from being beauty itself, because something characteristic is needed for beauty. But one can encounter this characteristic even in a face without beauty, in which expression is of advantage to the owner, though in some other respect (perhaps moral or aesthetic). One may, for instance, find fault with a beautiful face, with a slightly too narrow forehead, with a broad chin, or with the color of the hair,[42] and so forth, but one has to admit that this still remains more favorable to the individuality of the person than if regularity were complete, because this would generally also cause lack of character.

We should not charge any face with ugliness if in its characteristics it does not betray the expression of a mind degraded by vice or by a natural, though unfortunate, tendency to vice, for example, a certain characteristic of a person who has the tendency of sneering maliciously when he speaks, or of looking another person straight in the face with foolhardiness untempered by gentleness when he tries to convey that one does not take his judgment seriously. There are men whose faces are *rébarbaratif*[43] (as the Frenchman says); they have faces with which, it is said, one can drive children to bed; others have faces pockmarked and grotesque, or others who have, as the Dutch say, a *wanschapenes* face (a face perceived in delirium or in a dream). Nevertheless, people with such faces still show such good-naturedness and gaiety that they can make fun of their own faces, which therefore cannot be called ugly, because they would not be offended if a lady said of them (as was said of Pelisson[44] at the Académie Française): "Pelisson abuses the privilege men have of being ugly." It is more mischievous and at the same time[45] more stupid when persons, from whom one can   [299] expect correct behavior, behave like rabble by reproaching a handicapped person with his physical defects which often enhance his intellectual excellence. If this happens to one who has suffered an accident during early childhood (for example, if he is called "you blind dog," or "you lame dog"), such pronouncements are really wicked, and gradually embitter him toward well-formed people who imagine themselves to be superior.

Generally, people who have never left their country make fun of unfamiliar faces of strangers from other nations. Japanese children follow Dutch tradesmen, calling out: "What big eyes, what big eyes!" The Chinese react with aversion to the red hair of some Europeans who visit their country, while their blue eyes seem ridiculous to them.

The observations concerning only the skull and its structure which constitutes the basis of its shape, for example, the skulls of Negroes, Kalmucks,[46] South-Sea Indians, and so forth, as they have been described by Camper[47] and especially by Blumenbach,[48] belong more to physical geography than to pragmatic anthropology. A mean just between the two might be the observation that even the forehead of the male of our species is customarily flat, while that of the female is rather rounded.

Whether a hump on the nose reveals a satirist; whether the peculiarity of the shape of the Chinese face, of which we say that the upper jawbone projects somewhat beyond the lower, is an indication of their rigid minds; or whether the forehead of the American Indian, overgrown with hair on both sides, is a sign of an innate mental weakness, and so forth; all these are conjectures which permit only inconclusive interpretation.

b. *On Characteristics in Facial Features* [49]

It does no harm to a man, even in the judgment of the feminine sex, if his face has been disfigured and made unlovely because of the coloring of his skin or pockmarks. If good-naturedness shines in his eyes, and also if the expression of decency reveals itself on his face peacefully together with the consciousness of his power, then he can always be liked and be worthy of love; and this should be universally so regarded. One jokes with such people and their amiability *(per antiphrasin);* [300] and a woman can be proud of having such a husband. Such a face is not a caricature,[50] since a caricature is an intentionally exaggerated sketch (a distortion) of a face in excitement, devised for derision and belonging to mimicry. Such a face[51] must rather be counted as a variety inherent in nature, and must not be called a grotesque face (which would be terrifying). Without being beautiful such a face can inspire love, and although it is not lovely, it is still not ugly.*

* Heidegger, a German musician in London, was fantastically deformed, but a clever and intelligent person with whom aristocrats liked to associate for the sake of conversation. Once it occurred to him at a drinking party to claim to a lord that he had the ugliest face in London. The lord reflected and then made a wager that he would present a face still more ugly. He then sent for a drunken woman, at whose appearance the whole party burst into laughter and shouts: "Heidegger, you have lost the wager!" "Not so fast," he

c. On Characteristics in Facial Expressions[52]

Expressions are facial features put into action, and this action is controlled more or less by strong emotion, the tendency to such emotion is a trait of the person's character.

It is difficult to hide the impact of emotion from some facial expression; emotion[53] betrays itself by the careful restraint from gesticulation, or in the tone itself. And he who is too weak to control his emotion, will reveal his inner emotions through facial expression (much against his will), even if he would rather like to hide and conceal them from the eyes of others. Once they have been found out, those who have mastered this art are not considered the best people to deal with in confidence, particularly when they know how to fake expressions which contradict their real actions.

[301] The art of interpreting facial expressions which unintentionally reveal the interior, but which are used to deceive, can offer occasion for many proper remarks, but I wish to consider only one. When anybody who ordinarily is not cross-eyed tells a story and looks at the point of his nose and consequently looks cross-eyed, then the story he is telling is always a lie. But one must not count in this category anyone who squints because of defective eyesight, because he can be entirely free from this vice.

Moreover, there are gestures designed by nature, by which people of all races and from all climates understand each other without prior agreement. Among these

---

replied, "let the woman wear my wig, and let me wear her headdress; then we shall see." As this took place, everybody fell to laughing, to the point of suffocation, because the woman looked like a very presentable gentleman, and the fellow looked like a witch. This shows that in order to call anyone beautiful, or at least bearably pretty, one must not judge absolutely, but always only relatively. It also shows that no one ought to call a fellow ugly just because he is not handsome. Only repulsive physical defects of the face can justify such a verdict [A: such a claim—Ed.].

gestures are nodding the head (in affirmation), shaking the head (in negation), lifting up the head (in objection), shaking the head (in wonder), turning up one's nose (in mockery), smiling ironically (in grinning), having one's countenance fall (upon the refusal of a request), knitting the brows (in vexation), rapidly snapping and locking the jaws (bah!), beckoning toward and away from oneself with the hands, throwing up one's arms (in astonishment), clenching the fist (in threatening), bowing, laying a finger on the mouth *(compescere labella)*[54] in order to command silence, hissing, and so forth.

Random Remarks[55]

Often-repeated facial expressions, which involuntarily accompany emotion, gradually become fixed features which only disappear in death. Consequently, as Lavater noticed, the terrifying face that revealed the scoundrel in life refines itself (negatively) in death. Because all muscles are relaxed in death, nothing remains but the expression of repose, which is an innocent expression. Thus it may even happen that a person who has not worn himself out during his youthful years, in later years, despite his good health, may take on a new face because of debauchery. From this, however, nothing should be concluded about his natural disposition.

One also speaks of a common face in contrast to one that is aristocratic. The aristocratic signifies nothing more than an arrogant importance combined with a courtly manner of ingratiation, as it prospers only in big cities where people cause friction among each other and wear off their crudeness. Therefore, when civil servants, born and brought up in the country, are transferred with their families to important municipal positions,   [302] or when they only qualify for such service in accordance with their rank, they show something common, not merely in their manners, but also in their facial expression. Having dealt almost entirely with their subordinates, they felt unchallenged in their sphere of activity, so that their facial muscles did not develop the flexibility necessary for all situations involving the treatment of superiors, inferiors, and equals. They would not have lost their dignity if they had stooped to cultivate the play of facial expressions which is required in order to be well received in society. On the other hand, people accustomed to urban manners and who are of the same rank are well aware that they have an advantage in this respect over other people. When this consciousness of superiority becomes habitual by long practice, it is stamped upon their faces with lasting outlines.

Devotees of a predominant religion or cult, when disciplined for a long time in mechanical exercises of devotion and, so to speak, petrified by them, attribute characteristics to the people of an entire nation which became representative of that nation's physiognomy. Herr Fr. Nicolai[56] says this of the awkward, hypocritically pious faces in Bavaria; whereas John Bull of old England, wherever he may go, carries in his face the license to be impolite to strangers, be it either abroad or in his own country. There is, therefore, something like a national physiognomy, but it should not necessarily be thought of as innate. There are characteristic marks in groups of people whom the law has brought together for the purpose of punishment. About the prisoners in Amsterdam's Rasphuis, Paris' Bicêtre, and London's Newgate, an able traveling German physician has remarked that they were mostly skinny fellows who were conscious of their superiority. But there were none about whom it would be permissible to say with the actor Quin:[57] "If this fellow is not a scoundrel, then the Creator does not write a legible hand." In order to pass such hard judgment, we would need to distinguish, more clearly than any mortal can presume to claim, between the purposes of the game that Nature plays with the forms of its creation only to generate a variety of temperaments, and what this does or does not do for morality.

[303]   B.   THE CHARACTER OF THE SEXES[58]

ALL machines, designed to accomplish with little[59] power as much as those with great power, must be designed with art. Consequently, one can assume beforehand that Nature's foresight has put more art into the design of the female than the male, because Nature has equipped the male with greater strength than the female in order to bring both, who are also rational beings, together in intimate physical union for the most innate purpose, the preservation of the species. Moreover, for this capacity of theirs (as rational animals) Nature provided them with social inclinations so that their sexual partnership would persist in a domestic union.

A harmonious and indissoluble union cannot be achieved through the random combination of two persons. One partner must subject himself to the other, and, alternately, one must be superior to the other in something, so that he can dominate or rule. If two people, who cannot do without each other, have identical ambitions, self-love will produce nothing but wrangling. In the interest of the progress of culture, one partner must be superior to the other in a heterogeneous way. The man must be superior to the woman in respect to his physical strength and courage, while the woman must be superior to the man in respect to her natural talent for mastering his desire for her. Under still uncivilized conditions, on the other hand, superiority is on the man's side only. Therefore in anthropology the nature of feminine characteristics, more than those of the masculine sex, is a subject for study by philosophers. Under adverse natural conditions one can no more recognize those characteristics than the characteristics of crab apples or wild pears, which disclose their potential only through grafting or innoculation. Civilization does not establish these feminine characteristics, it only causes them to develop and become recognizable under favorable circumstances.

Feminine traits[60] are called weaknesses. People joke about them; fools ridicule them; but reasonable persons see very well that those traits are just the tools for the management of men, and for the use of men for female designs. The man is easy to fathom; but the woman [304] does not reveal her secret, although she keeps another person's secret poorly (because of her loquacity). He loves domestic peace and gladly submits to her rule, so that he does not find himself hindered in his own affairs. She does not shy away from domestic strife which she carries on with her tongue, and for which Nature has provided her with loquacity and passionate eloquence which together[61] disarm the man. He builds on the right of the stronger to give orders at home because he has the obligation to protect his home against outside enemies. She builds on the right of the weaker to be protected by her masculine partner against men, and she disarms him with her tears of exasperation by reproaching him with his lack of generosity.

In primitive cultures this is quite different.[62] There the woman is a domestic animal. The man leads the way with weapon in his hand, and the woman follows him, laden with his household belongings. But even in a barbaric civilization with legal polygamy, the most favored woman in the prison-yard (called harem) knows how to win control over a man; and he has his hands full with bringing about a tolerable peace in the quarrel of many women about the one[63] (who is to dominate him).

In a civil society the woman does not submit herself without marriage to the desires of a man, and if she is married, then only in monogamy. Where civilization has not yet reached the level of feminine freedom in gallantry (that is, where the wife may openly admit to having lovers other than her husband), the man punishes the wife who threatens him with a rival.* But when gallantry

* The old Russian story that wives suspect their husbands of keeping company with other women unless they are beaten now and then, is usually considered to be a fable. However, in Cook's travel book one finds that

has become fashionable and jealousy ridiculous (as happens when a certain degree of luxury is reached), [305] the feminine character reveals itself. By extending favors toward men, the feminine character lays claim to freedom and simultaneously to the conquest of the entire male species. Although this inclination is in ill repute, under the name of coquetry, it is not without a real justifiable basis. A young wife is always in danger of becoming a widow, and this leads her to distribute her charms to all men whose fortunes make them marriageable; so that, if this should occur, she would not be lacking in suitors.

Pope[64] believes that one can characterize the feminine sex (the cultivated element of it, of course) under two headings, the inclination to dominate and the inclination to gratify. By the latter, however, must not be understood gratification at home, but gratification in public, which can work to her advantage and distinction. Then the inclination to gratify also dissolves into the inclination to dominate, and instead of giving in to her rivals' preoccupation with gratifying, she conquers all of them with her taste and her charm, wherever possible. However, even the inclination to dominate, like any inclination, cannot be used for characterizing the relationship of one class of people to another. The inclination to what is beneficial to them is common to all people; and the same also holds true for the inclination to dominate, as far as this is possible. Consequently, inclination

---

when an English sailor on Tahiti saw an Indian chastising his wife, the sailor, wanting to be gallant, began to threaten the husband. The woman immediately turned against the Englishman and asked him how it concerned him that her husband had to do this! Accordingly, one will also find that when the married woman practices obvious gallantry and her husband pays no attention to it, but rather compensates himself with drinking parties, card games, or with gallantry of his own, then not merely contempt but also hate overcomes the feminine partner, because the wife recognizes by this that he does not value her any longer, and that he leaves her indifferently to others, who also want to gnaw at the same bone. [On margin of MS: The woman wishes to be liked by all men, because if her husband should die, she will set her hopes on another man who likes her—Ed.]

does not characterize people. The fact that this female species is in a continual feud with its own kind, whereas it remains on rather good terms with the opposite sex, could be taken for a characteristic if it were not merely the natural consequence of rivalry among women for the favor and devotion of men. The inclination to dominate is the real goal, while public gratification, by which the field of their charm is extended, is only the means for providing the effect for that inclination.

We can only succeed in characterizing the feminine sex if we use the principle which served as Nature's end in the creation of femininity, and not what we[65] have devised ourselves as its end. Since this end must still be wisdom according to Nature's design, despite the foolishness of men, these assumed ends will also be able to reveal their underlying principle which does not depend on our own choice, but on the higher design for the human race. These ends are   1) the preservation of the species,   [306] 2) the improvement of society and its refinement by women.

1.   As Nature entrusted to the woman's womb her most precious pledge, namely, the species, in the shape of the embryo by which the race was to propagate and perpetuate itself, Nature was concerned about the preservation of the embryo and implanted fear into the woman's character, a fear of physical injury and a timidity toward similar dangers. On the basis of this weakness, the woman legitimately asks for masculine protection.

2.   Since Nature also wanted to instill the finer sensations, such as sociability and propriety, which belong to the culture, she made this sex the ruler of men through modesty and eloquence in speech and expression. Nature made women mature early and had them demand gentle and polite treatment from men, so that they would find themselves imperceptibly fettered by a child due to their own magnanimity; and they would find themselves

brought, if not quite to morality itself, then at least to that which cloaks it, moral behavior, which is the preparation and introduction to morality.

Random Remarks[66]

The woman wants to dominate, the man wants to be dominated (particularly before marriage). This was the reason for the gallantry of medieval knights. Early in life, the woman acquires confidence in her ability to please. The young man always manages to displease and, consequently, is embarrassed (feels awkward) in the company of ladies. By virtue of her sex, she maintains a feminine haughtiness in order to restrain all importunities of men through the respect which haughtiness instills; and she claims the privilege of respect even without deserving it. The woman is unwilling; the man is insistent; her yielding is a favor. Nature wants that the woman be sought after; therefore she does not have to be so particular in her choice (in matters of taste) as the man, whom Nature has built more coarsely, and who already pleases the woman if only his physique shows that he has the strength and ability to protect her. If she were repelled with respect to the beauty of his body, and fastidious in her choice, then she would have to do the courting in order to fall in love; while he would have to show himself unwilling. This would entirely degrade the dignity of her sex, even in the eyes of the man. [307] She must appear cold, while the man must appear ardently in love. Not to respond to an amorous advance seems to be shameful to a man, whereas responding readily appears outrageous to a woman. A woman's desire to let her charms play upon all gentlemen is coquetry; whereas boasting of being in love with all women is gallantry. Coquetry and gallantry may both be merely fashionable affectations without any serious consequence. This was the case with *cicisbeism*,[67] an unnatural freedom of the married woman, or with the courtesan system which previously also existed in Italy (in the *Historia Concilii Tridentini* it is reported, among other things; *Erant ibi etiam 300 honestae meretrices, quas cortegianas vocant*).[68] It is said about the courtesan system that it contained more cultural refinement as to moral public behavior than was contained in mixed company in private houses. In marriage the husband woos only his own wife, but the wife has an inclination for all men. Out of jealousy she dresses up only for the eyes of her own[69] sex, in order to outdo other women in charm or pretended distinguished appearance. The man, on the other hand, dresses up only for the feminine sex; if this can be called dressing, it goes only so far as not to shame his wife by his clothes. The man judges feminine mistakes leniently, whereas the woman judges very severely (in public); and young ladies, if they had the choice to have their trespasses judged by a male or a female jury, would certainly choose a male jury for their judge. Whenever the refinement of luxury has reached a high point, the woman shows herself well-behaved only by compulsion, and makes no secret in wishing that she might rather be a man, so that she could give larger and freer latitude to her inclinations; no man, however, would want to be a woman.

The woman does not ask about the man's continence before marriage; whereas to him the woman's continence is infinitely important. In marriage, women mock at men's intolerance (jealousy), but it is only done by them jokingly; the unmarried woman, however, passes judgment on intolerance with great seriousness. As for scholarly women, they use their books somewhat like a watch, that is, they wear the watch so it can be noticed that they have one, although it is usually broken or does not show the correct time.[70]

Feminine virtue or vice is very different from masculine virtue or vice, not only in kind but also in motive. She is expected to be patient; he must be tolerant. She is sensitive; he is perceptive.[71] The man's business   [308] is to earn; the woman's is to save. The man is jealous when he is in love; the woman is also jealous without being in love, because any lover gained by other women is one lost from the circle of her admirers. The man develops his own taste while the woman makes herself an object of everybody's taste. "What the world says is true, and what it does is good" is a feminine principle which is hard to relate with character in the narrow sense of the word. However, there have been valiant women who, in connection with their own household, have developed their specific and proper character with honor. Milton was encouraged by his wife to take the position of Latin Secretary, which was offered to him after Cromwell's death, although it was contrary to his principles now to declare a regime lawful which he had previously labeled unlawful. He replied, "Well, my dear, you and others of your sex[72] want to travel in coaches, but I must remain an honorable man." The wife of Socrates (and perhaps also Job's wife) were similarly driven into the corner by their virtuous husbands, but masculine virtue asserted itself in these men's characters without diminishing the credit due to the feminine character as posited in their relation.

Pragmatic Consequences[73]

The feminine sex has to develop and discipline itself in practical matters; the masculine sex does not understand this.

The young husband rules over his older spouse. This is based on jealousy according to which the party that is subordinate to the other in sexual capacity guards himself against encroachment on his rights by the other party and thereby finds himself obliged to give in to being compliant and attentive toward the other party. Therefore every experienced wife will advise against marriage to a young man, even if he is just of the same age, because with the passing of years the woman ages earlier than the man. Even if one disregards this dissimilarity, one cannot safely count on the harmony, which is based on equality. A young, intelligent wife will have better luck in marriage with a healthy but, nevertheless, noticeably older man. However a man   [309] who perhaps has carelessly dissipated his sexual power before marriage, will be the fool in his own home because he can have domestic domination only so far as he does not fail to fulfill any reasonable demands.

Hume remarked that women (even old maids) are most disturbed by satires on marriage than by sneers against their sex.[74] Sneers can never be meant seriously, but satires could very well become serious if the difficulties of the state of being married are correctly emphasized with respect to what the unmarried person is spared. But eccentric thinking along this line would only have bad consequences on the whole feminine sex, because it would degrade the woman to a mere means of satisfying the desires of the other sex; and this might easily result in ennui and unsteadiness. The woman becomes free by marriage; whereas the man loses his freedom thereby.

To make a point of detecting the moral properties in a man, especially a young man, before the wedding, is never the proper business of a woman. She believes that she can improve him; an intelligent woman, she says, can correct a man's bad habits; but in this judgment she frequently finds herself deceived in the most lamentable manner. This also applies to the opinion of the naïve woman who believes that the debaucheries[75] of her husband before marriage can be overlooked, because this instinct, if he has not yet indulged enough, will now be sufficiently provided for by his wife. But those good children do not realize that sexual debauchery consists just in the variety of pleasure, and that monotony in marriage will soon drive a man back to his former way of life.*

Who, then, should have the highest authority at home? Indeed, there can be only one who harmonizes all transactions under one concept which agrees with his own purposes. I should say in the language of gallantry (though not without truth): the woman should reign and the man should rule; because inclination reigns and reason rules. The husband's behavior must show that to him the welfare [310] of his wife is closest to his heart. But since the husband must know best how he stands and how far he can go, he becomes like a cabinet minister who wishes, first of all, to express his dutiful compliance to a monarch who is only intent on pleasure, and who has begun a festivity or the construction of a palace. The most high and mighty monarch can do everything he wants under the provision that the minister will lend him a helping hand in carrying out his wishes, even if at present there is no money in the treasury and even if certain more urgent needs must first be attended to.

Since the woman is to be sought after (this is required for the refusal necessary to her sex), she will in marriage be generally seeking to please, so that, if perchance she should become a widow while young, she will find suitors. The man gives up all such claims when he gets married. Therefore jealousy caused by a woman's desire to please is unjust.

Conjugal love, however, is intolerant by its nature. Women sometimes ridicule this intolerance; but, as already mentioned above, they do so in jest; because if a husband would be tolerant and lenient toward the incursion of a stranger into his own rights, the result would be contempt aroused in his wife and also hatred toward such a husband.

The fact that fathers generally spoil their daughters,

* The consequence of this is, as in Voltaire's *Voyage de Scarmentado:* "At last," he says, "I returned to my fatherland, Candia, took a wife there, soon became a cuckold, and found that this is the most comfortable life of all."

and mothers their sons, and that the wildest son, if he is only daring enough, is spoiled by the mother, seems to be caused by the prospect of each parent's needs at the time when one of them has died. If the wife dies before the husband, the father receives caring support from his eldest daughter; but if the wife loses her husband, then the grown-up, kindly-disposed son has the duty, as well as the natural inclination, to honor her, to support her, and to make her life as a widow pleasant.

I have dwelt longer on the subject of characterization than may seem proportionate to the other divisions of anthropology. But Nature has also stored into her economy such a rich treasure of arrangements for her particular purpose, which is nothing less than the maintenance of the species, that in the case of closer   [311] researches there will be for a long time enough material for admiring within the problems the wisdom of Nature's gradually unfolding designs and for putting this wisdom to practical use.

c.   THE CHARACTER OF NATIONS[76]

BY the word people *(populus)* we mean the number of inhabitants living together in a certain district, so far as these inhabitants constitute a unit. Those inhabitants, or even a part of them, which recognize themselves as being united into a civil whole through common descent, are called a nation *(gens);* the part which segregates itself from these laws (the unruly group among these people) is called rabble *(vulgus),** and their illegal union is called a mob *(agere per turbas),*[77] a behavior which excludes them from the privileges of a citizen.
    Hume is of the opinion that, whenever each indi-

---

* The insult *la canaille du peuple* probably has its origin in *canalicola,* a loafer going to and fro along a canal in ancient Rome, and teasing the working people *(cavillator et ridicularius. Vid. Plautus, Curcul.).*

vidual in a nation is intent upon developing his own particular character (as is the case with the English), the nation itself has no character.[78] To me it seems that he is mistaken, because the individual character's affectation is exactly the general character of the people to which the individual himself belongs, and it is also expressing contempt for all foreigners, especially since the English nation believes that it alone can boast of a constitution which combines genuine domestic civil freedom with protective power against anything foreign. Such a character is one of haughty rudeness which contrasts with trust-inspiring civility; it is a spiteful behavior toward every other person, which arises from imagined self-sufficiency because they believe that one has no need of anybody else and that, consequently, one can excuse oneself from extending civilities toward others.[79]

In this way England and France, the two most civilized nations on earth,* who are in contrast to each other because of their different characters, are, perhaps chiefly for that reason, [312] in constant feud with one another. Also, England and France, because of their inborn characters, of which the acquired and artificial character is only the result, are probably the only nations who can be assumed to have a particular and, as long as both national characters are not blended by the force of war, unalterable characteristics.[80] That French has become the universal language of conversation, especially in the feminine world, and that English is the most widely used language of commerce† among tradesmen, probably reflects the difference in their continental and insular geographic situation. But as to their present-day charac-

---

* It is understood that the German nation is omitted from this character analysis, because otherwise the praise by this author, who is German, would be self-praise.

† The mercantile spirit shows certain modifications of its pride in the difference of tone used in bragging. The Englishman says, "The man is *worth* a million"; the Hollander, "He *commands* a million"; the Frenchman, "He *owns* a million."

teristics and their formation by means of language, we should derive our findings from the indigenous character of the ancestral people in their lineage; but the documents for such a study are not available. However, in an anthropology from a pragmatic point of view, we are only interested in presenting the characters of both, as they are now, in several examples, and, as far as possible, systematically. These examples would permit judgment about what each has to know about the other, and how each could use the other to its own advantage.

Hereditary maxims, or those which have become second nature through long usage, as well as those maxims grafted upon them, which express the disposition of a people, are only so many risky attempts to classify the varieties in the natural tendencies of entire peoples more empirically for the geographer than rationally for the philosopher.[81]*

[313] To claim that the character of a nation is determined by its form of government is an unfounded assertion that clarifies nothing. Because from where does government itself derive its own peculiar character? Climate and soil also cannot furnish the key, since migrations of entire peoples have shown that they do not change their character because of the new location. Instead they have only adapted their character to the new

---

* If the Turks, who call Christian Europe *Frankestan,* would travel in order to learn about people and their national character (this is done by no other people but Europeans, which proves the provinciality in spirit of all others), they would perhaps classify the European peoples according to the defects shown in their characters as follows: 1) The land of fashion (France). 2) The land of moods (England). 3) The land of ancestry (Spain). 4) The land of splendor (Italy). 5) The land of titles (Germany, together with Denmark and Sweden taken as Germanic peoples). 6) The land of lords (Poland), where every citizen wants to be a lord; but none of these lords, except one who is not a citizen, wishes to be a subject. Russia and European Turkey, both largely of Asiatic lineage, would lie outside Frankestan; the first is of Slavic, the other of Arabian origin, both are descended from two ancestral races which once extended their reign over a larger part of Europe than any other people; and they have hit upon a constitutional system without freedom, where, therefore, no one is a citizen.

circumstances, while language, type of business, and even type of dress always reveal the traces of their origin, and consequently also their character. I shall sketch their portrait somewhat more from the side of their flaws and deviations from the rule than from the more flattering side (but, nevertheless, not in caricature), because criticism leads to improvement, while flattery perpetuates corruption. In this way the critic offends less against the self-love of people, when he merely confronts them, without exception, with their flaws, rather than stirring up the envy of those judged by praising some more and others less.

1. The *French* nation stands out among all others by its taste for conversation, in which it is the model for all the rest. It is a courteous nation, especially toward foreigners who visit there, even if it is now out of style to be courtly. The Frenchman communicates his thoughts not because of interest but rather because of an immediate feeling of good taste. Since this taste applies primarily to the world of women of high society, the language of ladies has become the language shared by all high society. It cannot be disputed at all that an inclination of such a nature must also have influence on the ready willingness in rendering services, helpful benevolence, and the gradual development of human kindness according to principles. An inclination of such a nature must make a people amiable as a whole.

The reverse of the coin is not sufficiently kept in check by considered principles; and, seen in the cold light of reason, it is imprudence not to let certain forms endure for long, which have proven quite satisfactory, just because they are old or have been praised excessively. There is also a contagious spirit of freedom which, probably, also affects reason itself, and, as to the relation of the people to the state, creates   [314] an enthusiasm which sends its shock waves into everything and beyond all bounds. The peculiarities of this people, sketched in black and white but according to life, easily permit without further description the emergence of a whole by merely naming disconnected fragments as materials for characterization.

The words *esprit* (instead of *bon sens*), *frivolité, galanterie, petit maître, coquette, étourderie, point d'honneur, bon ton, bureau d'esprit, bon mot, lettre de cachet,* and so forth, cannot be translated easily into other languages because they reflect more the peculiar disposition of the nation which uses them than the object which the thinking person is talking about.

2. The *English* people. The old stock of Britons[82]* (a Celtic people) seems to have been a race of sound people; but the immigrations of tribes of Germans and French (the brief presence of the Romans left no noticeable trace) have destroyed the original characteristics of this people as their mixed language proves. Because of the insular situation of their land, which protects them well against foreign invasions, and rather invites them to become aggressors, they have turned into a mighty nation of maritime commerce. So the English people has a character which is has acquired for itself since it actually has none by nature. Consequently, the character of the Englishman cannot signify anything other than the principle learned from early teaching and example, that he must make a character for himself, that is, see to it that he acquires one.[83] An inflexible disposition to insist on a voluntarily adopted principle, and not to deviate from a certain rule (no matter which), gives a person the assurance of knowing for certain what one can expect from him and what he can expect from others.

It is evident that this character is more directly contrasted to that of the French people than to any other, because it renounces all kindness to others and even to

---

* As Professor Büsch correctly spells it (from the word *britanni* not *brittanni*). [Johann Georg Büsch (1728–1800), professor of mathematics at the Hamburg Handelsakademie—Trans.]

230 ANTHROPOLOGICAL CHARACTERIZATION

people of their own; while kindness has been the most prominent social quality of the French. The English merely claim respect for themselves, so that, by the way, everybody can live according to his own will. For his own countrymen the Englishman establishes great [315] benevolent institutions unheard of among all other peoples. But the foreigner who has been driven to England's shores by fate, and has fallen into dire need, will be left to die on the dunghill because he is not an Englishman, that is, not a human being.

But even in his own country the Englishman isolates himself when he pays for his own dinner. He prefers rather to dine alone for the same money in a separate room than at an inn's table together with others, because some politeness is required at an inn.[84] And abroad, for example, in France, whither Englishmen (like Dr. Sharp)[85] travel only to decry all roads and inns as abominable, they gather in inns only for the sake of companionship among themselves. Since the French generally love the English nation, and praise it respectfully, it is strange that the Englishman (who has never traveled outside his own country) usually hates and despises the French. This is probably not caused by rivalry among neighbors (for in this respect England considers herself indisputably superior), but by the mercantile spirit in general, which makes English merchants very unsociable when they attempt to portray the most prominent social class.* Since both nations are close to each other with respect to their coasts and are separated only by a channel (which could very well be called a sea), their rivalry creates a political character modified by various manifestations of conflict. Concern[86] on one side, and hatred on

---

* The mercantile spirit is generally unsociable in itself, just like the aristocratic spirit. One *house* (as the merchant calls his establishment) is separated from the other by its business affairs as a castle is separated by a drawbridge from the other. Friendly relations without ceremony are proscribed, except with those establishments protected by the house, which then, however, would not be regarded as subsidiaries of it.

the other are two forms of incompatibility; one aims at self-preservation,[87] the other at domination; in the case of warfare the aim is extinction.

We can now more briefly draw the character sketch of the others, whose national pecularity cannot only be deduced, as in the preceding two cases, mostly from their different types of culture, but also from their natural disposition resulting from mixture of originally distinct racial stock.

[316]   3.   The *Spaniard,* who evolved from the mixture of European blood with Arabian (Moorish) blood, displays in his public and private behavior a certain solemnity; and even the peasant expresses a consciousness of his own dignity toward his master, to whom he is lawfully obedient. The Spanish grandeur and even the grandiloquence evident in colloquial conversation point to a noble national pride. For this reason the intimate roguishness of the French is entirely repulsive to the Spaniard. He is moderate and wholeheartedly obedient to the laws, especially those of his ancient religion. This seriousness does not hinder him from gratifying himself on days of amusement (for example, bringing in the harvest with song and dance); and whenever the fandango is played on a summer evening, there is no lack of laborers at leisure at this time who dance to this music in the streets. This is the Spaniard's good side.

The Spaniard's bad side is that he does not learn from foreigners; that he does not travel in order to get acquainted with other nations;* that he is centuries behind in the sciences. He resists any reform; he is proud of not having to work; he is of a romantic quality of spirit, as the bullfight shows; he is cruel, as the former auto-da-fé

---

*   The provincial spirit of all nations, which is not moved by disinterested curiosity to learn about the outside world with one's own eyes, and still less willing to be transplanted thither (as a world citizen), is something characteristic of such nations. In this respect the French, English, and Germans favorably differ from other nations.

shows; and he displays in his taste an origin that is partly non-European.

4. The *Italian* unites French vivacity (gaiety) with Spanish seriousness (constancy); and his aesthetic character is a taste that is linked with emotion. The view from his Alps down into the charming valleys offers stimulation to his courage on one side, and quiet enjoyment on the other. Temperament is not involved in this process in a mixed or aimless way (for thus it would yield no character), but it is a tendency of the senses toward attuning to the feeling of the sublime as far as it is also compatible with the feeling of the beautiful. His countenance reflects his strong play of sensations, and his face is full of expression. The pleading of an Italian advocate before the bar is so emotional that it resembles a declamation on the stage.

Just as the Frenchman excels in his taste for conversation, so the Italian excels in his taste for art. The Frenchman prefers private amusement; [317] the Italian prefers public entertainment like pompous pageantries, processions, great spectacles, carnivals, masquerades, splendor of public buildings, painting with a brush or wrought in mosaic, Roman antiquities on a grand scale, in order to observe and to be seen in high society. Along with these (so that we do not forget the Italian's self-interest) he invented letters of credit, banks, and the lottery. That is his good side; and this also extends to the independence, which *gondolieri* and *lazzaroni*[88] venture to display toward those of higher social rank.

A worse side is that the Italians converse, as Rousseau says,[89] in halls of splendor, and sleep in rats' nests. Their *conversazioni* resemble the stock exchange, where the lady of the house offers something to eat to a large number of people, so that they can share with each other the latest news as they wander around without the necessity of friendship. Later she will dine with a select few chosen from the multitude. But the evil side is knife-drawing, or brigandage, assassins taking refuge in sacred sanctuaries, neglect of duty by the police, and so forth, all of which should not be blamed on the Roman citizens but rather on their two-headed type of government.[90] However, these are accusations whose truth I cannot prove. They are of the kind with which the English commonly concern themselves because they will not approve of any other constitution but their own.

5.   The *Germans* are renowned for their good character; they have the reputation of honesty and domesticity; both are qualities which are not suited to splendor. Of all civilized people, the German subjects himself most easily and permanently to the government under which he lives; and he very much dislikes the rage for innovation and the opposition to the established order. His character is phlegm combined with understanding, he does not question the established order, nor does he try to invent a new one himself. And still he is a person of all lands and climates; he emigrates easily, and is not passionately fettered to his fatherland. But if he arrives in foreign lands as a colonist, he will soon form with his compatriots a sort of social club which, as a result of unity of language, and, partially, of religion, makes him part of a little clan, which under the higher authority of the government distinguishes itself in a peaceful and moral way through industry, cleanliness, and thrift from the settlements of other nationalities.   [318] This is how even the English praise the Germans in North America.

Phlegm (taken in its good sense) is the temperament of cold deliberation and perseverance for the purpose of accomplishing one's end, as well as the tolerance of hardship resultant from pursuing that end. Thus one can expect as much from the talent of the German's correct understanding and his deeply reflecting reason as from every other great nation which is capable of the highest culture. The only exception lies in the domain of wit and artistic taste, where, perhaps, he may not be equal to the

French, English, and Italians. This has been his good side, where things can be accomplished through unflagging industry, and for which genius* is certainly not required. Genius, anyway, is by far not as useful as the German's industriousness which is linked with a sound talent for understanding. In his contact with others the German is characterized by modesty. More than any other people, the Germans learn foreign languages; they are (as Robertson says) wholesale dealers in erudition,[91] and in the field of sciences they are the first on the trail that is later followed by others with much ado; they have no national pride; and they are too cosmopolitan to be deeply attached to their native region. However, in their own country, they are more hospitable to strangers than any other nation (as Boswell admits); they strictly discipline their children toward moral behavior, just as they rather submit to despotism, because of their propensity to order and regulation, than venture upon innovations (especially when unauthorized reforms in government are concerned). That is their good side.

The German's unflattering side is his propensity to imitation, and his low opinion of his own ability to be original (which is just the opposite of the stubborn Englishman). [319] Most unfavorable of all is a certain mania for method, which does not make the individual strive for the principle of reaching equality with the rest of the citizens, but rather asks for classification by de-

---

* Genius is the talent for discovering what cannot be taught nor learned. One can be taught by others how to make good verses, but not how to make a good poem, because that must come spontaneously from the author's nature. Therefore one cannot expect that a poem be made to order, and be procurable as a product for a high price; instead, a good poem must be conceived as an inspiration of which the poet himself cannot say how it was conceived, that is, a haphazard disposition whose very source is unknown to him (scit genius natale comes, qui temperat [A: temperet—Ed.] astrum). Genius, therefore, glitters like a momentary phenomenon which appears and disappears at intervals, and vanishes again. It is not a light that can be kindled at will and kept burning for a period of one's own choosing, but rather it is like a spark-scattering flash which a happy seizure of the spirit entices from the productive imagination.

grees of superiority, and by regulations regarding hierarchy. In this scheme of ranking, he is inexhaustible as to
the invention of titles *(Edlen* and *Hochedlen; Wohlgeboren*
and *Hochwohlgeboren;* sometimes also *Hochgeboren);*[92] and
thus he is servile out of mere pedantry. All this may very
well have resulted from the nature of the German constitution, but it must be noticed that the creation of this
pedantic form itself has resulted from the nation's spirit
and the natural propensity of the Germans. Accordingly,
they have devised a ladder reaching from the one who is
to rule down to the one who is to be ruled; each rung is
marked with the degree of prestige attributed to it. The
person who has no profession, and hence no title, is, as
they say, "a nobody." The state, which confers these
titles, realizes some profit from this; but also, without
paying attention to side effects, it arouses demands of a
different significance[93] among its subjects, which must
appear ridiculous to other nations. In fact, this mania for
painstaking exactitude and this need for methodical classification for the purpose of subsuming an entity under a
single concept reveals the limitations of the German's
innate talent.

Since *Russia* has not yet developed definite characteristics from its natural potential; since *Poland* has no
longer any characteristics; and since the nationals of
European Turkey never have had a character, nor will
ever attain what is necessary for a definite national
character, the description of these nations' characters
may properly be passed over here.[94]
Anyway,[95] since we are speaking here about innate,
natural character which, so to speak, lies in the composition of the person's blood, and since we are not talking
about the artificially acquired (or affected) characteristics
of nations,[96] we must be very cautious in sketching them.
In the character of the *Greeks* under the harsh oppression
by the *Turks,* and under the not much gentler pressure
from the *Caloyers,*[97] no change of temperament (vivacity

and lightheartedness), nor any change in the structure of their bodies, their shapes, and facial features has occurred. These qualities [320] would actually persist if their form[98] of religion and government would, under miraculous circumstances, grant them the freedom to regenerate themselves. Among another Christian people, the *Armenians,* a certain commercial spirit of a special kind prevails. In order to trade they journey on foot from the borders of China to Cape Corso on the coast of Guinea. This points to a separate origin of these wise and industrious people, who journey across almost the whole sketch of the ancient continent in a line from North East to South West, and who know how to be received peacefully by all the peoples they encounter on the way. This proves that the Armenian's character is superior to the modern Greek's[99] fickle and flattering character; but the origin of the Armenian's character can no longer be uncovered. Thus we can judge with probability that the intermixture of races (caused by large-scale conquests), which gradually extinguishes their characteristics, does not seem beneficial to the human race—all pretended philanthropy notwithstanding.

D. ON THE CHARACTER OF RACES[100]

As to this subject I can refer to what Girtanner[101] has stated so beautifully and carefully in explanation and further development (of my principles); I shall only add something on the classes of families, the varieties, or mutations which can be observed in one and the same race.

Instead of assimilation, which was intended by the melting together of various races, Nature has here made a law of just the opposite. In a nation of the same race (for example, of the white race), instead of allowing the characters to develop constantly and progressively toward resembling one another, whereby ultimately only one and the same portrait would result as in prints taken from the same copperplate, Nature has preferred to diversify infinitely the characters of the same stock, and even of the same family as to physical and spiritual characteristics. Nurses may flatter one of the parents by saying, "The child has inherited *this* from his father; and *that* from his mother"; but, if this were true, all variations of human procreation would have long been exhausted; [321] and, since the fertility of matings is regenerated by the heterogeneity of the individuals, reproduction would have been brought to a standstill. Ash-colored *(cendrée)* hair, therefore, does not result from the mixture of a brunette with a blond, but rather indicates a particular family stamp. Nature has sufficient supply at her disposal so that she does not have to send, for want of forms in reserve, a person into the world who has already been there.[102] Also, we notice that close kinship notoriously leads to infertility.[103]

E.   ON THE CHARACTER OF THE SPECIES[104]

IN order to sketch the character of a certain creature's species, it is necessary that the species be compared with and referred to in terms of other[105] species already known to us. What makes the species different from each other has to be quoted and referred to as the differentiating reason for its properties *(proprietas)*. But if one kind of creature[106] which we know (A) is compared to another kind of creature which we do not know (non-A), how, then, can we expect or demand to sketch the character of A, when we have no middle term for the comparison *(tertium comparationis)?* The highest concept of species may be that of a terrestrial rational being, but we will not be able to describe its characteristics because we do not know of a nonterrestrial rational being which would enable us to refer to its properties and consequently classify that terrestrial being as rational. It seems, therefore, that the problem of giving an account of the character of the human species is quite[107] insoluble, because the problem could only be solved by comparing two species of rational beings on the basis of experience, but experience has not offered us a comparison between two species of rational beings.[108]

Consequently, in assigning man his place within the system of animate nature, and thereby characterizing him, all that is safe for us to say is that he has a character which he himself creates, because he is capable of perfecting himself according to purposes which he himself adopts. Consequently, man as an animal endowed with capability of reason *(animal rationabile)* can make himself a rational animal *(animal rationale)*. On these grounds he first preserves himself and his species; secondly, [322] he trains, instructs, and educates his species for social living; thirdly, he governs the species as a[109] systematic whole (arranged according to principles of reason) which belongs to society. But in comparison with the idea of potential rational beings on earth, the characteristic of the human species is that Nature has planted in the species the seed of discord, and that Nature has willed that the human species, through its reason, turn discord into concord or at least create a constant approximation of it. Concord contains its purpose in its idea, whereas discord as action contains, within the plan of Nature, the means of a supreme and for us unfathomable wisdom. This wisdom is to affect the perfection of man through cultural progress, even if this should mean some sacrifice of the pleasures of his life.

Among the living inhabitants of the earth, man is markedly different from all other creatures, because of his technical gift for manipulating things (mechanically-connected with consciousness), his pragmatic gift (being clever in the use of others for his own purposes), and his moral gift of character (so that he can act toward himself and others according to the principle of freedom under the law). Any one of these three levels can by itself alone distinguish man characteristically from other inhabitants of this earth.

1. The *technical gift*. Whether man was originally intended for walking on all fours (as Moscati[110] proposed, perhaps only as a thesis for his dissertation) or on two feet; whether the gibbon, the orangutang, the chimpanzee, and other apes were so intended (which is a matter of contention between Linné and Camper);[111] whether man is a herbivorous or (since he has a membranous stomach) a carnivorous animal; whether he is by nature a predator or a peaceable animal because he has neither claws nor fangs, and consequently (without reason) he would have no weapons, these are all questions whose answer requires no hesitation. Eventually the question could be raised whether man is by nature a sociable animal or hermitlike and shying away from neighbors. The latter[112] is apparently the more probable.

The assumption that an already fully developed first human couple was placed by Nature in the midst of food supplies, and not provided at the same time with a natural instinct which we in our present natural condition do not have, is difficult to reconcile with Nature's provision for the maintenance of the species. The first man would drown   [323] in the first pool he saw, because swimming is an art which one has to learn; or the first man would eat poisonous roots and fruits, and thus be in constant danger. But, if Nature had implanted this instinct into the first couple, how, then, was it possible that the instinct was not passed on to their children, something which never happens nowadays?

Songbirds, it is true, teach certain songs to their offspring and pass them on by tradition, so that a bird taken from his nest while still blind, and brought up by hand in isolation, will have, after he has grown up, no song save a certain innate sound of his vocal organ. But where did the first song come from?* Since it was not learned, and if it had originated instinctively, why was it not inherited by the young?

The characterization of man as a rational animal is found in the form and organization of the human hand, its fingers, and fingertips. Nature has made them partly through their construction, and partly through their sensitivity, not only for manipulating objects in one particular way, but also in an open-ended way. Nature has made them, therefore, fit to be used by reason, and thereby Nature has indicated the technological gift, or the gift for skill, of this species as that of a rational animal.

2. The *pragmatic gift* is one level higher. It refers to becoming civilized through culture. It particularly has to do with the cultivation of social qualities and the natural tendency of this species to advance in social matters from the crudity of mere self-reliance to a well-mannered (but not yet moral) being bent on concord. Man can be and must be educated through instruction as well as correction (discipline).   [324] The question arises (either with or against Rousseau)[113] whether the character of this species with respect to its natural talent is happier with the crudity of man's nature than with the arts of culture where no end is in sight. Above all, it must be noted that all other animals left to themselves reach as individuals their full destiny, but human beings reach their full destiny only as a species. Consequently, the human species can work itself up to its destiny only through continuous

* We can accept Linné's hypothesis about the archeology of nature, which says that out of the universal ocean, which covered the entire earth, an island first emerged below the equator, like a mountain, upon which gradually developed all climatic stages of warmth, from the heat on the lower shore of the island to the arctic cold on the summit, together with all suitable plants and animals. Concerning the birds of all kinds, it is assumed that the songbirds imitated the native, audible sounds of many different birds. As far as their own voices permitted, they united every sound with others, whereby each species formed its own distinct song which one bird later taught to the other (forming a tradition). This is supported by the fact that finches and nightingales in various countries have slightly different songs.

progress within an endless sequence of many genera-
tions. The goal of man's efforts will always remain within
his view, and while the dedication to reach this final goal
may frequently weaken, it can never be entirely re-
versed.[114]

3. The *moral gift*. Here the question is whether man is
good by nature or bad by nature, or whether by nature he
is equally susceptible to one or the other, depending
upon which guiding hand he happens to fall into *(cereus in
vitium flecti etc.)*;[115] in this last instance the species itself
would have no character. But this last instance is contradictory in itself because a being endowed with the
faculty of practical reason and with consciousness of
free-will (a person) sees himself in this consciousness,
even in the midst of the darkest imaginings, subject to a
moral law and to the feeling (which is then called moral
feeling) that he is treated justly or unjustly or that he is
treating others justly or unjustly.[116] This is the intelligible character of humanity as such, and thus far man is
good (by nature) according to his inborn gift. But experience also shows that in man there is an inclination to
desire actively what is unlawful, although he knows very
well that it is unlawful. This is the inclination to evil
which arises as unavoidably and as soon as man begins to
make use of his freedom. Consequently the inclination to
evil can be regarded as innate. Hence, according to his
sensible character, man must be judged as being evil (by
nature). This is not contradictory when we are talking
about the character of the species because it can be
assumed that the species' natural destiny consists in continual progress toward the better.[117]

The[118] sum total of findings generated by pragmatic
anthropology as to the classification of man and the
characterization of his development is as follows: Man is
destined by his reason to live in a society of other people,
and in this society he has to cultivate himself, civilize

himself, and apply himself to a moral purpose by the arts and sciences. No matter how great [325] his animalistic inclination may be to abandon himself passively to the enticements of ease and comfort, which he calls happiness, he is still destined to make himself worthy of humanity by actively struggling with the obstacles that cling to him because of the crudity of his nature.

Man must, therefore, be educated to the good. But he who is to educate him is again a human who still finds himself in the crudity of nature. This human, now, is expected to bring about what he himself is still in need of. This accounts for man's continuous deviation from his destiny and his ever-repeated return to it. We shall now refer to the difficulties of solving this problem, and to the obstacles which have to be overcome.

A. As an animal species, the first physical criterion concerning this problem consists in man's impulse to maintain his species. But here the natural phases of his development do not coincide with the civil phases. According to the natural phase, man in his natural state is, at least from his fifteenth year on, driven by sexual instinct, and he is also capable of procreating and preserving his kind. According to the civil phase, he can (on the average) hardly venture upon this reproduction before his twentieth year. Even if the youth as a citizen of the world has the ability early enough to satisfy his own desire and his wife's as well, he, nevertheless, has as a citizen of the state not yet the ability to provide for wife and children. In order to start a household with his wife, he must learn a trade and become known as a craftsman. In the more refined classes his twenty-fifth year may very well have passed before the youth has matured for his vocation. How does he fill this interval of compulsory and unnatural abstention? Scarcely with anything else but vices.

B. The motivation to acquire scientific knowledge, understood as a cultural achievement that ennobles humanity, has in the entire human species no proportionate relation to the duration of life. When he has advanced in culture, to the stage of being able to make an original contribution, the scholar is called away by death, and his place is taken by a freshman who shortly before the end of his life, after he too has just taken a step forward, again yields his place [326] to another. What a mass of knowledge, what discoveries of new methods would now be on hand if an Archimedes, a Newton, or a Lavoisier[119] with their industry and talent would have been favored by Nature with hundreds of years of continuous life without the loss of vital power! The advancement of the species in sciences, however, is always only fragmentary (according to time) and affords no certainty against regression which always threatens because of interfering revolutionary barbarism.

c. The human species seems to fare no better in achieving its destiny with regard to happiness, which man's own nature constantly impels him to strive for, while reason limits the condition of what is to be the value of happiness (that is, morality). One certainly need not accept the hypochondriac (ill-tempered) picture which Rousseau paints of the human species. It is not his real opinion when he speaks of the human species as daring to leave its natural condition, and when he propagates a reversal and a return into the woods. Rousseau only wanted to express our species' difficulty in walking the path of continuous progress toward our destiny. These problems do not exist in thin air. Experience gathered in ancient and modern times must fill every thinking person with embarrassment and doubt as to whether our species will ever fare better.[120]

Rousseau wrote three works on the damage done to our species by 1) our departure from Nature into culture, which weakened our[121] strength; 2) civilization, which resulted in inequality and mutual oppression;

244 ANTHROPOLOGICAL CHARACTERIZATION

and 3) presumed moralization, which caused unnatural education and distorted thinking. I say, these three works,[122] which present the state of Nature as a state of innocence (the gatekeeper of Paradise[123] with a fiery sword prevents our return) should serve only as preludes to his *Social Contract,* his *Émile,* and his *Savoyard Vicar* so that we can find our way out of the labyrinth of evil into which our species has wandered through its own fault. Rousseau did not really want that man go back to the state of nature, but that he should rather look [327] back at it from the stage which he had then reached. He assumed that man is good by nature (as far as Nature allows the good to be passed on), but he is good in a negative way. He is good by his own decision and by intentionally not wanting to be evil. He is only in danger of being infected and ruined by evil or inept leaders and examples. Since, however, good men, who must themselves have been trained for it, are required for moral education, and since there is probably not one among them who has no (innate or acquired) depravity himself, the problem of moral education for our species remains unsolved. It remains unsolved not only with regard to the degree, but even as to the quality of the principle, because an innate, evil tendency in our species may be censured by common human reason, and at best also be controlled, but it will thereby still not have been extinguished.

In[124] the civil constitution of a state, which represents the highest degree of artifical enhancement of the good characteristics in the human species toward final purpose of its destiny, animality still manifests itself earlier and basically stronger than pure humanity. Domesticated animals are only more useful to man than wild animals because they have been weakened. Man's own will is always ready to turn hostile toward his neighbor. He never fails to press his claim to an unconditional freedom; he does not merely want to be independent, but he even wants mastery over others who are equal to him by nature. This tendency can be observed in the smallest child* because in him, starting from culture toward morality, and not [328] (as reason dictates) from morality and its laws, Nature strives to establish a culture which conforms with morality. This inevitably establishes the wrong tendency which does not answer the purpose. For example, one would try in vain to deduct morality if religious instruction, which should necessarily be a moral cultivation, starts with the historical, which is only memory training.

Man only expects from Providence the education of the human species in its entirety, that is, collectively *(universorum),* and not individually *(singulorum),* where the multitude does not represent a system, but merely an aggregate collected at random. He only expects from Providence that he be guided toward a civil constitution based on the principles of freedom, but at the same time he expects that this constitution be based on a coercive principle of statuatory quality. He expects this from Providence, that is, he expects this from a wisdom which

---

*   The cry of a newborn infant does not sound like distress, but like indignation and articulated anger; not because something hurts, but because something bothers him. Presumably he wants to move about, and his inability to do so feels to him like fetters that take away his freedom. What might have been Nature's intentions in letting a child come into the world with loud cries, which are extremely dangerous for himself and for his mother in the crude state of Nature? The crying could attract a wolf or even a pig which might eat him if the mother is absent or exhausted from the delivery of her offspring. But no animal except man (as he is now) will announce loudly his existence at the time of birth, which seems to have been so arranged by the wisdom of Nature in order to maintain the species. It must, therefore, be assumed that in the first stage of Nature (namely, in the period of crudity), the children of this class of animals did not cry at birth, and only later the crying began in the second stage when both parents had already reached the level of culture necessary for domestic life. But we do not know how, or through what contributing causes, Nature determined on the course of such a development. This observation involves more thinking and it suggests, for example, the question, whether this second stage is followed by a third, as in the case of major revolutions of Nature when an orangutang or a chimpanzee developed the organs used for walking, touching of objects, and speaking, into human forms whose interior housed an organ for the employment of the understanding and which developed gradually through social culture.

is not his, but which is still (through his own fault) an impotent idea of his own reason. I say, such education, coming from above, is wholesome but harsh and severe because of great hardship and cultivation of Nature, which lead close to the destruction of the entire species. This education consists in producing the good which man has not intended, but which perpetuates itself once it has come into existence, because the evil is always internally at odds with itself. Providence refers exactly to that same wisdom which we observe with amazement at work in the preservation of a species of organized natural beings that constantly busies itself with self-destruction, and still finds itself always protected. Nevertheless, we do not assume a higher principle in such providential care than we assume to be at work already in the maintenance of plants and animals. By the way, the human species should and can create its own good fortune. That he will   [329] do so, however, cannot be determined a priori from what is known to us about man's natural tendencies. It can be determined only from experience and history, with expectations as well-founded as necessary, that we should not despair about our species' progress toward the better, but instead further (each to his best ability) with all good sense and moral inspiration the approach to this goal.

We can therefore say the first characteristic of the human species is man's ability,[125] as a rational being, to establish character for himself, as well as for the society into which nature has placed him. This ability, however, presupposes an already favorable natural predisposition and an inclination to the good in man, because the evil is really without character (since it is at odds with itself, and since it does not tolerate any lasting principle within itself).[126]

The character of a living being enables us to determine its destiny in advance. Regarding the purposes of Nature, we can assume the principle that she wants every creature to arrive at its own destiny through the proper development of all inherent tendencies, so that at least the species, if not every individual, accomplishes Nature's purpose. Among the irrational animals this actually happens, reflecting Nature's wisdom. But regarding man only, the species reflects this principle. On earth we know of only one species of rational beings, the human species, in which we also recognize only one natural tendency for this purpose, namely, to bring about sometime in the future the development of the good out of the evil through its own efforts. This is a prospect which can be expected with moral certainty (sufficient certainty for the duty of working toward that purpose), unless it is suddenly cut off by upheavals in nature. Then there are men, truly ill-natured men, who nevertheless are gifted, rational beings endowed with an inventive and a moral capacity as well. As their culture grows, they become more and more aware of the wrongs which they themselves selfishly inflict upon each other. And since they see no other remedy for them than subordinating the private interest (of the individual) to the public interest (encompassing all), they subject themselves, reluctantly though, to the discipline (of civil restraint) which they only obey, however, by following the laws which they themselves have given. They feel themselves ennobled by the knowledge that they belong to a species which fits the [330] calling of man as reason represents it to him in the ideal.[127]

Basic Features Concerning the Description of the Human Species' Character[128]

1. Man was not meant to belong to a herd like the domesticated animals, but rather, like the bee, to belong to a hive community. It is necessary for him always to be a member of some civil society.

The simplest and least artificial way to establish such a society is to have one queen bee[129] in this hive (the monarchy). But many such hives next to each other will soon carry on feuds as robber bees do (war). But robber bees do not do this for the same reason as men, namely, to strengthen themselves by uniting with others—for here the comparison ends—but, rather, merely to use by cunning or force the industry of others for themselves. Each people seeks to strengthen itself by the subjugation of its neighbors, either through the desire to expand or the fear of being swallowed up by the other unless one could not outdo him. Therefore civil or foreign war in this species, as great an evil as it may be, is yet at the same time the mainspring for the transition from the crude state of nature to the civil state. War is like a mechanical device of Providence in which the struggling forces weaken each other through friction, but, nevertheless, they are still maintained for a long time on a regular course by the push and pull of other mainsprings.

2. Freedom[130] and law (by which freedom is modified) are those two pivots around which civil legislation revolves. But, so that the law can be effective and not merely recommended, a third term,* namely, authority, must be added. If authority is combined with freedom and law, the principles of freedom and law are ensured with success. There are four conceivable combinations of authority with freedom and law. A. Law and freedom, without authority (anarchy). B. Law and authority, without freedom (despotism). [331] C. Authority, without freedom and law (barbarism). D. Authority, with freedom and law (republic).

It is clear that only the last combination deserves to be called a true civil form of government. It should be noted, however, that we do not aim at establishing one of the three forms of government (democracy) but, instead, we understand by *republic* only a state as such. The old

---

* This is analogous to the *medius terminus* in a syllogism, which, when linked with subject and predicate of the judgment, yields the four syllogistic figures.

proverbial rule, *salus civitatis* (not *civium*) *suprema lex esto*,[131] does not mean that the psychological welfare of the common citizen (the happiness of the citizens) should serve as the highest principle of the political constitution. Such well-being, which each individual envisions for himself according to his own personal inclination in this way or that, is worthless for any objective principle such as universality requires. That proverb says only, the rational welfare, expressing itself in the maintenance of the political constitution that was once established, is the highest law of civil society as such; after all, society lasts only because of that constitution.[132]

The character of the species, as is well known from the experience of all times and all nations, is as follows. The human race taken collectively (as the entire human species) is a great number of people living successively and simultaneously. They cannot be without peaceful coexistence, and yet they cannot avoid continuous disagreement with one another. Consequently, they feel destined by nature to develop, through mutual compulsion and laws written by them, into a cosmopolitan society *(cosmopolitanismus)* which is constantly threatened by dissension but generally progressing toward a coalition. The cosmoplitan society is in itself an unreachable idea, but it is not a constitutive principle (which is expectant of peace amidst the most vigorous actions and reactions of men). It is only a regulative principle demanding that we yield generously to the cosmopolitan society as the destiny of the human race; and this not without reasonable grounds for supposition that there is a natural inclination in this direction.

If we now ask whether the human species can be considered a good or a bad race (it can be called a *race* only when one thinks of it as a species of rational beings on earth, compared to those rational beings on other planets, sprung as a multitude of creatures from one demiurge),[133] then I must confess that there is not much to boast about. Nevertheless, anyone who considers   [332] human behavior not only in ancient history, but also in recent history will often be tempted to coincide with Timon's[134] misanthropic judgment, but far more often and more to the point, he will coincide with Momus,[135] and find foolishness rather than evil the most striking characteristic of our species. But, since foolishness combined with traces of evil (when it is called madness) cannot be ignored in the moral physiognomy of our species, it is obvious from the concealment of a good part of our thoughts, which every clever person deems essential, that everyone in our race finds it advisable to be on his guard,[136] and not to reveal himself completely. This behavior betrays the tendency of our species to be evil-minded toward one another.

It could well be that on another planet there might be rational beings who could not think in any other way but aloud. These beings would not be able to have thoughts without voicing them at the same time, whether they be awake or asleep, whether in the company of others or alone. In what kind of different behavior toward others would this result, and what kind of effect would it have in comparison with our human species?[137] Unless they are all as pure as angels, we cannot conceive how they would be able to live at peace with each other, how anyone could have any respect for anyone else, and how they could get along with each other. Hence, it is part of the original composition of a human creature, and it belongs to the concept of the species, to explore the thoughts of others, but to conceal one's own. This nice quality, then, does not fail to deteriorate gradually from pretense to intentional deception, and finally to lying. This, then, would result in a caricature of our species, and not only justify* good-natured ridicule of the species but

* Frederick II once asked the excellent Sulzer [Johann Georg Sulzer (1720–79), translator of Hume—Ed.], whom he valued for his merits, and whom he had made Superintendent of Schools in Silesia, what he thought about the character of man. Sulzer replied, "Since we have built on [Rousseau's] principle that man is good by Nature, things are going better." "Ah"

also contempt for what constitutes its character. This would also lead to the admission that this race of terrestrial rational beings deserves no honorable place among other rational beings of the universe (unknown to us). On the other hand, such a condemning judgment reveals [333] a moral capacity of the species, an innate summons of reason, to work also against that tendency. Thus we tend to present the human species not as evil, but as a species of rational beings, striving among obstacles to advance constantly from the evil to the good. In this respect our intention in general is good, but achievement is difficult because we cannot expect to reach our goal by the free consent of individuals, but only through progressive organization of the citizens of the earth within and toward the species as a system[138] which is united by cosmopolitical bonds.

[said the king], "mon cher Sulzer, vous ne connaissez pas assez cette maudite race à laquelle nous appartenous." It is also a characteristic of our species that, in striving for a civil constitution, it requires discipline from religion, so that what cannot be attained through external compulsion can be effected by internal constraint (of conscience). Legislators use the moral capacity of man for political purposes, this is a tendency that belongs to the character of the species. If, however, morality does not precede religion in the disciplining process of the people, religion makes itself lord over morality, and statutory religion becomes an instrument of state administration (politics) under religious despots. This is an evil which inevitably upsets and misguides the character it governs by deception (called political wisdom). While publicly professing that he was merely the first servant of the state, Frederick II could not conceal the contrary in his agonizing private confession, but he excused his own role by attributing this depravity to the evil race called the human species.

NOTES / INDEX

NOTES

Introduction — FREDERICK VAN DE PITTE

1. *Kants gesammelte Schriften,* ed. Königlich Preussische Akademie der Wissenschaften (23 vols. 1–7, 14–16, Berlin: Georg Reimer, 1905–14; 9–13, 17–23, Berlin: Walter de Gruyter & Co., 1922–56), 2, 286. Cited hereafter as *Akademie Ausgabe,* abbrev. *Akad. Ausg. Kant: Selected Pre-Critical Writings and Correspondence with Beck,* trans. and intro. by G. B. Kerferd and D. E. Walford (Manchester: University Press, 1968), p. 17.

2. This comment belongs to the notes written into Kant's own copy of *Observations on the Feeling of the Beautiful and the Sublime* (1764). *Akad. Ausg.,* 20, 46.

3. Ernst Cassirer gives eloquent expression to the influence of Rousseau on Kant in his brief work *Rousseau-Kant-Goethe,* trans. James Gutmann, Paul Oskar Kristeller, and John Herman Randall, Jr. (Princeton: Princeton University Press, 1945).

4. *Akad. Ausg.,* 20, 44.

5. Ibid., 2, 311.

6. Ibid., 312.

7. Ibid., 20, 58.

8. *Rousseau-Kant-Goethe,* p. 20.

9. *Akad. Ausg.,* 5, 61. *Critique of Practical Reason and Other Writings in Moral Philosophy,* trans. Lewis White Beck (Chicago: University of Chicago Press, 1949), p. 170. Cited hereafter as Beck trans.

10. See Kant's letter to Moses Mendelssohn, April 8, 1766, *Akad. Ausg.,* 10, 70. *Kant: Philosophical Correspondence 1759–99,* ed. and trans. Arnulf Zweig (Chicago: University of Chicago Press, 1967), p. 55.

11. *Akad. Ausg.,* 20, 181.

12. Ibid.

13. Ibid., p. 57.

14. Ibid., p. 153.

15. *Akad. Ausg.,* 20, 46–47. *Observations on the Feeling of the Beautiful and the Sublime,* trans. John T. Goldthwait (Berkeley: University of California Press, 1960), p. 51.

16. *Critique of Practical Reason. Akad. Ausg.,* 5, 31; Beck trans., p. 143. It should be noted, however, that the recognition of the dignity and worth of human nature is clearly preserved in one of the formulations of the "Categorical imperative."

17.   Ibid. *Akad. Ausg.*, 5, 3; Beck trans. p. 118.
18.   Kant defines "nature" in the broadest sense as "the existence of things under laws." *Critique of Practical Reason. Akad. Ausg.*, 5, 43; Beck trans. pp. 153–54.
19.   Ibid.
20.   Ibid. *Akad. Ausg.*, 5, 3–4; Beck trans., p. 118.
21.   *Akad. Ausg.*, 5, 176. *Critique of Judgment*, trans. J. H. Bernard (London: Macmillan and Co., 1914), p. 14.
22.   For a more complete consideration of this interpretation and a more thorough examination of the evidence on which it is based, see *Kant as Philosophical Anthropologist* (The Hague: Nijhoff, 1971).
23.   *Akad. Ausg.*, 10, 136–38. Zweig, *Correspondence*, p. 78.
24.   A840:B868. *Immanuel Kant's Critique of Pure Reason*, trans. Norman Kemp Smith (London: Macmillan and Co., 1958), p. 658. Italics added.
25.   *Akad. Ausg.*, 20, 45.
26.   A317:B374. Kemp Smith trans., p. 312.
27.   "Die Kantliteratur 1965–1969," in *Proceedings of the Third International Kant Congress*, ed. Lewis White Beck (Dordrecht: D. Reidel, 1972), p. 5.
28.   "Notice Historique," in *Anthropologie du point de vue pragmatique*, trans. Michel Foucault (Paris: J. Vrin, 1970), p. 10.

ANTHROPOLOGY

The following notes are arranged in numerical sequence as they appear in the Parts and Books contained in *Anthropologie in pragmatischer Hinsicht*, vol. 7 (Berlin:Reimer, 1907) of *Kants gesammelte Schriften*, edited by Oswald Külpe for the Königlich Preussische Akademie der Wissenschaften, hereafter referred to as *Anthropology*. The following abbreviations in the notes refer to different versions of Kant's text.

MS: The only existing manuscript of the *Anthropologie in pragmatischer Hinsicht*, held by the Rostock University Library (call number MSS. var. 32). This manuscript came from the estate of Jakob Sigismund Beck (1761–1840) and dates from about 1796/97. It probably served as basis for the manuscript used for the printing of the first edition. References to different wording, deletions, and remarks found on the margin of the manuscript have been supplied by the editor when this information might serve to clarify the understanding of the text.

A: First edition of the *Anthropology*, published in 1798.

B: Three versions (B1, B2, B3) of the second edition of the *Anthropology*, published in 1800, and classified by Arthur Warda, *Die Druckschriften Immanuel Kants,* Wiesbaden: Staadt (1919), p. 47, as B₁, B₂, B₃. The B edition is a stylistically revised version of the first edition, probably revised by Kant himself and further corrected by Christian Gottfried Schütz (see *Akademie Ausgabe,* vol. 12, p. 307). The B versions differ from each other only slightly; B₂ is identical with B₁, except on sheets L through T.

Akad. Ausg.: Anthropologie in pragmatischer Hinsicht, vol. 7, edited by Oswald Külpe.

Cassirer: *Anthropologie in pragmatischer Hinsicht,* vol. 8, edited by Otto Schöndörffer (Berlin: Cassirer, 1923), of Immanuel Kant, *Werke,* general editor Ernst Cassirer.

The explanatory notes relating to material contained in Kant's text were prepared by Victor L. Dowdell, and the notes relating to the meaning of the text and its different versions were prepared by Hans H. Rudnick.

Introduction

1. Kant's term for "he knows the world" is *die Welt kennen;* and for "he knows his way about the world" Kant used *Welt haben.* The latter idiom implies that a person is experienced and civilized.
2. Kant's words for "high society" are *grosse Welt.*
3. Kant's terms are *Generalkenntnis* and *Lokalkenntnis. Generalkenntnis* is knowledge based on universals, whereas *Lokalkenntnis* means knowledge obtained from particulars. Kant uses these terms in order to maintain the general imagery of his argumentation, which refers to the general and particular environment from which an individual draws his experience.
4. A: but when he observes himself, then the impelling forces are at rest.

Part One: Anthropological Didactic
First Book: *On Cognitive Faculty*

1. MS, Cassirer: "comfort *(Wohltun)*" instead of "injustice *(Unrechttun).*"
2. B: "makes both of them so well disposed *(und diese geneigt macht)*" was added.
3. MS, on the margin: The cognition [of one's self] consists of two

parts. Perception and thought. Being aware of one's self with both in mind is not to perceive one's self, but to perceive the concept of the Ego in thought. In order to know one's self, one has to perceive of one's self (*perceptio* [simple perception], to which *apperceptio* [conscious perception] has to be added).

4. MS: has been united under no concept.

5. This translation here follows the text of the MS, which was also adopted by the *Akad. Ausg.* and Cassirer. The MS reads: "with . . . in order to" *(um mit)*, whereas B reads: "and with" *(und mit)*.

6. Trans.: an external criterion for truth.

7. MS, Cassirer: somehow.

8. A: Are there not also . . .

9. Kant uses "to deem" *(dünken)*.

10. MS and Cassirer: every writer who . . . important views stands isolated and just because of that is suspected by the public of . . .

11. Kant opposes unusual *(seltener)* with odd *(seltsamer)*.

12. Abailard: "I say no, even if all other fathers say yes."

13. Between "which" and "truly" MS reads: can only be found with regard to purpose, in the motives of the free will which must be valid for everyone.

14. A: by I and Thou.

15. The translation follows the A edition.

16. Kant uses *Er und Sie.*

17. A: "someone absent," which this translation follows.

18. B: "be . . . more" was added.

19. B: saw to it that.

20. B: down to.

21. The German term is *du.*

22. A: "the investigation of one's self is . . ." Kant's term is *Vorstellungen*, here translated as "sense impressions" in this context. The term is closely related to what is usually understood as "ideas." But since ideas are associated with reason and not with sense perceptions, it appears advisable to use "sense impressions" as a viable English translation for what Kant refers to as "ideas perceived by the senses." At the beginning of sec. 5 Kant also uses *Vorstellungen*, but there it seems appropriate to translate it as "ideas" because he speaks of *"Vorstellungen* which we have without being aware of them." Another problem relating to the translation of Kant's terminology is the English custom, followed in this volume, of translating *Vernunft* as "reason," *Verstand* as "understanding," and *Anschauung* as "intuition." Kant's attempt to name and describe the complicated world of man's experience and cognition loses some of its clarity in translation. The most problematic of the above terms is "understanding," a term which in English does not maintain the dichotomy between *Vernunft* and *Verstand* as clearly as in the original. The gerundial form of the word "understanding," together with the word's identity with the progressive form, frequently creates grammatical complications, and it does not have the same broad range of meaning that *Verstand* has. A more adequate English word for *Verstand* would be "intellect," readily recognizable as a term in opposition to "reason."

23. MS: and power of the soul.

24. MS, on the margin: as a whole . . . the condition of the sense impressions: has to be mastered.

25. A: for a *diary of the observer*.

26. A: even though it may not be without the fine arts and the cultivation of taste.

27. MS: the open [i.e., naïve].

28. MS: supposed interior inspirations (of the soul) without our [conscious] help.

29. Antoinette Bourignon (1616–80), a voluminous writer of mysticotheosophical books. Blaise Pascal (1623–62), a gifted mathematician and physician, as well as a notable mystic. Jacobi is not named, but is doubtless meant to be included with Pascal and others. See Ernst Troeltsch, "Das Historische in Kants Religionsphilosophie," *Kantstudien,* vol. 9 (1904), pp. 21–154.

30. A: does not contain "with terrifying and frightful implications"; MS: "terrifying implications."

31. Albrecht Haller (1708–77), *Tagebuch seiner Beobachtungen über Schriftsteller und über sich selbst,* vol. 2, ed. J. G. Heinzmann (Bern, 1787), pp. 219 ff.; as cited by Oswald Külpe in his notes appended to vol. 7 *(Anthropology)* of the *Akademie Ausgabe.* Subsequent references to Külpe's notes will be referred to as Külpe.

32. MS.: does not contain the name D. Less.

33. Anticyra was a coastal city on the Gulf of Corinth, in Phocis. Another Anticyra was in Thessaly. Both were famous sources of hellebore, regarded as a cure for insanity. See Horace *Sermones* 2. 3. 83, 166; *De arte poetica* 360.

34. MS: "are" instead of "appear"; A: "appear" deleted, and after "fixed" "thus providing experience" was added.

35. John Locke (1632–1704), *An Essay Concerning Human Understanding,* ed. Alexander Campbell Fraser, 2 vols. (New York: Dover, 1959), vol. 1, pp. 127 ff., 137–39; vol. 2, pp. 9 ff., 18 f., hereafter cited as *Essay.* Furthermore, see Gottfried Leibniz (1646–1716), "Nouveaux Essais" in *The Philosophical Works,* 2d ed., trans. George Martin Duncan (New Haven: Tuttle, 1908), pp. 170 ff.; hereafter cited as *The Philosophical Works.*

36. "Obscure . . . clear"; see David Hume (1711–76), *A Treatise of Human Nature,* ed. L. A. Selby-Bigge (Oxford: Clarendon Press, 1896), pp. 33, 72; hereafter cited as *Treatise.* Also see David Hume, "An Inquiry Concerning Human Understanding," *Essays and Treatises on Several Subjects,* vol. 3 (Basle: Tourneisen, 1793), pp. 66 f., hereafter cited as *Inquiry.*

37. "Optical instruments"; cf. Hume, *Treatise,* p. 28: "A microscope or telescope, which renders them visible, produces not any new rays of light, but only spreads those, which always flow'd from them; and by that means both gives parts to impressions, which to the naked eye appear simple and uncompounded, and advances to a minimum, what was formerly imperceptible." Cf. *Inquiry,* pp. 66 f. Kant's love of nature was kindled by his mother who taught him the names of plants and what she understood of the skies and planets. See William Wallace, *Kant* (Edinburgh: Blackwood, 1882), p. 12; cf. Thomas Kingsmill Abbott, *Kant's*

Critique of Practical Reason (London: Longmans, 1923), pp. xx–xxiv. Many eighteenth-century writers referred to the planets, often drawing upon Virgil who has 516 lines in the *Aeneid, Eclogues,* and *Georgics* which refer to the stars, sun, and moon. The two things which always filled Kant's soul with admiration and reverence were "the starry heaven above me, and the moral law within." Further references to the moon and stars will be found in secs. 4, 5, 11, and 71.

38. This translation follows A. B reads: "belongs only to physiological, not to pragmatic anthropology with which we are properly concerned." MS reads: "with which [physiological anthropology] we are not concerned."

39. Cf. William Wallace, *Kant,* pp. 48 f.: "From his celibate vantage-ground Kant made his observations on womankind and the relations between the sexes. His remarks are not unkindly or on the whole unfair, but they suffer from the effect of distance and of antithesis. He had a keen eye for the foibles of the sex, and a strong sense of the illusions and conventionalities which throw a 'beautiful sham'—a spiritual fig-leaf—over the nakedness of the spiritual attractions. His remarks are all from the exclusively masculine standpoint. Unlike Plato, he directs his view solely to the diversity between the sexes, instead of to the identity of human nature." Cf. Hume, *Inquiry,* sec. 4, p. 271: "Among nations, where an immoral gallantry, if covered with a thin veil of mystery, is, in some degree, authorized by custom, there immediately arises a set of rules, calculated for the conveniency of that attachment."

40. MS, Cassirer: motto.

41. For literature on the secret of secrets, see R. Foerster, *De Aristotelis quae feruntur secretis secretorum commentatio* (Kiel: Universitätsbuch-handlung, 1888).

42. See Abbott, "Memoir of Kant" in *Kant's Critique of Practical Reason,* p. xxxiii: " 'Besides,' said he, 'it flatters the vanity of the reader to find perplexities and obscurities here and there, which he can solve by his own acuteness.' "

43. See Leibniz, "Thoughts on Knowledge, Truth and Ideas," in *The Philosophical Works,* p. 28: "Thus knowledge is either *obscure* or *clear,* and clear knowledge is farther either *confused* or *distinct,* and *distinct* knowledge is either *inadequate* or *adequate,* or again, *symbolical* or *intuitive;* and if it is at the same time *adequate* and *intuitive,* it is perfect in every respect."

44. Joseph Addison (1672–1719), *Spectator* 132 (August 1, 1711), ed. Henry Morley (London: Routledge, 1896), p. 198: "Thy drum is a type of thee, it soundeth because it is empty."

45. See George Berkeley (1685–1753), "Introduction to the Principles" in *Selections from Berkeley,* ed. A. C. Fraser (Oxford: Clarendon Press, 1910), p. 15: "I proceed to examine what can be alleged in defence of the doctrine of abstraction, and try if I can discover what it is that inclines the men of speculation to embrace an opinion so remote from Common Sense as that seems to be."

46. Kant says *gesunder Menschenverstand;* literally, *sound* human understanding.

47. The word "represent" was transferred into this text from B.

48. Immanuel Kant (1724–1804), *Critique of Pure Reason,* trans. Nor-

man Kemp Smith (New York: St. Martin's Press, 1965), B 363, p. 305: "In the first place, reason in the syllogism does not concern itself with intuitions, with a view to bringing them under rules (as the understanding does with categories), but with concepts and judgments." Also see William Hamilton, *Lectures on Metaphysics and Logic,* vol. 2, ed. Henry L. Mansel and John Veitch (Boston: Gould and Lincoln, 1873), p. 149: "There is another law, which Kant promulgates in the *Critique of Pure Reason,* and which may be called the law of Logical Affinity, or the law of Logical Continuity. It is this,—That no coordinate species touch so closely on each other, but that we can conceive other or others intermediate."

49. MS reads only: in a practical.

50. A: "Section Two" precedes the heading. MS contains a subtitle: "A. On the Sensuous Perception of One's Self in Contrast to the Intellectual Perception." Kant crossed out the subtitle.

51. MS, crossed-out definition on the margin: "Sensibility is the imaginative power of the subject, if affected." *Critique of Pure Reason,* Kemp Smith, trans., A 285, p. 292: "Even if we were willing to assume a kind of intuition other than this, our sensible kind, the functions of our thought would still be without meaning in respect to it." See also Leibniz, *The Philosophical Works,* p. 195: "I have always favored, as I do still, the innate idea of God, which M. Descartes maintained, and consequently other innate ideas which cannot come to us from the senses." Christian Wolff (1679–1754) adopts Leibniz's view of the apparent interaction between body and soul as a preestablished harmony.

52. MS, crossed-out passage, very rough and grammatically awkward: Since learning about the objects through the lower faculty of cognition depends only on the subjective quality of being affected by impressions which have come from the object (by imagining it in a certain way), a power that just cannot be identical in all subjects, it is said that the lower faculty of cognition presents the objects of our senses to us only as they appear to us, not according to what they are by themselves. (But since these appearances are most intimately connected with the law of understanding, cognition [of objects of the senses], that which is called experience is, therefore, not less certain, as if we were dealing with the objects themselves. Because there can be no other knowledge for us than knowledge of objects which can be presented to our senses, there may always be notions in our understanding which have objective reality transgressing their own limits, only however, with a practical intention [the idea of freedom]. We are here only concerned with those objects which can be exposed to our senses.) *Note.* Section Two. On Sensuousness. The claim that this axiom also applies to the inner self and that man, who observes his inner self on the basis of impressions caused by whatever imaginings, can only recognize as he appears to himself, but not as he actually is, represents a bold metaphysical axiom *(paradoxon)* which cannot be dealt with in an anthropology. But if he obtains inner experience from himself, and if he pursues this investigation as far as he can, he will have to confess that self-knowledge would lead to an unfathomable depth, to an abyss in the exploration of his nature ("Man, you are such a difficult problem to yourself." Pope, as translated by Brock), this is relevant to

anthropology. All cognition depends on the understanding as a prerequisite. Beasts, which have no intelligence, may have something similar to what we call imagination (because its effects are very similar to the imagination found in man), but which may be radically different; in any case, they have no cognition of objects. This faculty needs understanding, a faculty of imagination with the awareness of action, whereby this relationship is thought through. But we do not understand anything correctly unless we are able to put it together ourselves as long as the material to do so is supplied to us. Consequently, understanding is a faculty of spontaneity within our cognition; it is a higher faculty of understanding because it submits ideas a priori to certain laws. Also, understanding itself makes experience possible. In the self-cognition of man through inner experience he does not put together what he has observed on himself, because that depends on the impression (concerning the matter of the idea) which he has received. He is enduring something so far as he has an idea of himself derived from his own self. According to form, this idea depends merely on the subjective condition of his nature which should not be interpreted as belonging to the object, even though he has also the right to attribute it to the object (here his own person). But this is only permissible under the condition that he can recognize himself through experience only as an object with this idea, as he appears to himself, and not as he, the observed one, really is. If he wished to recognize his real self, he would have to rely on an awareness of pure spontaneity (the notion of freedom). Such an awareness is possible but it still could not be perception of the inner sense and empirical cognition of his self (inner experience) based thereon. It can only be awareness of the laws of his ways and doings, without thereby acquiring a theoretical (physiological) cognition of his nature, which is psychology's real goal. The empirical self-cognition, therefore, presents man to the inner sense in the way in which man appears to the inner sense, not as he really is, because every cognition refers only to the affectability of the subject and not to the inner condition of the subject as object. How, then, can the great difficulty be solved in which the consciousness of one's self represents only the appearance of one's self and not the person himself? And why does it not represent a second person when there is a second consciousness of this person, first the consciousness of the mere thinking, and second the consciousness of inner perception (something rational and empirical); that is discursive and intuitive apperception, the first belongs to logic, the other belongs to anthropology (as physiology). Logic is without content (matter of cognition), anthropology is supplied by the inner sense with content. An object of the (exterior or inner) sense, as far as it is recognized, is called appearance *(phaenomenon)*. The cognition of an object as an appearance (i.e. *as* phenomenon) is experience. Consequently appearance is that representation whereby an object of the senses is given (an object of perception, i.e., empirical awareness). But experience or empirical cognition is that representation whereby the object as such is thought at the same time. Therefore, experience is the activity (of the imagination) whereby appearances are subsumed under the notion of one object of experience; and experience is obtained by making observations (intentional perceptions) and by reflecting about how to combine the experiences under one notion. We acquire and widen our cognition with experience by supplying our understanding with appearances of the exterior or even inner sense as material. Nobody doubts that we could not as well make inner observations of our selves and experiences in the same way, but if we dare now to speak of objects of the inner sense (which as a sense provides appearances only), it must be stated that the inner sense cannot provide us with cognition about ourselves as we are, but as we appear (internally) to ourselves. There is something upsetting in this statement and we must look at it more closely. We allow such judgment about objects outside us, but it looks quite absurd to apply it to what we perceive inside us. The falsification that some distorters take appearance as identical with semblance and say that their statement means as much as "it seems to me that I exist and have such and such idea" is not worth any objection. This difficulty rests entirely on the confusion of the inner sense (and the empirical self-awareness) with apperception (the intellectual self-awareness), which are usually taken to be identical. The self in every judgment is neither perception nor notion, and particularly no definition of any object, but it is an act of the understanding of the judging subject. Being conscious of his own self, pure apperception by itself, merely belongs to logic (without any matter and content). However, the self of the inner sense, which is the perception of one's self, is not the subject of the judgment, but an object. The consciousness of the one who observes himself is a very simple idea of the subject while performing the judgment. One knows everything about it, if one merely thinks it. But the self which has observed itself is the embodiment of so many objects of the inner perception that psychology has its hands full in tracing everything that lies hidden in it. Psychology cannot ever hope to complete this task and satisfactorily answer the question "What is man?" We must distinguish, therefore, pure perception (of the understanding) from empirical perception (sensuousness). When the subject attends to itself, empirical perception activates itself at the same time, thereby creating sensations, that is bringing ideas to consciousness. These sensations correspond with each other according to the form of their relation, the subjective and formal condition of the sensuousness, namely perception in time (simultaneously or in succession) and not only according to the laws of the understanding. Since this form can be assumed to be valid not for every creature that is conscious of its self, the cognition which is caused by the inner sense of man, cannot imagine with his inner experience how he himself is (because the condition is not valid for all thinking creatures since otherwise it would be an idea of the understanding), but it is only an awareness of how man appears to himself in his inner observation. The recognition of one's self according to the constitution of the self cannot be acquired through inner experience and it does not come from knowing man's nature, but it is merely and solely the awareness of his freedom which reveals itself to him through the categorical imperative of duty, the highest level of practical reason. B. On the Field of the Sensuous in Relation to the Field of the Understanding. Section 8. Division. The spirit of man, as the totality of all ideas which can be accommodated within it, has a range (sphaera) which comprises the three premises of the faculty of cognition, the feeling of pleasure and displeasure, and the faculty of desire. Each of these premises is split into two divisions, the field of sensuousness and the field of the intellect (the field of sensuous and intellectual cognition, pleasure or displeasure, desire and rejection). The sensuousness can be considered as a weakness or as a strength also.

53.   *Critique of Pure Reason,* Kemp Smith, trans., A 31, p. 75. "Time is not a discursive, . . . but a pure form of sensible intuition."

54.   MS, *Akad. Ausg.,* and Cassirer only read: "consciousness of activity."

55.   MS: "a rule of the consciousness of unity" with "of the consciousness" crossed out.

56.   On "Identity," see Locke, *Essay,* vol. 1, pp. 439–70, vol. 2, p. xxvii. See also *Critique of Pure Reason,* Kemp Smith, trans., A 263, pp. 278 ff.

57.   "Thing-in-itself," for *"Ding an sich,"* see *Critique of Pure Reason,* Kemp Smith, trans., B xx, p. 24: "This situation yields, however, just the very experiment by which, indirectly, we are enabled to prove the truth of this first estimate of our *a priori* knowledge of reason, namely, that such knowledge has to do only with appearances, and must leave the thing in itself as indeed real *per se,* but as not known by us."

58.   George Berkeley (1685–1753), "A Treatise Concerning the Principles of Human Knowledge" in *The Works of George Berkeley, Bishop of Cloyne,* ed. T. E. Jessop (London: Nelson and Sons, 1949), vol. 2, sec. 30, pp. 53 f.: "Now the set rules or established methods wherein the mind we depend on excites in us the ideas of sense, are called the *Laws of Nature;* and these we learn by experience, which teaches us that such and such ideas are attended with such and such other ideas, in the ordinary course of things."

59.   Trans.: Who has ever criticized virtue, you fool! See Plautus *Miles gloriosus* 3. 2. 139–40: *"Qui deorum consilia culpet, stultus inscitusve sit. Quique eos vituperet."* [Whoever would reject the advice of the gods, and he who would reproach them, is foolish and ignorant.]

60.   *Critique of Pure Reason,* Kemp Smith, trans., A 294, p. 298: "In the senses there is no judgment whatsoever, neither a true nor a false judgment." On the confusion between judgment and sensation, see Hume, *Treatise,* pp. 112 ff.

61.   MS reads: "animating," crossed out.

62.   Text follows B. MS, *Akad. Ausg.,* and Cassirer read after "often": "embarrass the understanding as far as its rational employment is concerned. The understanding often falls into confusion where it ought to make clear and set forth all the acts of reflection which it actually employs, no matter how obscurely."

63.   MS, Cassirer: "judge's verdict" for "tribunal."

64.   This edition follows the numbering of sections as established by the *Akad. Ausg.* The MS does not count this as a new section.

65.   Kant says: "[the sea's] distant part."

66.   Cf. Hume, *Treatise,* p. 393: "A great difference inclines us to produce a distance. The ideas of distance and difference are, therefore, connected together."

67.   MS: this section is found originally at the end of sec. 11, which corresponds to *Akad. Ausg.* sec. 13; Kant changed the location and the

numbering later. The last six paragraphs are not contained in the MS; there is only a reference to another part of the MS which has not been preserved. Following the numbering of the *Akad. Ausg.*, the subsequent section will be 12, although the MS continues sec. 10 here.

68. A: *ponderosum* instead of *grave*. "Light and heavy." Cf. Aristotle *De Caelo* 1. 3. 269b23.

69. MS: (subjectively) impracticable.

70. MS, crossed out: I want to do something that I can do.

71. MS, crossed out after "virtue": by which it is easy for the subject to act according to the law.

72. MS: "virtue" preceding "moral" crossed out.

73. "My commandments," 1 John 5:3.

74. Trans.: gasping in vain; occupied with many things, but accomplishing nothing. See C. Valerius Catullus 63. 31: *Anhelans vaga vadit, animam agens* [Gasping the woman went, moving her mind (thinking)]. The context of the passage refers to the self-mutilation of Attis.

75. For the effects of habit, cf. Hume, *Treatise,* p. 422: "But nothing has a greater effect both to increase and diminish our passions, to convert pleasure into pain, and pain into pleasure, than custom and repetition. Custom has two original effects upon the mind, in bestowing a facility in the performance of any action or the conception of any object; and afterward a *tendency or inclination* toward it; and from these we may account for all its other effects, however extraordinary; . . . The facility takes off from the force of the passive habits by rendering the motion of the spirits faint and languid." See also Hume, *Inquiry,* p. 45.

76. MS: sec. 11.

77. Cf. sec. 5. Anton Raphael Mengs (1728–79) was the author of *Gedanken über die Schönheit und über den Geschmack in der Malerei,* ed. J. C. Füssli (Zurich, 1774). He praised Raphael's *School of Athens;* cf. Gotthold Ephraim Lessing (1729–81), "Laokoön," in *Sämtliche Werke,* ed. Karl Lachmann (Berlin, Leipzig: de Gruyter, 1924), vol. 14, p. 383; or *Laokoön Selections,* ed. W. Guild Howard (New York: Henry Holt, 1910), p. 144.

78. MS and Cassirer: "for a moment" instead of "constantly."

79. Claude Adrien Helvétius (1715–71), *De l'esprit: or Essays on the Mind* (London: M. Jones, 1807), pp. 11–13.

80. Gassnerists, i.e., tricksters, from Johann J. Gassner (1727–79), a priest in Switzerland, who healed diseases by exorcism of the Devil. Mesmerists, from Franz Mesmer (1735–1815), who produced an abnormal condition, similar to sleep, in another person, during which time the victim was passive to the mind of the hypnotist.

81. Cf. Hume, *Treatise,* p. 112: "No weakness of human nature is more universal and conspicuous than what we commonly call credulity, or a too easy faith in the testimony of others." Ibid., p. 113: "A remarkable propensity to believe whatever is reported, even concerning apparitions, enchantments, and prodigies."

82. MS: sec. 12.

83. MS, Cassirer: praiseworthy.

84. Jonathan Swift (1667–1745), *A Tale of a Tub,* ed. A. C. Guthkelch and D. Nichol Smith (Oxford: Clarendon Press, 1958), preface, p. 40.

85. Abbott, *Kant's Critique of Practical Reason,* p. 43, n. "Kant distin-

guishes 'Hang (propensio)' from 'Neigung (inclinatio)' as follows: 'Hang' is a predisposition to the desire of some enjoyment; in other words, it is the subjective possibility of excitement of a certain desire which precedes the conception of its object. When the enjoyment has been experienced, it produces a 'Neigung' (inclination) to it, which accordingly is defined 'habitual sensible desire.'—*Anthropologie*, secs. 72, 79 [i.e., secs. 73, 80]; *Religion*, p. 31."

86. "Modesty," cf. Hume, *Treatise*, pp. 570–73.

87. "Politeness," cf. Hume, *Inquiry*, pp. 328 f.

88. Külpe refers to Aristotle *Eudemian Ethics* 1245b20 and Diogenes Laërtius 5. 1. 21.

89. Swift, *Tale of a Tub*, sec. 2, p. 78. See Külpe's note in *Anthropology*, which refers to *Satyrische und ernsthafte Schriften von Dr. Swift*, trans. Heinrich Waser, vol. 3, 2d ed. (Hamburg and Leipzig, 1759), p. 86.

90. Johann Peter Hofstede, *Des Herrn Marmontels herausgegebener Belisar beurtheilt, . . .* (Leipzig: Brockhaus, 1769); cited in Külpe.

91. A: "perceptions" instead of "pretenses."

92. Hume, *An Inquiry Concerning the Principles of Morals* (London: printed for A. Miller, 1751), sec. 8, p. 331: "Men have, in general, a much greater propensity to over-value than to under-value themselves; notwithstanding the opinion of Aristotle." Hereafter cited as *Principles of Morals*.

93. MS: On the Five Senses [Belonging to the Cognitive Faculty]. Cf. Locke, *Essay*, vol. 2, pp. 402–5; Hume, *Treatise*, pp. 235–37.

94. MS: sec. 13.

95. MS: sec. 14.

96. The *Spectator* 419:604: "They bring up into our memory the stories we have heard in our childhood, and favor those terrors and apprehensions to which the mind of man is naturally subject."

97. MS: sec. 15.

98. B: "senses of the first class" was added.

99. MS: sec. 16.

100. MS: sec. 17.

101. A: of an infinitely cruder liquid (the air).

102. MS: sec. 18.

103. B: "the body . . . organ" was added.

104. MS: The beginning of this sentence had been crossed out.

105. MS: sec. 19. B: entire section was added.

106. Kant's word is *Vitalempfindung*.

107. B: "finds repugnant" was added.

108. B: "is the man" was added.

109. Kant's term is *zärtliche Empfindlichkeit* which is opposed to *zarte Empfindsamkeit* (delicate sensitivity).

110. MS: sec. 20. B: entire section was added.

111. MS: sec. 21. B: identical section was added.

112. A: are felt but not enjoyed.

113. A: Appendix. *On the Inner Sense*.

114. A: sec. 19. MS: sec. 22.

115. B: "or even for inspiration" was added.

116. MS: intentional fiction.

117. See note 29 above.
118. Ibid.
119. A: Section Three. On . . .
120. MS: sec. 23. B: section was added.
121. B: "the perfect completion" was crossed out.
122. MS: a contradiction in the tone of the doctrine of truth.
123. Henry Fielding (1707–54).
124. Johann Aloys Blumauer (1755–98), *Virgils Aeneis . . . travestiert,* 3 vols. (Vienna: Gräffer, 1784–88).
125. Samuel Richardson (1689–1761), *Clarissa, oder die Geschichte eines vornehmen Frauenzimmers,* 8 vols (Göttingen, 1748–52).
126. Literally, "Termination is not variation."
127. MS: "purposively arranged"; not found in other editions.
128. MS: satisfaction of the senses.
129. A: sec. 20. MS: sec. 23 continued.
130. A: does not contain this sentence; a similar definition appears in A, sec. 22.
131. MS contains the following crossed-out section: If one feels tired when one goes to bed, but for some unknown reason cannot fall alseep, one may realize by carefully observing one's physical sensations that there is some spasm not only in the muscles of the legs but also in the brain. At the moment of falling asleep a relaxation is felt which is a very pleasant sensation. The phenomenon that waking is a condition of tension and contraction of all fibers can be proven by measuring draftees. Those who have just been awakened measure half an inch longer than those who are already getting up on their own. They would have measured half an inch shorter if those just awakened had been lying awake in their bed for a long time. Sleep is not only a necessity for the relaxation of exhausted powers, but also an enjoyment of pleasure at the beginning (at the moment of falling asleep) as well as at the end (at the moment of awaking). With this enjoyment, however, one has to be necessarily frugal because enjoyment exhausts sensitivity and along with it vitality. It is the same with this as with the Mohammedan's moderation of eating. The Moslem believes that it has already been determined at the birth of every person how much he should eat. If he is eating much, he will have consumed his portion, and will have to die early. If he eats moderately, he has food to eat for a long time and, consequently, he will live for a long time. Just the same could also be said of sleep; he who sleeps much while young and still vigorous will have little sleep when he is old; which is a sad lot. The Kalmucks call sleeping during the day shameful, and the Spaniards' *siesta* does not shed a favorable light on their activity.
132. A: *Tramontano* is a troublesome north wind similar to the sirocco which is an even more ferocious southeast wind. Friedrich Wilhelm Schubert adds a footnote: "Therefore in his first edition Kant appended, because he took for granted that the Tramontano was a troublesome north-wind, the following explanation. 'When an inexperienced young man enters a gathering, principally of ladies, which is more brilliant than he anticipated, he easily gets in a state of embarrassment, as to how he ought to start his conversation. It would be unseemly to begin with a news-item because the others would not see what led him to speak of it.

But, since he has just come from the street, the bad weather would be the best introduction to his conversation; and, if this does not occur to him, the Italian would say: He has lost his Tramontano.' "

133.   A: sec. 21. MS: sec. 24. This entire paragraph follows A, sec. 22, pp. 75 f. (i.e., B, sec. 26). Using B as the basis for orientation, the MS has the sequence of secs. 23, 26, 24, 25, 27.

134.   MS: Unconsciousness and death, the former of both which usually follows . . . is a prelude to the latter, i.e., a ceasing of all sensation even though it is not the cause of the latter.

135.   Michel Eyquem de Montaigne (1533–92), *The Complete Works,* trans. Donald M. Frame (Stanford: Stanford University Press, 1957), "Essays," bk. 1, chap. 13, pp. 54 f.

136.   Kant also held that "I think" is equivalent to "I am." See Norman Kemp Smith, *A Commentary to Kant's Critique of Pure Reason,* 2d rev. ed. (London: Macmillan, 1923), pp. 322 ff., hereafter cited as Kemp Smith, *Commentary.*

137.   A: "The Second Chapter on the Sensibility of the Faculty of Cognition. On the Imagination."—Joseph Addison was the first to try to give the limits of art and taste in his eleven essays on the "Pleasures of the Imagination" in the *Spectator* 411–21 (June 21–July 3, 1712). See also Mark Akenside (1721–70), *The Pleasures of Imagination* (London, 1744); Hume, *Treatise,* passim; Berkeley, "A Treatise Concerning the Principles of Human Knowledge," sec. 33; Leibniz, *De modo distinguendi phenomena realia ab imaginariis;* Locke, *Essay,* vol. 2, pp. 185 ff.

138.   A: sec. 21. MS: sec. 25.

139.   B: (satiation) was added.

140.   MS, Cassirer: non-sense.

141.   The German word is *Sinnspruch.*

142.   MS: sec. 26.

143.   Cf. the General Observation appended to sec. 79, Second Book.

144.   B: "with such excess . . . experience" was added.

145.   B: "or intoxicated" was added. Also cf. definition of drunkenness in sec. 26.

146.   Kant says, "no moderation in."

147.   Trans.: as a satisfied guest.

148.   MS: and he deems himself happy and bold in his weakness.

149.   Kant says "Jews" in all texts.

150.   "Separatistic character" refers to a social group's self-consciousness which makes the group proud of its own heritage and difference from others.

151.   Cato, as orator, was more eloquent under the influence of wine. Horace *Carmina* 3. 21. 11–12: "Narratur et prisci Catonis saepe mero caluisse virtus." [The virtue of even the old Cato is said to have often been inspired by wine.]

152.   Külpe cites Tacitus *Germania* 22.

153.   Trans.: wine makes eloquent.

154.   Jean Jacques Rousseau (1712–78), *Héloïse* 1, letter 23.

155.   Hume, *Principles of Morals,* sec. 4, p. 271: "I hate a drinking-companion, says the Greek proverb, who never forgets. The follies of the

last debauch should be buried in eternal oblivion, in order to give full
scope to the follies of the next."
156.　B: this sec. added. MS: sec. 27.
157.　Paragraph beginning with "It is not advisable" is found in A, sec.
24 as the third paragraph following the words "were forced on him" (A:
pp. 86 f.).
158.　Kant uses the term "onlooker" *(Zuschauer)* instead of the maga-
zine's title. The *Spectator* 77 treats of absentmindedness; cf. Jean de La
Bruyère (1645–96), *Caractères,* especially the picture of the ab-
sentminded man.
159.　The German proverb is, "Er hat den Faden verloren."
160.　A: sec. 23. MS: sec. 28. The German term for "sensory productive
faculty" is *sinnliches Dichtungsvermögen.*
161.　MS: *affinitatis.* Cassirer: *imaginatio affinitatis.*
162.　B: "If the artist . . . natural" was added.
163.　About the year 1775, Prince Palagonia began the construction of a
villa near Palermo. See Johann Wolfgang von Goethe (1749–1832),
Italienische Reise (April 9, 1787).
164.　B: "fantastic . . . like" was added.
165.　Trans.: Chimeras are created like the dreams of a sick person.
166.　MS contains the additional sentence: It is an association caused by
vicinity.
167.　MS: "give" stricken out.
168.　B: "whatever" was added.
169.　Külpe refers to Descartes, *Ueber die Lehre von den materiellen Ideen.*
Hermann Samuel Reimarus (1694–1768), cf. his detailed critique in
Göttingisches Magazin der Wissenschaften und Litteratur, ed. by G. Chr.
Lichtenberg and G. Forster, vol. 1 (1780), pp. 27 ff. and 351 ff.
170.　MS, on the margin: The digression from the subject of conversation *(facultas signatix)* belongs to the accompanying imagination. However, if we experience real sense perceptions (not imaginations) which
are related to each other by a rule called experience, which means that we
perceive our imaginations as being interconnected with each other, then
we realize that all this happens within time and that it is associative.
171.　A: sec. 24, entitled "Explanations with Examples." MS: sec. 29.
172.　Trans.: "We are at home where we are doing well," probably from
Pacuvius; cf. Cicero *Tusculanae Disputationes* 5. 37. 108.
173.　See sec. 13, n. 79.
174.　Christian Friedrich Michaelis (1754–1804), "Tollheit aus Mit-
leidenschaft," in *Medicinisch-praktische Bibliothek* (Göttingen, 1785), vol. 1,
pp. 114 ff.
175.　A: "to them"; all other versions read "him" (i.e., the person who
explains something emotional).
176.　MS: have.
177.　Trans.: The similar ones are pleased by each other.
178.　*Henry IV* 1. 2. 4. See Wallace's *Kant,* p. 51: "The name of Shakespeare does not occur in Kant's works."
179.　A: sec. 25, On the Means for Animating and Controlling the Play
of the Imagination. MS: sec. 30.

180. Külpe cites Leopold von Dessau (1693–1747), i.e., Leopold I.
181. Trans.: "the mask falls, and the essence remains."—Lucretius *De Reum Natura* 3. 58.
182. "Ras-Sem"; Külpe refers to "Abhandlung von einer versteinerten Stadt in der Landschaft Tripoli in Afrika" in *Neues hamburgisches Magazin* 19 (1757): 631–53.
183. Lodovico Ariosto (1474–1533). Külpe refers to C. L. Fernow, *Ariosto's, des göttlichen Lebenslauf* (Zurich: Gessner, 1809), p. 97.
184. Trans.: the world wants to be deceived.
185. A: sec. 26. MS: sec. 31.
186. A: irregular imagination.
187. Trans.: wags just do not have a trustworthy memory.
188. Karl von Linné (1707–78), the Swedish botanist.
189. MS, Cassirer add: *(loci topici)*.
190. Giovanni Pico della Mirandola (1463–94). See John E. Sandys, *A History of Classical Scholarship* (Cambridge: Cambridge University Press, 1908), vol. 2, p. 82: "While he was still absorbed in planning a vast work, which was to form a complete system of Platonic, Christian, and Cabbalistic lore, he passed away at the early age of thirty-one."
191. Külpe refers to Julius Caesar Scaliger (1484–1558), the father of the famous Joseph Justus Scaliger (1540–1609). See Sandys, *History of Classical Scholarship*, vol. 2, p. 199: "In four months he perused all the Greek poets." Ibid., p. 204. "Casaubon says of Scaliger, 'nihil est quod discere quisquam vellet, quod ille docere non posset; nihil legerat, quod non statim meminisset.' " [There is nothing that anyone would want to learn that he could not teach; he had read nothing that he did not remember immediately.] Cf. sec. 59, n. 321.
192. Angelo Poliziano (1454–94) wrote poems in Greek at the age of seventeen.
193. Antonio Magliabechi (1633–1714) has been described as "a walking museum and a living library."
194. MS, Cassirer: carried.
195. Trans.: we know as much as we carry with us in our mind.
196. See Plato *Phaedrus* 275A. Of course Socrates was relating a tale, and it is not clear that either he or Plato intended the point stated so baldly as their own.
197. B: section was added. MS: sec. 32.
198. For Kant's knowledge of the Caribs, Külpe cites Johann Wilhelm von Archenholz (1743–1812), "Über die Religion, Sitten und Gebräuche der Karaiben" in *Litteratur und Völkerkunde*, vol. 6 (1785), pp. 473 ff.
199. Kant uses the word *Ahndung*. Modern German uses *Ahnung*. *Ahnen* means to have presentiment of something; *ahnden* was once semantically identical with *ahnen* but gradually acquired the meaning "punishing someone for a committed crime."
200. Epoptae were those who received the highest grade of initiation at the Eleusinian mysteries. Cf. Plato *Symposium* 210A.
201. B: section was added. MS: sec. 33.
202. A: does not contain "or."
203. "Sortes Vergilianae"; see Charles Knapp, *The Aeneid of Vergil*

(Chicago: Scott, Foresman, 1923), Introduction, p. 62: "Convincing testimony to the unique position of Vergil in Roman estimation is to be found in the so-called *Sortes Vergilianae*, i.e., the practice, in vogue as early as the time of Hadrian's reign (117–138 A.D.), of seeking to learn the future by opening at random a volume of Vergil and taking as an omen of coming events the first line on which the eyes fell. Even emperors consulted Virgil in this way and the custom lasted many centuries. Aside from the famous Sibylline books only two other books—the Homeric poems and the Bible—have been thus venerated."

204. B: "parts of" was added.
205. A: "that" instead of "as if."
206. Trans.: Oh, what troubles man makes for himself!
207. MS, Cassirer, *Akad. Ausg.* only contain "sacred."
208. A: sec. 27. MS: sec. 34.
209. A: rule.
210. A: "but sleep . . ." which, logically, is not as clear as B version.
211. Kant says, "thoughtless sleep."
212. The phrase "tries . . . again" is a free translation of the literal "is again set into action."
213. A: sec. 28. MS: sec. 35.
214. MS contains between "notions. . . . symbolic cognition": like the words of a language which are meaningless sounds for the ear of a stranger, just because of that lead to more definite notions, and the . . .
215. MS, Cassirer, *Akad. Ausg.:* presentation.
216. Emanuel Swedenborg (1688–1772). See Wallace, *Kant,* p. 132: Kant's "interest, indeed, was strong enough to make him spend seven pounds on a copy of Swedenborg's great work . . . and to study the alleged visions as well as the theories of the author. His investigations were talked about, and the importunity of friends drew from him a book—'Dreams of a Visionary, explained by Dreams of Metaphysics'—in its mixture of sympathy and scorn, spiritualism and materialism, the strangest of his works."
217. MS contains a final sentence, crossed out: "For the purpose of designating thoughts, and not mere sensation, man at first uses mimical signs, then sound-signs in language, and finally allegorical signs of the [visible reproductions] images which are to contain an analogy to [nonvisible] merely thinkable objects." Kant's deletions have been indicated by brackets. Another lengthy remark found on the margin at this point in the MS seems also worth our attention: "Most of the Indians who live on the Malabar Coast belong, according to Sonnerat, to a very secret organization, whose symbol (a round tin coin) is hanging from a band around the neck directly on the bearer's skin. They call this their *tali* which is accompanied during their initiation ceremonies by a mystical word which they whisper into another person's ear only on their deathbed. The Tibetans cover hills with certain sacred objects like consecrated stones and flags embroidered with certain sacred words which they call *mani*. A combination of both words has probably resulted in the word *talisman* which appears to correspond in word and sense to *manitou* of the American savages."

218.   A: sec. 29. MS: sec. 36.
219.   On the miraculous, as opposed to the natural, cf. Hume, *Treatise*, p. 474, and sec. 10 "Of Miracles," pp. 119–45.
220.   MS: does not contain "and astonishment."
221.   MS: does not read "physical."
222.   B: "nations" was added; before addition, the referent was "things."
223.   A: memory. MS: memories.
224.   A, beginning of sentence reads: The interpretation of signs with regard to future events concerning the world is most reliable . . .
225.   B: "human" was added.
226.   MS: before.
227.   The phrase "critical days" refers to menstrual pains and discomfort.
228.   A, after "Yet": "the position of the stars at the birth (the horoscopus), or . . ." MS reads after "Yet": "the position of the stars at the birth (the horospicus) . . ."
229.   B, inserted before "seven": as well as.
230.   The "grand climacteric" is one's sixty-third year.
231.   See Daniel 9:24: "Seventy weeks are determined upon thy people and upon thy holy city." The 490 years would begin in 586 B.C., at the fall of Jerusalem, and end in 96 B.C., by exact chronology; but Daniel's knowledge of history was not accurate.
232.   See [Frederick Shobel], *Frederick the Great*, ed. Thomas Campbell (Philadelphia: Lea and Blanchard, 1843), vol. 2, pp. 334–35: "The inventory of the personal affects of the great king . . . eleven silver tea-spoons."
233.   B: "Germany, and other places perhaps" was added.
234.   Some are superstitious because of Judas, the traitor.
235.   MS, Cassirer: Much worse still . . .
236.   A: sec. 30. MS: sec. 37, preceded by the subtitle, Classification of Terms.
237.   MS, Cassirer add: but sensitivity is more necessary and more indispensable.
238.   MS: sec. title is preceded by Part One: The Understanding.
239.   A: sec. 31. MS: sec. 38.
240.   MS, Cassirer: real.
241.   Kant says he quotes Juvenal, but he actually has taken the quotation from Persius 3. 78: "What I know is enough for me, I do not long to be what Arkesilaos and the troubled Solon [were]."
242.   MS, on the margin: 1.) What do I want to do? 2.) What matters? 3.) What do I gain? . . . Real understanding.
243.   A: sec. 32. MS: sec. 39.
244.   MS: makes for himself.
245.   Trans.: the concept has to be adequate to the object.
246.   MS: satisfies without trickery its . . .
247.   MS: Kant had originally written "characteristic" instead of "way of thinking" but crossed it out.
248.   Kant has quoted from Voltaire, *La Henriade* (Paris: Lecointe, 1835), p. 91.

249.   John Wilmot, Earl of Rochester (1647–80), *The Works of the Earl of Rochester* (London: printed for Edmund Curll, 1707): "Here lies our Sovereign Lord the King, / Whose Word no Man rely'd on; / Who never said a foolish thing, / Nor ever did a wise one" (p. 156). The authentic version of this epigram is to be found in *The Complete Poems of John Wilmot, Earl of Rochester,* ed. David M. Vieth (New Haven and London: Yale University Press, 1968), p. 134: "God bless our good and gracious King, / Whose promise none relies on; / Who never said a foolish thing, / Nor ever did a wise one." See also "Rochester on Charles II" in the *London Times Literary Supplement,* 4, 18, 25 October, 1 November 1934, pp. 675, 715, 735, 755 respectively.

250.   MS: does not contain "French."

251.   A: *theoretical.*

252.   The translation follows the more grammatically correct MS version.

253.   A: sec. 33. MS: sec. 40.

254.   A: direction of thoughts.

255.   B: or.

256.   See also sec. 41.

257.   MS, on the margin: Preliminary judgments.

258.   The word "perfect," meaning "with regard to principles."

259.   See also sec. 57.

260.   MS: "should" crossed out; reads "could."

261.   A: sec. 34. MS: sec. 41.

262.   B: "called" was added.

263.   B: the heading "A. General Division" was added, as well as the first two sentences. MS: sec. 42; the *Akad. Ausg.* begins sec. 45 here, whereas A, sec. 35 begins with the third sentence, slightly different in wording.

264.   MS: involuntary.

265.   A: a poetic attack.

266.   Laurence Sterne (1713–68), *The Life and Opinions of Tristram Shandy* (1760), vol. 1, chap. 7.

267.   A: sec. 36, headed A. MS: sec. 43.

268.   On the difference between clever (*klug*) and wise (*gescheut*), see Kant's "Fundamental Principles of the Metaphysic of Morals," in Abbott, trans., *Kant's Critique of Practical Reason,* p. 33.

269.   This reference could not be found in Hume.

270.   A: sec. 37. MS: sec. 44.

271.   A: (*dissipatio*).

272.   A: sec. 38. MS: sec. 45.

273.   Adam Smith (1723–90), *An Inquiry into the Nature and Causes of the Wealth of Nations* (London, 1776), bk. 2, chap. 3.

274.   A: "at the time of" instead of "after."

275.   A: sec. 39, entitled, B. On Differences in the Degree of Mental Weakness. MS: sec. 46.

276.   MS: this entire sentence in parentheses.

277.   A: after he has just come home. MS: when he has returned again.

278.   A: sec. 40. MS: sec. 47. B: entitled, B. On Mental Ailments.

279.   B: "as . . . above" was added.

280. See sec. 45.
281. The German word *Grillenkrankheit* has been translated as "melancholia."
282. See note by Friedrich Wilhelm Schubert, ed., in *Anthropologie in pragmatischer Hinsicht abgefasst*, vol. 7 of *Immanuel Kants sämmtliche Werke* (Leipzig: Voss, 1838), p. 121: "Compare the discussion of the power of the mind to master ill feelings merely by resolution, which is included in *Contest of the Faculties*, i.e., the Academic Faculties." Abbott says of Kant: "Yet by dint of careful attention and great regularity he was able, without medical aid, to maintain such good health on the whole, that at a later period he used to say to himself on going to bed, 'Is it possible to conceive any human being enjoying better health than I do?' . . . At the age of seventy he wrote an essay, 'On the Power of the Mind to Master the Feeling of Illness by Force of Resolution.' . . . Afterwards included in the *Streit der Facultäten*." "Memoir of Kant" in *Kant's Critique of Practical Reason*, p. xliii and n.
283. MS: business.
284. MS, Cassirer: "are emotional moods" for "is . . . moods."
285. C. A. Hausen (1693–1745), professor of mathematics in Leipzig.
286. A: sec. 41, MS: sec. 48.
287. A: sec. 42, entitled, Classification of Derangement. MS: sec. 49.
288. A: "outside the *sensorium commune*" [common sense] instead of "from . . . *communi*."
289. B: "place" was added.
290. MS: "outside of itself" following "object" stricken out.
291. Johann Baptist von Helmont (1578–1664). Monkshood (*Aconitum napellus*) is a poisonous plant which yields the drug aconite.
292. A: sec. 43; its opening sentence reads "There is no deranged child." MS: sec. 50.
293. This translation follows the A version. MS: so that. B: as if.
294. MS contains the following crossed-out paragraph: But this is only a saying of people completely unfamiliar with geography; the businessman who has to do with the sea knows better. Even the fact that some have embarked on the way to India because they were possessed by the crazy idea that they would not fail to amass riches there just because someone once succeeded to do so. The germ of folly to weather blindly the adventure of becoming rich without effort began to grow with time and matured at the moment of return.
295. James Harrington (1611–77), *The Oceana, and Other Works*, ed. John Toland (London, 1737). Hume says that Harrington's *Oceana* is the "only valuable model of a commonwealth that has yet been offered to the public."
296. MS contains the following crossed-out section: On the Talents of Cognition Which are Available to the Understanding. Sec. 39. These talents are cleverness, gift of scholarship, originality of talent (a clever, intelligent and original mind is a *genius*). All are gifts of nature which further the development of what is contained in the concepts of the mind. The ability (*habilitas*) to do this cannot be acquired. Nature must have equipped man with it. However, it can be cultivated and one does not only understand it as a faculty but also as an inclination (instinct)

toward using one's talents. If the word genius is understood literally as the inborn talent, then the first talent would refer to the skill (*promptitudo*), the second to the cleverness, and the third to the originality of a mind as to the arrangement of its thought. Imagination provides the material which may be identical in different minds. But the talent to ready this material for use by the understanding can result in great difference. The faculty of uniting heterogeneous conceptual ideas through understanding is the creative intelligence (*perspicacia*).

297.   A: sec. 44. MS: sec. 51.

298.   Cf. sec. 56, sagacity. See Locke, *Essay*, vol. 2, p. 179: "A quickness in the mind to find out these intermediate ideas (that shall discover the agreement or disagreement of any other) and to apply them right, is, I suppose, that which is called sagacity." Cf., however, Thomas Hobbes (1588–1679) in "Human Nature or the Fundamental Elements of Poetry," *The English Works of Thomas Hobbes,* ed. William Molesworth, vol. 4, chap. 4, sec. 4, pp. 15 ff.: "Another sort of discursion is, when the *appetite* giveth a man his beginning; as in the example before, where honour to which a man hath appetite, maketh him think upon the next means of attaining it, and that again of the next, etc. And this the Latins call *sagacitas,* and we may call hunting or tracing, as dogs trace beasts by the smell, and men hunt them by their footsteps; or as men hunt after riches, place, or knowledge."

299.   Trans.: we grant and plead for mutual goodwill.

300.   On judgment, see Locke, *Essay*, vol. 1, p. 203. The MS contains the following crossed-out section: Sagacity, or the gift of intellectual exploration, is also a gift of nature. It means that someone knows how to search (with luck) successfully (answers about nature and other men). It is a talent which can make preliminary judgments about where and how the truth might be found. Francis Bacon, Baron of Verulam, has provided us in his *Organon* with a brilliant example of the art of making preliminary judgments (*iudicii praevii*) about ourself. As a result he has put the method of the natural sciences back on its proper tracks. The genius, however, is the originality which concerns the generation of results as to the faculty of cognition; it is the faculty of thinking and acting in an exemplary manner in full independence from any other pattern.

301.   A: sec. 45. MS: sec. 52; in the title Kant had first used "comparative" instead of "productive," but then crossed it out.

302.   Kant's term *Witz* is translated as "intelligence."

303.   Georges Louis Leclerc, Comte de Buffon (1707–88), *Histoire Naturelle* (1749).

304.   Abbé-Trublet (1697-1770).

305.   Pope made this statement. See Robert Kilburn Root (1877–1950), *The Poetical Career of Alexander Pope* (Princeton: Princeton University Press, 1938), pp. 128–29: "On March 8, 1728, appeared *The Last Volume* of the *Miscellanies* of Pope and Swift. The most important piece included in the collection was Pope's prose essay 'Peri Bathous, Or The Art of Sinking in Poetry,' a deliciously witty piece of sustained irony in which are given grave instructions for the writing of dull poetry. . . . The satire is pointed by copious illustrations from bad poets." Swift was not directly associated with this prose treatise even though it is a work to which

several members of the Scriblerus Club may have contributed, Arbuthnot in particular. The final form of this treatise is, however, almost entirely Pope's work ("I have entirely methodized, and in a manner, written it all"). The piece was included into the third volume of the *Miscellanies,* apparently because it could be read as a prelude to the *Dunciad.* Swift is believed to have seen the work for the first time after its publication.

306.   Samuel Butler (1612–80), *Hudibras.* See H. A. Taine (1828–93), *History of the English Literature,* trans. H. van Laun (New York: Holt and Williams, 1871), vol. 1, p. 462: "How mean is the wit, with what awkwardness and dulness he dilutes his splenetic satire!"

307.   Edward Young (1684–1765), *The Universal Passion* (1725–27), a collection of seven satires.

308.   Kant's word *Witz* is translated as "cleverness."

309.   Külpe's note reads: "He doubtless praised many whom he would have been afraid to marry; and, perhaps, married one whom he would have been ashamed to praise." Boswell (1859), vol 3, pp. 47 f.

310.   MS: utter.

311.   A: sec. 46. MS: sec. 53.

312.   Francis Bacon, Lord of Verulam (1561–1626), whose *Novum Organum* (1620) is a collection of scientific decrees, written in aphorisms.

313.   A: sec. 47. MS: sec. 54.

314.   Cf. *Kant's Critique of Judgment,* trans. Bernard, sec. 46: "*Genius* is the talent (or natural gift) which gives the rule to Art. . . . Genius is the innate mental disposition (*ingenium*) *through which* Nature gives the rules to art."

315.   MS: "by others" added.

316.   B: "however" added.

317.   Kant's word is *Geist.*

318.   MS: arise from Nature.

319.   A: sec. 48. MS: sec. 55.

320.   A: sec. 49. MS: sec. 56.

321.   See sec. 34, n. 191. Here again Joseph Justus Scaliger might have been named. See Sandys, *History of Classical Scholarship,* vol. 2, p. 204: "His main strength lay in a clear conception of ambiguity as a whole, and in the concentration of vast and varied learning on distinctly important works."

322.   MS: (like Leibniz). Sir Isaac Newton (1642–1727) was acclaimed by Voltaire in his *Lettres sur les Anglais,* letter no. 12, as the greatest man who ever lived. For his influence on Kant, see Kemp Smith, *Commentary,* pp. lv–lvi, 140–42, 161 ff., 539. Ibid., p. 605: "Kant's first-hand knowledge of Leibniz' teachings was very limited. He was acquainted with it chiefly through the inadequate channel of Wolff's somewhat commonplace exposition of its principles."

323.   Christian Heinrich Heinecke (1721–25).

324.   Jean Philippe Baratier (1721–40), infant prodigy; at seven he knew German, French, Latin, Greek, Hebrew.

325.   B: statement in parentheses was added and refers back to sec. 43.

326.   Trans.: Nobody is forced to follow the words of the master.

Second Book: *On Pleasure and Displeasure*

1. A: Second Chapter.
2. A: sec. 50. MS: sec. 57. A reads: Pleasure. Section One.
3. Trans.: contradictory or logically opposed.
4. Trans.: contrasted or truly opposed.
5. Pedro, Count of Veri (1728–97), author of *Meditazione sulla economia politica.*
6. MS at this point contains on the margin and on the next page a lengthy but not completely elaborated passage on contentedness, the usual misjudgment of distances, and the duration of time sensed during different states of mind.
7. A: sec. 51. MS: sec. 58.
8. Külpe, in a note in the *Anthropology,* says the reference is to l'Abbé le Blanc, *Lettres* (1751), vol. 1, p. 259.
9. MS, *Akad. Ausg.,* Cassirer: open spaces.
10. Trans.: extend life through activity.
11. MS: or.
12. MS: "or the dulling of" does not appear.
13. For discussion of desire, see sec. 73.
14. A: sec. 52. MS: sec. 59.
15. Butler, see sec. 55, n. 306; Sterne, see sec. 45, n. 266.
16. A: and, what is worse, a.
17. B: "oneself" was added.
18. A: sec. 53. MS: sec. 60.
19. B: "as . . . above" was added. Cf. sec. 25.
20. B: phrase in parentheses was added.
21. A: sec. 54. MS: sec. 61.
22. A: sec. 55. MS: sec. 62.
23. MS: for *himself.*
24. A: sec. 56. MS: sec. 63.
25. Trans.: opposites become clearer when they are juxtaposed.
26. MS, Cassirer: greater; all other editions read great.
27. A: Second Part. On the . . . ; instead of i.e., A reads or. Much has been written on Kant's views of the Beautiful, of Taste, and of the Sublime. His *Critique of Judgment* and *Essay on the Sublime and the Beautiful* can well be supplemented with this section in the *Anthroplogy.* Attention has already been called (sec. 27, n. 137) to Joseph Addison, *Spectator* 411–21, translated into German in 1745. Kant was also familiar with Francis Hutcheson's (1694–1747) *Inquiry into the Ideas of Beauty and Virtue* (1725), translated into German in 1762; Thomas Robertson's (d. 1799) *An Inquiry into the Fine Arts* (Edinburgh, 1784), which treats of music; Mark Akenside's (1721–70), *The Pleasures of Imagination,* which shows the influence of Shaftesbury, Hutcheson, Longinus, Plato, and Dr. Young. He may have read "Of Beauty: Philosophical Opinions of it: Directions for Improving and Preserving it," the *Mirror* 1 (London, 1779), 13–19; also "An Epistle upon the Cultivation of Taste," in *Instructions for a Young*

Lady (Edinburgh: Donaldson, 1723), pp. 185–93. David Hume's *Of the Standard of Taste* appeared in German translation by Sulzer, in 1754–56. *Elements of Criticism* by Henry Home, Lord Kames (1696–1782), was published in 1762 and shortly afterward was translated into German. Edmund Burke's (1729–97) *Philosophical Enquiry into the Origin of Our Ideas of the Sublime and Beautiful* (1756) was translated into German in 1773. Alexander Pope's (1688–1744) essay, *Of Taste,* may also be mentioned. Kant's general view of taste and his concept of sublimity are well treated by E. F. Carrit, *The Theory of Beauty,* 2d enl. ed. (London: Methuen, 1923), where authorities are cited. There is an essay by the same writer in *Immanuel Kant: Papers Read at Northwestern University on the Bicentenary of Kant's Birth* (Chicago: Open Court, 1925), pp. 179–92.

28.   A: sec. 57. MS: sec. 64.
29.   B: "as . . . above" added.
30.   MS contains a longer, crossed-out passage here which deals with pleasure and taste.
31.   MS: *gustus reflectens apprehendens* with *apprehendens* crossed out.
32.   MS, Cassirer: dress himself up, decorate and . . .
33.   MS: "of beauty" added.
34.   MS, *Akad. Ausg.,* Cassirer: satisfying.
35.   MS contains one crossed out sentence preceding the definition: "Taste is the faculty which unites the free play of the imagination with the laws of the understanding." On the universal validity of aesthetic judgments, see *Critique of Judgment,* sec. 16.
36.   MS: represented.
37.   Thersites was an ugly and scurrilous Greek in Homer's *Iliad* 2. 212.
38.   MS: beauty of soul.
39.   A: sec. 58. MS: sec. 65 entitled, On Taste in Regard to the Sublime.
40.   A: sec. 59. MS: sec. 66.
41.   B: "the inclination" added.
42.   A: sec. 60. MS: sec. 67.
43.   A: sec. 61. MS: sec. 68 entitled, Taste, and crossed out is the following passage: Popular taste (in contrast to the exquisite one) is fashion. The question, "what, then, is fashion?" is not merely directed at elegant choice, which has become law through habit.
44.   MS: "the weaker person" instead of "man." Cf. sec. 14, n. 85 on "propensity."
45.   Trans.: poetry in a broad sense.
46.   Trans.: poetry in a strict sense.
47.   Kant's term is *Dichter,* which he has opposed to "Poet." The term "maker" (in the sense of ποιητής) seems to be the best possible rendering.
48.   This sentence differs in wording but not in sense from the A version. The reading given is the one in MS and B.
49.   Kant's word is *Naturmaler* (painter of nature).
50.   Kant's word is *Ideenmaler* (painter of ideas).
51.   Hugh Blair (1718–1800), *Lectures in Rhetoric* (1783), translated into German by Schreiter (1785–89). The word "mad" is not used, but see *Epistle to Dr. Arbuthnot,* line 188: "Not poetry but prose run mad."

52. MS continues: in modern poetry.
53. *Xenion,* a present to a guest or stranger; a New Year's gift; a kind of satirical epigram first introduced by Schiller and Goethe.
54. A: sec. 62. MS: sec. 69.
55. MS contains a crucial passage after "weaken the nation" which provides the verb "suppress . . . entirely" *(ganz zu unterdrücken)* for the subordinate clause.

Third Book: *On Faculty of Desire*

1. A: sec. 63, entitled, Section Three. MS: sec. 70.
2. A: sec. 64. MS: sec. 71.
3. MS, crossed-out section between "is" and "surprise" reads: "inundation caused by the breaking of a dam; passion, however, is a stream which, caused by the steepness of the terrain, persistently digs itself in deeper and deeper." In the MS "surprise" is the beginning of the new sentence.
4. Emotion and apathy are opposite terms. Kant's word for emotion is *Affekt,* and his word for apathy is *Affektlosigkeit.*
5. MS modifies man with "reasonable" which was later crossed out.
6. A: sec. 65. MS: sec. 72.
7. Cf. sec. 60.
8. A: sec. 66. MS: sec. 73.
9. A reads "and" instead of "with." John Brown (1735–88), *Elementa Medicinae* (1780). See William Wallace, *Kant,* p. 46.
10. A: "is the" instead of "accompanies."
11. A only reads "latter."
12. B: "laughing . . . weeping" added.
13. A: sec. 67. MS: sec. 74.
14. Charles XII (1682–1718), King of Sweden, was defeated by the Russians. See Voltaire, *Histoire de Charles XII;* see also Voltaire, *Dictionary,* article on "Characters": "Charles XII in his illness on the way to Bender was no longer the same man; he was as tractable as a child."
15. MS does not contain "only."
16. The German saying referred to (as is also evident in the MS) is *Das Herz rutscht einem in die Hosen,* translated literally as "one's heart falls into one's pants."
17. Kant derives the word "hallucinate" from the Latin word *allex* (the big toe) instead of the Greek ἀλάομαι.
18. This sentence is not in A; a sentence with similar content is found at the end of the next paragraph.
19. Kant uses the word *Dreustigkeit* in the MS, whereas the other versions spell the word in the usual way, *Dreistigkeit.* In his footnote Kant argues that the word should be spelled *Dräustigkeit* in order to convey the threatening character of such behavior to others.
20. A contains a new paragraph which does not exist in the other versions at this place: "Finally, determination belongs also to purely moral courage. It is the determination to do what duty demands even at

the expense of possibly being ridiculed by others. This takes a high degree of courage because the love of honor is the steady companion of virtue. He who is usually well equipped to withstand force rarely feels strong enough to endure ridicule if his claim of honor is sneeringly refused."

21.   Külpe refers to Frederick the Great, King of Prussia (1740–86), and military genius of the Seven Years War (1756–63).

22.   Jean Marie Roland de la Platière (1734–93), French statesman; he fell upon his sword, piercing his heart.

23.   Trans.: a mind that knows what is right.

24.   Trans.: the knight without fear and weakness. Pierre Terrail, Seigneur de Bayard (1493–1524), French nobleman, died in battle.

25.   Latin subhead: The disabled movements of the mind.

26.   A: sec. 68. MS: sec. 75.

27.   A reads only: The emotions are *anger* and *shame*. They are suddenly . . .

28.   Hume's essay "Of Impudence and Modesty." David Hume, *The Philosophical Works* (Edinburgh: printed for Adam Black and William Tait, 1826), vol. 4, p. 517.

29.   A: sec. 69. MS: sec. 76.

30.   A, sentence reads: These emotions are laughing and weeping.

31.   A and B_2: anger; all others: the anger.

32.   B: "her children and" added.

33.   MS: "and subject" added.

34. B_3: fatigue of vitality will . . .

35.   A, does not contain; who makes us laugh.

36.   A, sentence begins: However, . . .

37.   MS: Kant had originally written "of a joke" but crossed it out.

38.   MS, crossed-out phrase: "feelings related to a certain fictitious condition," after "they."

39.   On seasickness, see sec. 29 where Kant speaks of his own experience on the water.

40.   Abbé Jean Terrasson (1670–1750) is mentioned in *The Critique of Pure Reason,* trans. F. Max Müller (London: Macmillan, 1881), p. xxviii, and note; see also Kemp Smith, *Commentary,* p. 15, and note.

41.   MS: "the solemn person" is crossed out.

42.   A: sec. 70; heading reads, On the Faculty of Desire. MS: sec. 77.

43.   Cf. sec. 73.

44.   MS: they can never be completely.

45.   A: sec. 71. MS: sec. 78.

46.   Alexander Pope (1688–1744), *Essay on Man,* Epistle 2, line 108: "Reason the card, but Passion is the gale." Kant used Brockes' translation (1740).

47.   A: sec. 72. MS: sec. 79.

48.   MS: section B begins after this paragraph.

49.   Cassirer follows MS: "passions" instead of "inclinations."

50.   MS: last part of sec. 78 (sec. 81 of this edition) Division of the Passions begins with a classification of passions into   A) passions of external freedom concerning a negative enjoyment; and   B) passions of faculty concerning a positive enjoyment. At the end of MS sec. 82

another section (see n. 57 below) begins, On the Division of the Passions, in which it is stated that "passions are inclinations that are only directed by human beings toward human beings."

51. A: sec. 73. MS: sec. 80. Heading in B reads: On the Thirst for Vengeance, as a Passion; A and MS read: "Justice," instead of "Vengeance."

52. MS: in such a state.

53. A: sec. 74. MS: sec. 81. MS and Cassirer: "Out of Passion" added at the end of heading.

54. MS, on the margin: The possession of the means heightens the passion more than its use. Possessing the faculty itself is pleasant.

55. A: sec. 75. MS: sec. 82.

56. Kant uses the word *Vermögen* which has the dual meaning of faculty and fortune (wealth).

57. MS, new section follows here: On Formal Propensities Based on the Free Play of Vitality. Formal propensities are 1) the propensity to enjoy; 2) the propensity to work; 3) the propensity to be at ease. a. Because I am here abstracting from the object of our desire (i.e. matter), the aversion of nature to an empty feeling of existence, i.e. boredom, is by itself enough stimulus to every cultivated person to fill this emptiness. Demands for continuous enjoyment, be they physical or even aesthetic (when it is called luxury), are asking for a life of pleasure which is at the same time a waste of life, where you become the hungrier the more you enjoy. [At this point reference is given to the asterisk indicating Kant's footnote in the text following the phrase "makes one despised."] This is also true of the aimless hunger for reading. b. Occupying oneself during leisure time, which is, therefore, not called business but playtime, and which is designed for victory in the competition with others, contains a motivation to maximal stimulation of propensities; even if the stimulation is not directed toward acquisition (without interested intention). However, during gambling this stimulation is frequently intensified into the most furious passion, while [the following closing part of this section was crossed out by Kant] refined manners fake equanimity and even polite behavior in order to cover up skillfully the internally raging anger. Consequently, the ruined person feigns happiness while he is taken advantage of. It is not easy to explain why gambling exerts such an attraction among civilized and uncivilized peoples (Chinese and American Indians). It is even more difficult to explain that gambling as a means of maintaining social life is even praised as being beneficial to humaneness. People with obscure notions, like hunters, fishermen, and perhaps also seafarers, are usually simple lottery players, they are all superstitious. [On the margin Kant wrote "Brama" at this point.]

58. A: sec. 76. MS: sec. 83.

59. MS, Cassirer: "its" not "his."

60. MS: especially when the passion is intended for competition between human beings.

61. A: sec. 77. MS: sec. 84.

62. Italian: [*dolce*] *far niente*, [the sweetness of] doing nothing.

63. Külpe suggests that Kant may refer to Demetrius of Phalerum (345?–283 B.C.).

64.   Kant's terms are: *Liebe zum Leben* and *Liebe zum Geschlecht.*

65.   MS, on the margin: which should not lead to a higher rank of mankind, or even to a specifically different rank (like the one held by the Americans), but to a higher humanization *(humanisatio)*. Is mankind on a path of continuous progress toward perfection? Is mankind becoming progressively worse or better, or does mankind remain on the same moral level? From the first day the child is held in his nurse's arms until the days of old age, the exposure to trickery, deception, and malice is always the same. The answer to the question whether there should be war or peace continues to be given by the person holding the highest power in the state. The highest level of culture is achieved when the state of war between nations is in balance; and the remedy to this question is who shall determine whether there should be war or not.

66.   A: sec. 78. MS: sec. 85.

67.   MS, Cassirer: and partly moral (intellectual).

68.   Kant speaks of the mannerisms of egoism; A reads *feinen Manieren* (good manners) instead of *seinen Manieren* (his manners).

69.   MS, stricken passage continues the sentence: The candidness of conversation should neither be interferred with (as by being seated at the same table with the host), nor should there be any conversation without choice or context as at the Lord Mayor's banquet (because every overly large social gathering becomes a mob).

70.   MS, *Akad. Ausg.,* Cassirer do not contain "it need not be feared."

71.   A reads "and"; all other versions, "with."

72.   Trans.: the solitary person at the table.

73.   Kant uses the word *Exhaustion;* A reads *Exhaustation.*

74.   Trans.: to keep the people at the dinner table.

75.   Phrase "first appetite" refers to the appetite for news.

76.   MS, Cassirer: consequently, all others do not indicate a causal connection.

77.   Kant's word is *Gastmahl* which suggests the meaning of symposium.

78.   MS, Cassirer: in a more serious context.

PART TWO: ANTHROPOLOGICAL CHARACTERIZATION

1.   MS heading, Characterization; on the margin is written, Part One: Anthroplogical *didactic.* What is man? Part Two: Anthropological *characterization.* How can the particular nature of every man be discovered? The first part is an elementary doctrine so to speak, whereas the second part is a methodology of anthropology. For Character and Characterization Kant drew from many sources, notably from Anthony Ashley Cooper (1671–1713), 3d earl of Shaftesbury, *Characteristics of Men, Manners, Opinions, Times* (London, 1711). A German version of Shaftesbury was begun in 1738. See also John Brown (1715–66), *Essays on the Characteristics of Lord Shaftesbury* (London: printed for C. Davis, 1751); and Gustav Zart, *Einfluss der englischen Philosophen seit Bacon auf die deutsche Philosophie des 18ten Jahrhunderts* (Berlin: Dümmler, 1881), pp. 219, 231.

2.   A: sec. 79. MS: sec. 86. This is the last section of the *Anthropology* in which Kant identified sections by number.

3.   From here on, with the exception of Cassirer, all printed versions omit the identification of sections by number. The subsequent section numbers are Cassirer's; this is sec. 90. The heading, On Nature, refers to the nature of man.

4.   Cassirer: sec. 91.

5.   As to the middle term (*medius terminus*) see Kant, *Erweis der falschen Spitzfindigkeit der vier syllogistischen Figuren* (1762), which Wallace, in *Kant*, p. 124, calls "somewhat inept as a criticism of Aristotle, although it may be valid as against the formal logic of Kant's own time."

6.   A: can be neatly retained.

7.   A: whether according to.

8.   According to Külpe, "The chief representative of Humoral-pathology was C. L. Hoffman (1721–1807), and the chief representative of Nerves-pathology was W. Cullen (1712–90)."

9.   A: temperaments of sensation.

10.   MS, on the margin: "If one temperament is mixed with another, both will resist each other and neutralize one another. If, however, one temperament is to alternate with another, then it is mere whim and certainly not temperament. One does not know what to make of man. Happiness and recklessness; melancholy and insanity; high-mindedness and stubbornness; cold-bloodedness and constancy." The respective German terms for the opposites are: *Frohsinn und Leichtsinn; Tiefsinn und Wahnsinn; Hochsinn und Starrsinn; Kaltsinn und Beharrlichkeit.*

11.   A: temperaments of sensation.

12.   Cassirer: sec. 92.

13.   MS and Cassirer only read "full."

14.   Trans.: Three cheers for minutiae!

15.   Cassirer: sec. 93.

16.   MS: loves only himself.

17.   MS, crossed-out sentence: According to its intellectual signifi-cance phlegm is the happiest of all temperaments. The reader is re-minded that "phlegm" is used here as one of the four humors of early physiology. A phlegmatic person is dull, cold, and indifferent.

18.   Cf. sec. 16.

19.   Cf. sec. 91, n. 10. Only the last word of the opposites was changed. The German word for feeblemindedness is *Schwachsinn.*

20.   Cassirer: sec. 94.

21.   MS, Cassirer: even admirable.

22.   Kant's word is *Affektionspreis.*

23.   Cassirer: sec. 95.

24.   Kant's spelling is *Sylla.*

25.   MS: invincible.

26.   See sec. 77, n. 14.

27.   Kant's *Vorlesungen über Anthropologie* (1789–90), p. 130, contains the full proverb: *Noscitur ex socio, qui non cognoscitur ex se* [He who can not be characterized on his own merits, can be characterized by the company he keeps].

28.   MS: shallow or malicious.

29. B: "restraining" was added for clarity.
30. MS, last half of this sentence reads: and even if its influence has already acquired some weight, it appears nevertheless better, as people say, to be a fool in fashion than a fool out of fashion.
31. MS, Cassirer: philosophers themselves.
32. Kant's text reads "and" instead of the editor's "that can."
33. Cassirer: sec. 96. Physiognomy, see Johann Wilhelm von Archenholz, "Ein Scherflein zur Physiognomik," *Litteratur und Völkerkunde* 4 (1784), pp. 877 ff.; also *Spectator* 86 (June 8, 1711); and Giovanni Battista Della Porta (1535–1615), *Della Fisionomia dell' Huomo* (Padova, 1626). Kant also drew on Johann Caspar Lavater (1741–1801), *Physiognomische Fragmente* (Winterthur: Steiner, 1774–78), which contains over 400 engravings of faces, several silhouettes, and a few pictures of beasts.
34. A: "doctrine" instead of "art."
35. Trans.: This one is black-hearted; therefore, Roman, beware of him.
36. Phrase "two heterogeneous things" refers to body and soul.
37. Only MS does not contain "also."
38. B₃ contains the parentheses.
39. Cassirer: sec. 97.
40. B: "statues" added.
41. A: "gems" instead of "works of art."
42. The more detailed version of the MS is used here. The other texts include the nose as a faulty organ.
43. The correct French word is *rébarbatif*, which means crabbed, stern. See *Spectator* 17 (March 20, 1710): "women and children, who are at first frightened at him, will afterwards be as much pleased with him. As it is barbarous in others to rally him for natural defects . . ."
44. Paul Pelisson-Fontanier (1624–93), a French philosopher.
45. A only: at the same time.
46. The Kalmuck Province lies near the mouth of the Volga.
47. Pieter Camper (1722–89), Dutch anatomist and naturalist.
48. Johann Friedrich Blumenbach (1752–1840), German naturalist.
49. Cassirer: sec. 98.
50. A: These are not traits characteristic of caricature.
51. A: Such traits . . .
52. Cassirer: sec. 99. This section on facial expression *(Mienen)* was added in B.
53. *Akad. Ausg.* amends the personal pronoun *sie verrät* to *er verräth*, thereby referring it to emotion, whereas all other versions refer the personal pronoun *sie* to facial expression.
54. Trans.: to close the lips (with one's finger).
55. Cassirer: sec. 100.
56. Friedrich Nicolai (1733–1811), editor of the *Allgemeine deutsche Bibliothek*.
57. James Quin (1693–1766), English actor.
58. Cassirer: sec. 101.
59. MS: with less power.
60. A: These feminine traits.
61. The grammatical structure of the sentence implies "both" (loquac-

ity and passionate eloquence). Kant's text uses "disarm," which allows reference only to "passionate eloquence."

62. MS, on the margin: Why a woman like Venus marries the ugliest man (Vulcan) and why she is not ridiculed. The woman is the pack-animal in primitive tribes. Hearne of Hudson Bay. On the last favors of the cicisbeo; . . . Out of love and jealousy Russians beat others. See also n. 67 below.

63. MS: "one" does not refer to a woman but to the one man about whom the women quarrel.

64. Külpe cites Alexander Pope, *Moral Essays*, Epistle 2, lines 209–10.

65. B2: we.

66. Cassirer: sec. 102.

67. Külpe refers the reader to Samuel Sharp, *Letters from Italy* (London, 1767), pp. 18 ff., 73 ff., 257, concerning the cicisbeo or cavaliere servente. See *Cicisbeo* in *Encyclopedia Britannica,* 11th ed.: "The cicisbeo was the professed gallant of a married woman, who attended her at all public entertainments, it being considered unfashionable for the husband to be escort."

68. Trans.: There were also 300 kept mistresses, who are called courtesans.

69. MS only: own.

70. Kant says literally that the watch has not been set according to the sun.

71. In the two preceding sentences, Kant plays on the sound and meaning of related German adjectives. In the first sentence they are *geduldig* and *duldend;* in the second they are *empfindlich* and *empfindsam.*

72. A: and yours. MS: and the rest of your sex.

73. Cassirer: sec. 103.

74. For comparison, Külpe quotes the opening sentence of Hume's essay "Of Love and Marriage"; "I know not whence it proceeds, that women are so apt to take amiss every thing which is said in disparagement of the married state; and always consider a satire upon matrimony as a satire upon themselves." *The Philosophical Works,* vol. 4, p. 522.

75. MS: Kant modifies debaucheries as charitable or beneficial.

76. Cassirer: sec. 104.

77. Trans.: acting like rabble.

78. Hume essay "Of National Characters": "the English, of any people in the universe, have the least of a national character, unless this very singularity may pass for such." *The Philosophical Works,* vol. 3, p. 235.

79. MS, sentence is continued with: because everything can be bought for money.

80. MS, crossed out on the margin: war will be difficult to avoid because of the differences in their national character.

81. MS, crossed out: The Frenchman characterizes himself to his advantage through his excellent talent and his tendency toward pleasant-mannered, and philanthropic behavior. The foreigner is, because of these conditions, already under his protection. The Frenchman's liveliness makes him prone to change which can often be healthy, but more often also neck-breaking. He also participates in national pleasures and interests.

82.   It is believed that Kant's friend Joseph Green served as model for the description of the English character. See Abbott's "Memoir of Kant" in *Kant's Critique of Practical Reason*, p. xlvii.

83.   MS, Kant argues: since a people of tradesmen as such has no character but the one it has chosen to acquire for itself, such a nation of tradesmen has actually no natural character.

84.   MS, Cassirer read "the latter" (at the inn) whereas all other versions read "the former" (alone in a separate room), which seems not to make sense.

85.   Külpe refers to "Sharp in the *Neues hamburgisches Magazin,* pp. 259, 261." Sharp is called a splenetic doctor by Smollet in *Das deutsche Museum* (1786), vol. 1, p. 387.

86.   MS: "friendship" instead of "concern."

87.   A: self-preservation *(Selbsterhaltung).* All other versions read self-control *(Selbstverhaltung)* in the sense of self-containment.

88.   Neapolitan street loungers, lazybones.

89.   Kant applies these remarks to the Italians even though they were made by Rousseau with reference to the Spaniards. See *OEuvres de Jean Jacques Rousseau,* ed. V. D. Musset-Pathay (Paris: P. Dupont, 1823), vol. 5, "Du contrat social," bk. 3, chap. 8, p. 164: "in Madrid they have superb salons, but windows that do not close; and they sleep in rats' nests."

90.   "Two-headed" refers to the Vatican as one government and the Quirinal as the other.

91.   William Robertson (1721–93), Scottish historian.

92.   The English translation of these titles would be, approximately, The Honorable; The Most Honorable; The Right Honorable.

93.   A: it arouses demands of judging the significance of others.

94.   A, after "definite national character": this incomplete and insecure sketch of national characters must be judged with leniency because it rests on demonstrative, remembered, and prognostic evidence.

95.   B: "anyway" added.

96.   B: "of nations" added.

97.   Caloyer is a monk belonging to the Order of St. Basil.

98.   A: forms.

99.   A: Greeks'.

100.   Cassirer: sec. 105.

101.   C. H. Girtanner (1760–1800), *Über das Kantische Princip für die Naturgeschichte* (Göttingen: Vandenhoeck, 1796). Girtanner was a professor at Göttingen. See also Kant's "Bestimmung des Begriffes einer Menschenrasse," in Cassirer *Anthropology,* vol. 8, pp. 91–106.

102.   MS: who has been there once before.

103.   MS, written on margin: First stage: Man is an animal created not only for nature and instinct, but also for the liberal arts. Second stage: The judgment of Spaniards in Mexico.

104.   Cassirer: sec. 106.

105.   MS reads: a.

106.   Kant's word is *Wesen* which has been translated in this context with "creature." The word is ambiguous, its alternate meanings extend from "nature," "being," "characteristic," to "feature."

107.   MS: "absolutely" crossed out and replaced by "quite."

108. MS contains crossed-out passage: Man is conscious of himself not only as an animal capable of thought *(animal rationabile)*, but man is also conscious of himself as an animal without regard to being a rational animal *(animal rationale)*. In such a situation man does not know himself through experience, because experience can never teach him the absolute necessity of what he is supposed to be. Experience can only teach him empirically what he is or what he is supposed to be under empirical conditions. Man only knows about himself via pure reason (a priori), he recognizes the ideal of humanity, which, in comparison to him as a human being, makes the character of his species visible and describable through the frailties of his nature that limit the archetypal image. However, in order to appreciate the character of the species, a comparison is necessary with an entity which cannot be found anywhere else but in perfect humanity.

109. MS, *Akad. Ausg.*, Cassirer: as a; all other versions read, as in a.

110. On Dr. Moscati, see Wallace, *Kant*, p. 112: "Once more we have the natural man, and on all fours. . . . Dr. Moscati proves that the upright walk of man is forced and unnatural."

111. See First Book, nn. 181, 219.

112. MS: "the former" changed to "the latter."

113. Külpe cites Rousseau, *Discours sur les arts et les sciences* (1750).

114. MS, crossed out: Because the transition from the crude to the civilized state cannot be sudden, but rather an unnoticeable process of refinement, it is futile to warm against it and stop the flood with the pretense that natural evils and injustice will emerge by force from Pandora's Box and inundate the world. The quiet simplicity and satisfaction (of a shepherd's life) does not require much art of applied cleverness; it remains free. But such calculations about advantage and disadvantage are wrong. The increasing number of the human species that behaves well reduces the activity of those humans who try to further their means by war. Cultural progress of the human species provides such a rich advantage over the loss that the sum of virtues and pleasures always outweighs their drawbacks *in toto*. Over the course of centuries the virtues and pleasures promise a constantly increasing progress because wisdom seasoned with experience naturally knows how to guide progress on to better paths.

115. Trans.: like wax moulded toward evil.

116. MS, crossed out: Not one can also ask whether man could be called good or evil by Nature (i.e. before he can think about the motives of his free action or inaction; before he can think of a law). In other words, whether in his crude condition he has a stronger inclination toward what he knows to be evil than toward what he recognizes as good just because it is good and representative of the character of the human species. The stages of emerging from this crudeness are cultivation, civilization, and ultimately moralization. Being good or evil depends upon the inclination of a man, out of principle, to prefer motives of the moral law over impulses of sense impressions, which would make him evil by nature. However, man primarily inclined toward evil cannot simply be labeled evil, because this same freedom of will makes it also possible for reason to overshadow this inclination habitually by its maxims, but merely through

a particular determination made in response to every action without establishing a continuous inclination toward the good. MS, on the margin: The question whether the human nature is good or evil depends on the notion of what we call evil. It is the inclination to desire the illicit, even if one knows very well that this is wrong. A child is evil, it cries because its wish has not been fulfilled and will not be fulfilled by anybody else. The same holds true for the desire to rule over others.

117.   On the progressive improvement of the human species, see Abbott, trans., *Kant's Critique of Practical Reason*, p. 326*n*: "it is my duty to strive to promote this improvement." See also John Bagnell Bury (1861–1927), *The Idea of Progress* (London: Macmillan, 1920), pp. 243 ff., 258, 278.

118.   Cassirer; sec. 107.

119.   MS: "Galilei" replaced with "Lavoisier." Archimedes (287?–212 B.C.), Greek mathematician; Isaac Newton (1642–1727), English philosopher, mathematician; Antoine Laurent Lavoisier (1743–94), French chemist, was guillotined.

120.   MS, crossed out on margin: "The prosecutor [is] attorney and judge. The attorney is the one who is charged with defending any matter, be it true or untrue to him." Not crossed out is "despite all wars, there seems to be a cosmopolitan trait in the human species which gradually in the course of political matters wins the upper hand over the selfish traits of nations."

121.   MS: Nature's strength.

122.   The works referred to are *Discours sur les arts et les sciences* (1750), *Discours sur l'origine de l'inégalité des hommes* (1754), *Julie, ou la nouvelle Héloïse* (1761).

123.   MS: of that paradise.

124.   Cassirer: sec. 108.

125.   MS: "man's ability"; all other versions are "in the ability."

126.   MS, on the margin: Quite different is the answer to the question what one should do in order to provide conviction to moral laws than just access. . . .

127.   MS, on the margin: The character of the species can only be derived from history. The human species as a whole must possess a tendency toward an artistic skill by which the selfishness of all individuals (*singulorum*) turns out to be beneficial for the happiness of all (*universorum*) by means of the moral gift. It is the character of the species that the human species as a whole has a natural tendency toward continuous improvement. The species can collectively be considered as a whole or distributively as the logical entity representing the notion of man. The character of the species cannot be derived historically from his history alone. This refers only to the human species as an animal species. The character of the species can be derived from understanding as long as it subjectively understands and modifies not only itself but also puts itself into perspective with relation to others.

128.   Cassirer: sec. 109.

129.   Kant's word is *Weiser*, meaning "leader" here.

130.   MS: "Freedom under the law and . . ." Kant crossed out "under the law."

131.   Trans.: The well-being of the state (not of the citizens) is the highest law. Kant had written in the MS, *Salus rei publicae,* which he then crossed out. The proverb goes back to Cicero *De legibus* 3. 3: "Salus populi suprema lex esto," which states that the well-being of the people is the highest law.

132.   MS, crossed out: Concerning the character of the human species, history cannot reveal how other humans have behaved at different times and in other countries. With the mixture of good and evil, which they reveal at different occasions, the result would be at times favorable and at times unfavorable. The most large-scale investigation and the most careful interpretation of history can provide no safe instruction in this matter. But the attempt of an inner examination of one's self, particularly guided by how he wants to be judged by his fellow humans, reveals his character as not being willing to reveal himself, because, at least in the case of a negative impression, he wants to deceive others to his advantage in their judgment of him. Consequently, there is the tendency to lying, which not only proves a lack of candor, but also a lack of sincerity, which is the hereditary cancer of the human species. And so the character of the species consists in the attempt to make one's personal character not visible and to take any spying looks and investigations for insults.

133.   Demiurge, named by Plato in the Timaeus for God the Creator. In Gnosticism the demiurge is identified with the Jehovah of the Hebrews. Kant's interest in Swedenborg would naturally lead him to speculate on the demiurge in biblical and Gnostic thought.

134.   Timon was the son of Echecratides.

135.   Momus, meaning "blame," is personified as the Critic-God; cf. Plato *Republic* 487A: "the very Genius of criticism." Timon and Momus are named in Pope's *Moral Essays,* Epistle 3, "Of the Abuse of Riches," which Kant may have read.

136.   MS margin: There could be beings that would not be able to think without having to speak at the same time. They would only be able to think aloud. These creatures would have quite a different character from the human species.

137.   MS, *Akad. Ausg.,* Cassirer omit: and what kind of effect would it have?

138.   MS, crossed out: of mutual subordination.

INDEX

Absentmindedness: as involuntary distraction, 102, 104; *Spectator* on, 269n*158*
Abstraction: of sense impressions, 14–15; ability of 99; George Berkeley on, 260n*45*
Accomplishment: capacity for, 24
Acuteness: a faculty of judgment, 96
Addison, Joseph, 23
Admiration: result of having character, 203–5
Affability: an appearance of politeness, 39
Affection: result of politeness, 39
Affinity: Kant on, xx; faculty of, 67–68
Ailments: mental, 108–14
Albee, Ernest, ix
Ambition: a label for passion, 172; a passion as illness, 173; directed at a purpose, 175; as a human passion, 177; as a weakness, 179; related to arrogance, 180–81; a characteristic of choleric temperament, 200
Amusement: and boredom, 133–35; mentioned, 232
Anger: affection of rage, 118; the emotion of, 156, 169; and shame as emotions, 165–67; and phlegm, 202; mentioned, 162
Anguish: a degree of fear, 161
Anthropology: philosophical, xix, xxi; empirical, xxi; physiological, 3; pragmatic, 3–5, 6, 20, 81, 149, 211, 241; principles exhibited by, 128
Anticipation: empirical, 77
Antipathy: trait of presentiment, 99
Anxiety: expression of fear, 79, 161; causing suicide, 164
Apathy: as self-possession, 156; principle of, 158–59; signifying phlegm, 200

Appearance: faculty of intuition, 27; misjudging of, 31; faculty of, 32; deception by, 36; mentioned, 37
Apperception: and apprehension, 18n; spontaneity of, 25; inner sense and, 27, 49, 263; discursive and intuitive, 262
Apprehension: and apperception, 18n; faculty of, 22; of impressions, 27, slow, 99; and quality of mind, 99; and terror, 266n*96*
Archenholz, Johann Wilhelm von, 209
Archimedes, 243
Aristo, Lodovico, 72
Aristotle, 39
Arrogance: a mistaken ambition, 180 and n; of choleric person, 200
Art: mnemonic, 75–76; and taste, 147, 149–53; of judging physiognomy, 207; ideal structures in, 210; design with, 216; Italian's taste for, 232
Artificiality: opposed to simplicity, 107
Assimilation: of races, 236
Association: law of, 66; and imagination, 118
Astonishment: result of surprise, 167; as a gesture, 214
Astronomy: science of, 81; prognostic signs of, 86
Attribution: highest degree of designation, 83
Audacity: definition of, 163; and freedom of mind, 166
Authority: a result of influence, 179; lust of, 181, 182; freedom, law, and, 248
Autonomy: of pure reason, xvi–xvii
Avarice: an emotional passion, 175, 177, 179; causes of, 181–82
Awareness: attribute of distinctness, 21; of self, 55, 263; of spontaneity, 262

INDEX 295